My Country

by Pierre Berton

"Mr. Berton wrote *My Country*'s stories just like he did *The National Dream* and *The Last Spike* — with a journalist's eye for history. The result is an immensely readable — but not footnoted and fogbound — look into Canada's past — something for which Pierre Berton is famous. . . . Pierre Berton has done it once again."

Calgary Albertan

"*My Country, A Remarkable Past*, is a remarkable book. It should lay to rest the saying that Canadian history is as dull as ditchwater. Here, told in masterly style, are eighteen stories of amazing variety. . . . It is full of surprises, full of exploits so dangerous, of hardships so nearly unbearable, of courage and endurance so immeasurable, of triumphs so spectacular, that in some cases they would be incredible if they were not supported by impeccable evidence. It is a book to delight and inspire. This book gives the reader, as no formal text book can do, a deep and thrilling attachment to Canada."

The Hon. Eugene Forsey
(Senator of Canada, retired)

"Throughout, the Berton instinct for indispensable trivia seldom falters. (Why was a grand piano a "necessity" to the Franklin expedition? What earthly use would a box of carpet tacks be to a man who sails around the world alone? Berton, like The Shadow, always knows.) . . . *My Country* is popular entertainment and information on the grand scale."

Victoria Times

A Penguin Books Canada/McClelland and Stewart Book

My Country

Pierre Berton was born in 1920 and raised in the Yukon. He spent his early newspaper career in Vancouver, where at 21 he was the youngest city editor on any Canadian daily. He moved to Toronto in 1947 and at the age of 31 was named managing editor of *Maclean's* magazine. He was an associate editor and columnist at the *Toronto Star* from 1958 to 1962 and has written and hosted several national television programs. He is the author of thirty-six books and has received three Governor General's Awards for works of non-fiction including *Klondike*. He is a Companion of the Order of Canada and a member of the Canadian News Hall of Fame. Mr. Berton lives in Kleinburg, Ontario.

Canada
is a live country,
live,
but not, like the States,
kicking.
—*Rupert Brooke*

Pierre Berton

My Country

The Remarkable Past

A Penguin Books Canada/
McClelland and Stewart Book

PENGUIN BOOKS

Published by the Penguin Group

Penguin Books Canada Ltd, 10 Alcorn Avenue, Toronto,
Ontario, Canada M4V 1E4

Penguin Books Ltd, 27 Wrights Lane, London W8 5TZ,
England

Penguin Books USA Inc., 375 Hudson Street, New York,
New York 10014, U.S.A.

Penguin Books Australia Ltd, Ringwood, Victoria,
Australia

Penguin Books (NZ) Ltd, 182-190 Wairau Road, Auckland
10, New Zealand

Penguin Books Ltd, Registered Offices: Harmondsworth,
Middlesex, England

First published in Canada by McClelland and Stewart, 1976
Published in Penguin Books, 1991

1 3 5 7 9 10 8 6 4 2

Maps by Jack McMaster

All rights reserved

Manufactured in Canada

Canadian Cataloguing in Publication Data

Berton, Pierre, 1920-
My country

ISBN 0-14-013949-4

1. Canada — History.   2. Canada — Biography.
I. Title.

FC163.B47 1991   971   C90-095506-6
F1034.B47 1991

Contents

List of Maps

Preface

Many years ago, when I was conducting a half-hour interview program on television, I found myself without an interview; somebody, at the last moment, had begged off. To fill in the missing half hour, I decided to tell a story from the Canadian past. There was no film and few props; I simply sat in a chair and told the tale as one might tell it around a campfire. To my surprise this program brought more reaction than most of the interviews I had been conducting with internationally famous writers, politicians and movie stars. As a result, from time to time I continued the practice of digging into the past and spinning true yarns about my own country.

Eventually, this led to a new weekly half-hour program titled *My Country*, which is still being shown on the Global Television network in Ontario and on other stations in various parts of Canada. The stories in this book spring out of the research for that program. They are not told in the same way, of course. I had thought at first that I might use verbatim transcripts of my television shows (which were ad libbed from notes) as the basis for these published tales. To my chagrin, I discovered that when the spoken words were typed up they were almost incomprehensible. Each story had to be totally rewritten from the original research, in quite a different style and often from a different point of view.

13

Freed from the fetters of time I have also been able to enlarge on the original tales: the stories in this book are each almost three times as long as the television versions.

There is no particular theme here except the theme of country. My only guide in selecting the pieces that follow was that I enjoyed telling them and knew I would enjoy writing them. They are, I think, good, entertaining stories; but I hope they are more than that. The television series had one important criterion: each tale that we selected had to have some historical, social or geographical significance. I have followed this general rule and tried to enlarge upon it here. I hope that these stories, taken as a group, will give some insight into what kind of country we live in and what kind of people we are. If this is informal history it is also informal geography.

The producer of the television series, who worked on the concept with me and was responsible for the high quality of the result, is Elsa Franklin; she deserves a special note of praise. Our story editor for much of this period was Janice Patton. I am grateful to Peter Such for his valuable advice on The Last of the Red Indians. I wish also to thank my editor, Diane Mew, for her careful analysis of the manuscript and her many useful suggestions, my secretary, Ennis Armstrong for typing my various drafts, and my wife, Janet, for catching a variety of errors in the proofs, which only her eagle eyes were able to spot.

Kleinburg, Ontario
May, 1976

1

The Great Cross-Canada Hike

In the first six months of 1921 there occurred an extraordinary event, which made newspaper headlines from Halifax to Vancouver but which is now forgotten. Four men and one woman walked a distance of 3,650 miles from the Atlantic to the Pacific in a race that has never been copied or equalled. They did it for no particular gain or reward and for no particular reason except for personal satisfaction and, perhaps, for the fleeting fame that it gave them.

There was nothing remarkable about these five. If they had anything in common, apart from a determination to walk across the continent, it was that ordinary quality which is conjured up by such phrases as "average Canadian" or "man on the street." They were neither fanatics nor screwballs, as were the marathon dancers and flagpole sitters of the coming era. They were simply five unexceptional people who emerged from anonymous working class backgrounds, strode swiftly across a large stage, and then returned almost instantly to anonymity, none of them materially richer for the experience. One is reminded of Andy Warhol's remark that in the future everybody will be famous — for fifteen minutes.

The story begins with a 20-year-old Halifax labourer named Charles Burkman, laid off in January 1921 after a year in the shipyards. Burkman had no intention of racing across Canada. He and an out-of-work acquaint-ance, Sid Carr, simply decided they would walk west at their own pace, perhaps as far as Vancouver, to look for a job.

Canada that year was in the throes of a depression — the result of the winding down of the wartime boom and the swelling of the labour market by thousands of returned soldiers. Vancouver, then as later, was a kind of mecca for the jobless. In bad times people tend to head for the west coast which is, after all, the one part of Canada where you can sleep out under the stars for most of the year. As for walking — well, people walked a good deal more in those days. Children, especially in the rural areas, were used to walking several miles to school each day. Many men walked to work. Young men thought nothing of walking young ladies home of an evening. The country was on the edge of the automobile era but the motor car had not yet taken over. Radio was in its infancy; motion pictures had yet to become the universal entertainment. Walking was a pastime as well as a necessity. The Sunday afternoon drive had not yet replaced the Sunday afternoon walk.

Burkman and Carr planned to pay for their trip by selling specially made photographic postcards of themselves along the route at ten cents apiece, a respectable price at a time when newspapers could be purchased for two cents and some magazines for five. They also decided to offer regular dispatches to the Halifax *Herald*, an enterprising paper in those days, which specialized in stunts and contests. The newspaper responded with enthusiasm and offered to buy their dispatches.

The obvious route to take was that of the railways. There was, of course, no Trans-Canada Highway, and although the automobile was becoming popular (there were 1,150 *stolen* in Toronto the previous year), roads tended to be muddy, rutted and winding. In those days all the major Canadian communities (and many minor ones) were on the railroads, not the highways. Burkman and Carr planned to walk the CNR tracks to Maine, take a short cut across that state via the Maine Central right of way to Quebec and then follow the Canadian Pacific roadbed for the rest of the journey.

Neither man was in a hurry. They planned to take at least seven months to reach the west coast and they did not expect to travel more than fifteen miles a day in the winter, although they hoped they might increase the pace when they reached the prairies in the spring. What they envisaged was a kind of leisurely stroll, with time out to view the scenery or to linger in the towns and villages of rural Canada. It didn't work out that way.

The hike might easily have gone unnoticed if the *Herald* had not turned it into news by *saying* it was news — an early example of what the American sociologist Daniel Boorstin has called "the pseudo event." Carr and Burkman were featured on the front pages for two days before they actually set off in the wind and the rain on January 17, to the cheers of a large crowd and the good wishes of the mayor who gave them a personal letter for the mayor of Vancouver. Pathé News was on hand to film the start and in the months that followed Canadian movie audiences would get regular reports on the cross-Canada hike, along with Charlie Chaplin in *The kid,* Pola Negri in *Passion* and Mary Pickford in *The Love Light.*

All this publicity had its effect. After the first day, Carr, employing a phrase now long in disuse, reported back to the *Herald* that "continental hikers are some pumpkins." As the two men plodded into Windsor Junction at the end of their first fourteen miles they could hear cries of: "Here they come!" That night meals were free and so was lodging; they slept together in the spare bed of a family who requested and got anonymity.

17

Two days and fifty miles later they were in Truro, feeling a little stiff from the unaccustomed exercise. Again, everything was free: meals and a room at the Stanley Hotel, an evening at the Strand Theatre, and the ultimate accolade — two free suits of Stanfield's unshrinkable long johns.

The temperature was down to ten degrees Fahrenheit the next morning as they set off briskly in the heavy snows, pausing at station houses along the way for free meals and, on one occasion, to listen to the station master entertain them on the piano. It was pleasant, easy going. But then, after five days and ninety-eight miles, they received a piece of news that was to change a leisurely walk into a fierce and often bitter race. In Dartmouth, the rival community across the harbour from Halifax, two other men announced that they would duplicate the feat and that they meant to better the time of the original hikers.

All the publicity had been too much for Jack Behan and his son Clifford. On January 21, the two men appeared at the *Herald's* office, armed with a letter from Dartmouth's mayor, and demanded similar press attention. The *Herald* was delighted to give it to them. The elder Behan made no bones about the competitive aspects of the race: "We are out to overtake Burkman and Carr," he declared, "and I am convinced that we will do so before they reach Montreal."

Both the Behans were "returned men," having served in the front lines with the Halifax Rifles, the father rising to sergeant, the son wounded three times in action. Jack Behan, aged forty-four, was used to walking long distances for he was a letter carrier; he was also an amateur sculler, past president of a local rowing club. Neither man had any money but they planned, also, to sell postcards of themselves en route. The

Dartmouth Commercial Club outfitted them with breeches, boots and knapsacks.

Burkman and Carr took up the challenge at once, walking forty-three miles in two days: "You can tell the Dartmouth people that nobody will overtake us at any place between here and Vancouver unless we break our legs."

So now the race was on. Burkman and his partner turned down the luncheon proffered by the Amherst Commercial Club and plunged off into the driving snow before reaching Dorchester, "the hardest day we have had yet." The following day, under even worse conditions, they pushed twenty-seven miles to Moncton. "If we had the Behans along with us we would have shown them what hiking is," Carr wired back. Clearly, however, the fun was gone. The day, Carr wrote, had taken "some of the sap out of us." The Behans were already on the road, eight days behind, but announcing that they would make fewer stops; on their first day out they picked up a few miles on the leaders.

Now an odd thing happened. In spite of their bold reports to the *Herald,* Burkman and Carr slackened off. They loafed around Moncton until 3 p.m. and made only a few miles that day. Clearly, something was wrong. Later events suggest that a rift was developing between the two men — a rift that sprang from the changed complexion of the hike.

Arriving in Truro, the Behans waxed enthusiastic. "This hiking is great fun," Jack Behan reported. "I had no idea the kind of stuff that boy of mine is made of."

And on that same day, a *third* team of hikers, Frank and Jennie Dill, called on the *Herald* and announced that they, too, were prepared to walk at top speed across Canada. One can imagine the glee at the city desk when it was revealed that this was a man and wife team. Up to this point the story had had a whiff of the sports pages about it. Now it would attract a wider audience, especially at a time when women's aspirations were making news. By 1921, Canada's suffragette movement had managed to push votes for women through in every province except Quebec and Prince Edward Island. Before the year was out, Agnes Macphail, an unknown school teacher from rural Ontario, would become the first woman Member of Parliament.

The Dills had been married for a little less than two years. Frank was a foundry worker in Dartmouth and had been a runner of some distinction in his home town of Windsor, Nova Scotia. But the dominant member of the family was clearly his wife, Jennie, and it is her personality that overshadows that of the others who took part in the cross-Canada hike. She emerges, in fact, from the sere pages of the 1921 newspapers, as a diminutive tigress, the strongest of the lot; fiercely competitive, pushing her husband forward, cajoling, nagging and threatening whenever he seems to falter.

She was a dark little creature weighing 128 pounds at the start — all of it muscle: a fisherman's daughter from Petpeswick Harbour, fond of the outdoors and a good hunter. She was one of the fastest women skaters in the Maritimes. The *Herald* was careful to point out, however, that there was "not a single suggestion of the mannish in her personality."

There was never any doubt, then or later, about who had prompted the pair to enter the race. "It was I who first suggested the trip," said Jennie. "We have both worked hard since we were married and now we are going to see the world." She made it sound like a holiday excursion but it soon ceased to be that. "We have no home ties," said Jennie, "not a chick nor a child." But Frank had a mother to whom he *was* tied. He did his best to phone her regularly, especially during the early stages of the walk.

The Dills announced they would leave on February 1, a week behind the Behans and fifteen days behind Burkman and Carr. They, too, would peddle postcards of themselves at a dime apiece (the nickel had yet to be invented) to finance the journey.

But even before the Dills left, the team of Burkman and Carr had a falling out. The split occurred on the banks of the Petit-codiac River on January 28, and it was Carr who made the announcement. Events were pushing him into a position which he could not control. He had not planned on a mad scramble from sea to sea and he said so. "I won't be forced into racing across Canada," he declared and took the train back to Halifax. One can sympathize with him now; nobody did then. Burkman became the hero of the hour, "the lone hiker," as the press was to dub him for the next five months.

The loss of his partner was a considerable blow to Burkman. Events were to prove that two hikers could force the pace — something mile runners have always known. And then there was the loneliness; it is not much fun to walk thirty or forty miles a day through empty country with no one to talk to or to urge you on. Burkman felt Carr's loss immediately but he plunged ahead nevertheless, covering a record thirty-three miles that day At Sussex he announced his intention of continuing: "I have made up my mind to walk to Vancouver and if I have my health I will do it. . . . I have no hindrance now."

This attitude was much applauded and the public enthusiasm elated Burkman. Crowds gathered all along the way to wish him well en route to Saint John, which he reached the following evening. Scarcely pausing to rest his feet, he went to a dance and then the following morning hiked another twenty-four miles to Welsford, New Brunswick, totally confident of maintaining his

21

lead. In Halifax, a group of businessmen announced they'd give him five hundred dollars if he reached Vancouver in six months.

The date was January 31, and Charles Burkman at that point had covered 298 miles. The Behans had walked 158, but they had narrowed the final gap between themselves and the leader by 23 miles.

The following morning, two thousand Haligonians gathered before the *Herald* building to bid Godspeed to Frank and Jennie Dill. The pair did not make very good time at first, held back by heavy snow and continually delayed by curious onlookers, many of them women — far more than had turned out for the others. At Truro, twelve hundred people cheered them and they sold 220 postcards. There was, of course, more free underwear from Stanfield's.

On that same day, Charles Burkman crossed into Maine. He made twenty miles in heavy snow and slept that first night in a logging camp. The Behans gained another six miles on him. They were pushing very hard; the following day they managed to cover a record forty-four miles, increasing their pace in the last two hours of the day to four and a half miles an hour — a very fast clip indeed. (The U.S. Army recommends an average speed of three miles an hour for long marches.) By Saint John, the Behans had gained a full two days on Burkman.

The Dills were still being held up by admirers. All along the route people were pressing gifts of food upon them, but there was no time to accept them all. At East Mines, the station agent, a Mr. McManaman, was lying in wait for them with tea, cakes, chocolates and cigars and nothing would do but that they stop. They were, after all, celebrities, albeit instant ones, and everybody wanted to reach out and touch them in some way. So flustered was Mr. McManaman at the presence of real, live celebrities, munching cookies in his station house, that he quite forgot that he had prepared other refreshments for them. After the Dills left he could be seen trotting down the tracks, his arms laden with more gifts, urging them to slacken their pace.

The Behans had developed a system for walking along the rails in the snow. Jack walked on one rail, Clifford on the other; between them they carried a long spanner to maintain their balance. In Maine, Burkman got behind a snowplough, which made walking easier.

The Dills tried to adopt the Behan method but because Frank was tall and Jennie a little bit of a thing, they were forced to abandon it and walk on the ties. They were still losing ground. In Sackville there was an unscheduled delay; when the couple passed Mount Allison University, a covey of young women burst from that institution and fairly swamped Frank. Jennie, who wrote most of the dispatches to the *Herald*, commented with just a touch of acerbity that "I hope we do not pass any more girl college towns on this hike."

Back home, the wiseacres had been predicting that no woman could hike farther than Truro. Jennie was out to prove them wrong and that resolve gave her a competitive edge. "Tomorrow," she wired on February 3, "we will at least go as far as Moncton, twenty miles away, and perhaps *if Frank can stand it,* I'll take him further." That one sentence tells us a great deal about Jennie Dill.

On February 9, as the Behans entered Maine, Charles Burkman crossed the Quebec border and his pursuers gave up any hope of catching him before he reached Montreal. They were still setting the fastest pace: 23 miles a day, compared to 21.5 for Burkman and only 17.5 for the Dills. Burkman, because he was carrying on alone, was very popular. In Danforth, Maine, one pastor shooed his congregation out of the church and urged them to buy Burkman's postcards to help him on his way. "The fact that he has plugged along alone has won him a legion of friends," the *Herald* reported. There were fears for his safety in the lonely country west of Sherbrooke, Quebec, and one Springhill miner wrote in advising that he arm himself with a rifle to ward off wolves. But he reached Sherbrooke safely on February 15, having walked twenty-one miles that day. Said he: "I laugh when I think of the boast Jack Behan made about catching me before I reached Montreal. Already I can smell dear old Craig Street and hear the feet of the French girls skipping along St. Lawrence Main."

That day the Dills reached Saint John and were almost jailed as vagrants by a policeman who did not recognize Jennie in her breeches and knapsack until she was a few paces from him. He had heard all about her, of course — everybody had. A thousand people were waiting to welcome her farther down the line and one CNR trainman had even composed a poem to her:

And if your Frank gets weary
And talks of turning back,
Give him a dose of Nerveline
Or a bottle of Taniac.
Paint his spine with iodine
Put hemlock oil on, too,
But keep on going, Jennie,
Whatever else you do.

As the doggerel suggests, there was no doubt in the public's mind who was the stronger member of the Dill team. Women crowded about Jennie, asking questions, surprised by her diminutive size and astonished at her male attire (breeches and high boots), unusual in those circumspect days when dresses still trailed to the ankle. She was not in the least concerned about the slowness of the pace, confident that they could pick up the lost distance as the weeks went by. "By the time I get to Montreal I will be as hard as spikes," said she.

By this time, railwaymen along the route were placing wagers on the outcome of the race. Passengers on passing trains waved at the hikers, cheered and tossed out newspapers, candy, inspirational notes and sometimes letters from home (although most mail arrived quite legitimately at post offices along the route). All the walkers were offered rides on sleighs, cars and trains and all refused. Were they being tested? They couldn't be sure.

On February 19, one month and two days from the time he left Halifax, Charles Burkman reached Montreal, then a city of some six hundred thousand. It was, perhaps, the finest hour of his hike. The streets were black with people out to greet him on a crisp Saturday afternoon. The *Herald* had a man in Montreal to describe the triumph and he rose splendidly to the occasion:

"Bronzed like an Indian and aglow with radiant health, Charles Burkman, slim and boyish looking, strode into Montreal Saturday afternoon. As with head thrown back and chest out he marched through the streets he was a notable figure, youth and energy vibrated from him."

Burkman stayed at the Windsor, then Montreal's smartest hostelry and, in spite of his thirty-mile hike that day, spent the evening dancing. "He tripped the light fantastic for many hours and had no lack of admiration from his partners," was the way the press described it. Those, after all, were the dancing years. The one-step, the two-step and the waltz were giving way to new and faster steps and glides (such as the Gaby Glide) springing out of the music of ragtime and often imitating the struts of birds and walks of animals: the Alligator Crawl, the Turkey Trot, the Kangaroo Hop, the Bunny Hug and the longer-lasting Fox Trot. Newspapers were already referring to Burkman as "the smiling, happy-go-lucky daredevil" who was "dancing his way across the continent," and gushy letters were beginning to arrive from Halifax girls. "I have an appetite like a horse," Burkman declared, "and I sleep like a log." All that dancing held him up for a day. He slept well into Sunday and did not resume his hike until Monday morning.

At that juncture, the Behans, walking twenty-two miles in below-freezing weather, had already reached Sherbrooke, while the Dills had entered Maine. Burkman was holding to his average pace of 21.7 miles a day but the others had increased theirs slightly. The Behans were now making 24 miles a day while the Dills were averaging slightly more than 19 miles a day.

It was hard going in Maine. Jennie and her husband found themselves struggling through snow that often reached to their waists before the plough came through. It was so cold that one night frost formed on the comforter in the room in which they were sleeping. On a sharp downhill turn they were almost run over by a train that came coasting silently behind them. One day they made only eleven miles, but their spirits remained high. It was obvious that Jennie admired the lonely Burkman. "Good luck to him," she wired, when she learned that he was already en route to Ottawa.

But Burkman lost his way trying to take a short cut to the capital and the Behans gained another day. Now they were only four days behind. In Montreal they were fêted, as Burkman had been, and given gifts of tobacco and cigars from Benson and Hedges and new boots from the Knights of Columbus. Burkman, meanwhile, spent a full day in Ottawa being lionized by Nova Scotia members and senators. The new Conservative prime minister, Arthur Meighen signed his logbook; and the Honourable F. B. McCurdy, a Halifax business leader who was Minister of Public Works, played him a game of 100-up on his own billiard table.

The Behans were still pressing him hard. On February 28, they walked thirty-five miles to Burkman's seventeen. "We know we are closing the gap on Burkman and can almost hear him pant as he leads us in the race," Jack Behan reported. Burkman began to make extravagant prophecies that he could not hope to fulfill. He vowed to walk fifty-three miles to Pembroke "or bust," but rain and darkness frustrated that attempt. By this time the Behans were in Ottawa. The Dills, at Lac Mégantic, Quebec, were still losing ground.

Hampered by blisters, Burkman kept plugging along. At Chalk River, he reached the thousand-mile point in the walk after a hard thirty-two mile hike. He scoffed at reports that the Behans were on his heels. Said he: "if they are, my heels are much longer than I think." But the Behans, who thought nothing of walking until midnight, announced they'd catch him before he reached Winnipeg. In the empty, wolf-infested forests of northern Ontario, Burkman finally acquired a gun and lost a day at North Bay having it repaired. No one knew exactly where his pursuers were; for the first time since leaving Halifax they had failed to report.

The Dills, meanwhile, having celebrated their second wedding anniversary by plunging through heavy snow in the eastern townships of Quebec, had finally reached Montreal. Jennie was interviewed by a Miss M. J. Dewar, a society writer, to whom she confided that she considered the hike a honeymoon trip. "Rouge or powder would have been wasted on Mrs. Dill's healthy, tanned complexion," Miss Dewar wrote. "The financial cares of the trip weighed not at all on her as they did on her serious husband who perhaps realized more than she the gravity of the undertaking." Jenny had only one goal in mind: to prove that a woman could do whatever a man could do.

The Dills did not rest in Montreal, as the others had. Ahead of them the Behans had again stepped up the pace. At North Bay on March 10, they were only a day behind Burkman. A Halifax man bet a thousand dollars they'd catch him by March 12.

On March 11, the Behans were only nine miles behind their quarry. Burkman had devised an ingenious contraption that enabled him to walk on one rail while balancing himself with a stick that ran on a roller skate on the other. In this way he held off the Behans on the 12th and the Halifax plunger lost his money. But the gap remained narrow. At Sudbury, Burkman voluntarily gave up half a day visiting old cronies and didn't leave until half past one in the afternoon. The Behans moved into town later that same day and didn't stop.

Now the contest became heated. When he reached Chelmsford, Burkman asked a friendly telegraph operator to wire back to Azilda, a station between Sudbury and Chelmsford, to see if the Behans were planning to spend the night there. If so, Burkman would sleep at Chelmsford, secure in the knowledge that he held the lead. The Behans, however, fooled him. When they arrived in Azilda they told the operator they were stopping for the night. Instead they plunged on to Chelmsford. Burkman, meanwhile, went to bed in the Algoma Hotel. At two that morning the proprietor woke him to reveal that the Behans had arrived and were snoring away in the next room. Burkman dressed quietly and slipped off into the dark; but the Behans, who seemed alert to every possibility, soon learned of his escape and followed. In the faint light of dawn, five miles out of Larchwood, they finally caught up with him.

It was a memorable meeting. The rivals, strangers to each other, exchanged greetings and congratulations like old friends and then, in Jack Behan's words, "started off like three schoolgirls," the Behans walking on one rail (a remarkable balancing act) and Burkman on the other, keeping fairly even all the way. They stayed even for the rest of the day, arriving together at Cartier. Behan reported that "we hit a clip of 4 miles an hour for 5 hours but Burkman, with his patent, stuck like glue and beat us 2 yards at the finish."

The Dills had reached Ottawa. Here they met Prime Minister Meighen and also the Liberal leader, William Lyon Mackenzie King, who was already campaigning against the Conservative party on whom he would inflict a crushing defeat the following December. The hike to Ottawa had given the Dills "the best day yet." Though they had taken one day longer than Burkman and five days longer than the Behans to reach the capital, they were beginning to gain back some of the time lost in the East.

Now the Behans found themselves locked in a duel with Charles Burkman as the three men made their way across the lonely Pre-Cambrian desert of northern Ontario. Here, in a land of stunted trees, cracked grey rocks and muskeg, the rivals stayed even. Then, on March 18, Burkman opened up a slight lead and reached Woman River ahead of the Behans. They expected that he would sleep there, since it was late in the day; but he fooled them and trudged on to the camp of an Italian section gang. The following day the Behans were led astray by an Indian guide who promised, but did not deliver, a short cut. They lost two days, blamed Burkman for the deception and confessed to feeling glum

29

because their funds were low and their postcards weren't selling. In northern Ontario in 1921 there were few customers.

Somewhere in the dark forests to the east, the Dills had an adventure. A timber wolf sprang out of the bushes directly at Frank. Jennie downed it with a single shot. "I was by no means excited," she told her readers. She could not conceal her continuing admiration for Burkman who, though she had never met him, she now treated as an intimate friend: "We are hoping that Charlie wins and we only wish we had as many friends along the route as this boy has. Everywhere we go people speak in glowing terms of Burkman and state that they hope he beats the Behans." But the Dills were also stepping up the pace and increasing their average daily.

The Behans caught up with Burkman again at White River, traditionally the coldest spot in Canada. He had been keeping his whereabouts a secret, refusing even to wire the paper, to prevent his rivals finding him. That night all three men gave lectures describing their journey at the local YMCA. Two days later, at a little place called King, Burkman made another attempt to elude the Behans, slipping away before dawn in the bitter cold — minus 11 degrees Fahrenheit. He had not gone ten miles before he heard a familiar voice hailing him from the rear; it was Jack Behan. That day they walked an additional thirty-three miles to Heron Bay. The following morning the Behans managed to get off ahead of Burkman. Along the route people were saying that they slept like dogs — with one eye open.

Thus it came about that Jack Behan and his son Clifford were the first of the cross-Canada hikers to see the frozen expanse of Lake Superior. And here, at a watering station, they encountered the special train of the Governor General, Victor Christian William Cavendish, the 9th Duke of Devonshire, making the last of his cross-Canada tours before his term ended in July. Jack Behan made so bold as to approach a policeman to ask if the Duke would sign his logbook. The constable refused but Behan insisted on seeing the Duke's secretary who, having a more highly developed sense of public relations, immediately invited the hikers on board. The Governor General, a hefty, mustached figure, signed the book while the Duchess offered them a silver basket of fruit, urging them to take it all. This ritual complete, the vice-regal train puffed off, with the Duke and Duchess waving cheerily from the observation platform and the Behans, their mouths full of fruit, waving back until the train was out of sight.

Burkman had vanished again. "I found that sometimes telegraph wires leak," he explained later. "Jack Behan is pretty chummy with some of the folk up this way. I know that every day he arrived at a telegraph office he would try and locate me." On March 31, a dreadful blizzard hit the Middleton area. The Behans were warned not to attempt to move in the white-out but, having heard rumours that Burkman had passed them in the night, they set out anyway and managed to cover sixteen miles in spite of the raging storm. No living creature, least of all Burkman, crossed their path, which was hazardous in the extreme. At one stage they were forced to crawl nervously across a long trestle suspended sixty feet above a canyon. But where was Burkman? Had he been lost in the driving snows?

The following day was April Fool's Day: still no sign of Burkman. That day the Dills walked a record thirty-five miles with Jennie (by her own account) egging on her faltering husband for the last ten. The next afternoon, at Cavers, Ontario, Jack Behan and his son were picking up their mail at the post office when Burkman walked in and clapped them each on the back. He had hiked thirty-nine miles to catch them.

The rival hikers were glad enough of each other's company in the bleak nights that followed. They walked in the dark, always aware of the wolves lurking just beyond the dim circles cast by their flashlights. Stopping one night in an empty cabin, they shivered in the gloom as the wolves just outside the door howled at the moon.

The trio reached Port Arthur on April 6. This was Burkman's home town — his parents still lived here — and hundreds were at the station to welcome him. He had decided that nothing would prevent him from spending two full days with his friends and relatives: "I promised them that at home and I shall keep my promise. I had hoped, though, when I made that promise to have at least 7 or 8 days lead on the Behans, but since I have not there is no use to cry over spilt milk." He fully expected to make up the lost ground en route to Winnipeg because he knew all the short cuts from his boyhood days.

The Behans did not linger but moved right on to Fort William. "It may seem unfair of us to leave Burkman at Port Arthur," Jack Behan wrote, "but this is a race."

One does not have to read too deeply between the lines of the chatty newspaper dispatches to realize that Jennie Dill's admiration for Charles Burkman was causing domestic difficulties. In one of her earlier dispatches, Mrs. Dill had hinted at dissension when she wrote that Frank believed that Burkman was purposely lagging behind in order that he might walk the rest of the way with Jennie. Frank's suspicions had been aroused by the fact that Burkman was sending letters back to Mrs. Dill. "It's not often that I sigh," Jennie reported. "The other day I got a letter from Charlie Burkman and then today I got another one. . . . I told

[Frank] that he was silly but he said it looked fishy to him. . . ."

This titillating hint at a romance with a woman he had never met was dispelled by Burkman when he left his home town. "He [Frank] need have no fear of me," he wrote. "I did write twice to encourage her along, as I think she is the pluckiest woman in Canada. . . . However, I am not waiting for any woman." After two days' rest, he admitted, "it took quite a bit of courage to start again." That day the Behans reached Savanne, 1,851 miles from Halifax, the half-way point on the great hike.

The Behans enjoyed being in the lead. They were, reported Jack, "feeling like two jack rabbits." Once again, Burkman's reports ceased abruptly and it was assumed he was again attempting a short cut. Actually, he had injured his hip falling off a slippery rail. It took him eight days to struggle on to Ignace, Ontario, which he reached on April 16, the day Babe Ruth hit his first home run of the 1921 season; the Behans had covered the same distance in four. The Dills, meanwhile, had arrived in Port Arthur and were closing fast.

Now the prairies beckoned — Winnipeg, then the third-largest city in Canada and after that Regina and Calgary. They were small towns then; Winnipeg, by far the largest, had fewer than 180,000 people. There were no skyscrapers. (The tallest building in the whole country was the new Royal Bank headquarters at King and Yonge in Toronto, whose nineteen storeys had recently overshadowed the fifteen-storey Dominion Bank across the way. Bankers, then as later, indulged in a literal form of one-upmanship.) Prairie horizons were dominated by church towers and grain elevators. Suburbs, drive-ins, shopping centres, supermarkets, motels, stop lights and parking lots all belonged to the future. The Canada which the 1921 hikers saw was still a country of villages and farms. More people lived in the rural areas than in the cities and one-third of the work force was employed in agriculture. The railway, not the highway, was the lifeline of the nation and the names of the villages that turn up in the hikers' logbooks Nemegos, Cavers, Molson, Lydiat, Elkhorn, Wapella, Herbert, Enfold, Gleichen — have a musty, nostalgic ring to them; most of them are long gone, by-passed and left to shrivel away by later ribbons of asphalt.

The Behans reached Winnipeg on April 20 and promptly bathed their feet in the cold waters of the Red River. Burkman, recovered from his injury, had walked forty-five miles to Kenora that day and filed a report that had some of the flavour of a subtitle from one of William S. Hart's immensely popular western films: "I passed through several towns so early in the morning that the inhabitants were sleeping soundly, and the lone hiker departed without stopping to be greeted."

But Burkman's reports were growing terser as his daily mileage rates became more uneven. It became obvious that his morale was weakening and that he was reluctant to reveal how quickly he was falling behind. Even though the Behans took two days off to visit old army buddies in Winnipeg, Burkman was still a week behind them when he reached the prairie capital. The Dills, however, were picking up speed. The worst rain-storm of the trip did not stop them, as it had stopped Charles Burkman; they walked for twenty-seven miles and, according to the irrepressible Jennie, "had the grandest time."

It took Burkman 101 days to reach Winnipeg. The Behans made it in 86. The Dills managed to do it in 89 and were beginning to realize that they might win the race. "It is the Behans we are trying to catch," Jennie wrote. "I feel rather sorry for Burkman, who has been travelling in hard luck of late."

The days of blizzards and drifts were over. In the prairie spring, the snow patches vanished to reveal the glistening black of the world's richest soil. Soon there would be new obstacles: biting sandstorms, oppressive heat waves, maddening clouds of mosquitoes. But in spite of that, all five hikers made the fastest time of the trip crossing the plains. Burkman's feet were a real problem; his continuing blisters caused him to lose ground to the others. On May 9, while the Dills were passing through Whitewood, Saskatchewan, they were hailed by a telephone operator who connected them with Burkman only twenty miles ahead at Broadview. Unable to struggle on farther, the bottoms of both heels almost raw, he waited for them to catch up. For the past two weeks, he confided, he had barely been able to walk. They left him behind the following day and hiked fifty-one miles to Indian Head.

So now the contest was between the Dills and the Behans, who realized they were being pressed hard by the wiry little Jennie. "We will surely have to step out," was the way Jack Behan put it. Because of the heat, they travelled at night, reaching Medicine Hat on May 17 after a thirty-two mile hike. But the Dills were still gaining, having walked forty-four miles that day. They continued to gain in the days that followed; by May 22 they had cut the Behans' lead to sixty-one miles. It was Jennie who was forcing the pace and she was clearly proud of that role, as her dispatch from Bassano, on May 23, indicates:

"Race well in hand. Few will ever know what the struggle meant to me, although I feel fine. . . . Frank will never forgive me for the manner in which I have made him walk. When he wanted to rest I wanted to keep going, and while I do not think that Frank is a quitter, I pride myself with the thought that I have kept him going. . . . When we passed Burkman I felt sorry for him. Then I got to saying to myself, "Well; he is a man and he should be able to look after himself." I have often thought that if Burkman had a wife he would make better progress. . . . This wonderful hike has taught me a great lesson which I shall endeavour to teach my sex when the contest is over. The subject is not what men can do women can do, but what men have done women CAN MORE THAN DO."

There was a problem looming up, however. Frank Dill had a host of friends in Calgary, which the Behans reached on May 24, Victoria Day — a more important holiday then than July 1. The Dills were only two days behind them and Jennie was beside herself with fear that Frank might want to dally with his cronies: "I do hope that he will not stay longer than to get a bite to eat. I tell him that we will have lots of time to stay off and see our friends on the way back and that we should devote every minute of the time now to the hike."

Her worst fears were about to be realized. The Behans slipped out of the sleeping town, still bedecked with flags and bunting, at 7 a.m. on the 25th. They walked forty-one miles into the foothills and slept that night at Morley. At that point the Dills were still hiking along. They reached Calgary at two in the morning, having covered fifty-two miles. Jennie was still alert enough to dispatch a wire to Halifax: "This has been the longest hike we have made. . . . Frank would have been quite willing to stop at the 40 mile mark but I said, 'No, Frank, I am hungry to win the race, and there are Beans ahead.' 'All right, girlie, I am after the Beans if it takes all the pork out of me.' " Jennie admitted that she was tired but added, proudly, that she would soon be back in Halifax "where you can all see what hiking has done for 'poor, frail Mrs. Dill.' "

To Jennie's grinding frustration, Frank's friends, all former Haligonians seeking their fortune in the cattle town, bore him off to the Kiwanis Club and kept him there until late afternoon. The couple was hard put to make ten miles in an unseasonable hailstorm before seeking refuge in a section house. There is more than a little bitterness still lingering in the report that Jennie filed almost a week later: "I do not think that I will ever forgive Frank for the long stay he made in Calgary, when he 'went out with the boys.' I told him not to stay more than 10 minutes and he stayed almost that many hours, and we lost practically a day and allowed the Behans to get out of our clutches for the time being." One suspects that the male readers of the Halifix *Herald* might at this point have been viewing the plight of Frank Dill with the same kind of sympathy which they had hitherto reserved for Charles Burkman, still plugging along gamely in the rear.

The Behans, meanwhile, having reached Banff at midnight, "so tired that we could hardly step over a match," were suffering nosebleeds brought on by the unaccustomed altitude. They were so exhausted that they could not move on the next day. Jack Behan had lost fourteen of his original 152 pounds. On May 28, with the Dills in Banff, the Behans were sleeping on the station platform at Lake Louise. The next day they crossed the Great Divide. Burkman at this point had passed through Calgary and was more cheerful — "in the pink of condition and in great spirits."

The race grew tighter. The Behans left Field on the morning of May 30; the Dills arrived on the same afternoon. Charles Burkman wrote: "Some, I suppose, will criticize me for letting a woman pass me, but few know what I have done since I left Halifax. It has been a hard, long, lonesome grind and many times I would have felt different if I had company, but I decided to stick and stick I will until I reach Vancouver." Anybody reading those words could not help but admire Charles Burkman.

At Beavermouth, the Dills lost a full day to the Behans; the next sleeping place was several hours distant and they did not have the strength to go further. That same day, June 1, was Clifford Behan's finest. He and his father were nearing Albert Canyon, within twenty miles of Revelstoke, when he fell to the ground, a spasm of pain searing his back. He urged his father to continue alone while he took the train to Revelstoke. Jack Behan went on "almost at a trot" and found Clifford in bed at the Revelstoke YMCA. A doctor had diagnosed his ailment as a cold in the muscle, probably caused by sleeping on the open platform at Lake Louise, and had prescribed rest.

Clifford stayed in bed for a few hours and then, so he wouldn't be accused of cheating, took the midnight train back to Albert Canyon. In the early hours of June 2 he repeated the walk alone to Revelstoke, only then realizing how difficult it must have been for Charles Burkman, trudging on, day after day, without human companionship. He arrived at 7 a.m. and after a few hours' sleep headed west with his father.

With the end in sight, the pace again began to accelerate. On June 3, each team walked twenty-six miles. On June 4, the Dills walked twenty-nine miles to Sicamous, British Columbia, but it was not enough. The Behans, afraid to sit down for more than a few minutes for fear of falling asleep, pushed on for fifty miles to Kamloops. At this point the Behans were 250 miles from Vancouver, the Dills, 334.

By June 8, the Dills had again pulled within a day of the leaders, but the pace was taking its toll. "It was a terrible ordeal we went through today," Jennie wired. The Behans were also exhausted. "The trip is wearing us both down," Jack reported. The Dills had set out, in their own words, "to see the world," but that objective had long since been discarded. The scenery was magnificent — the green expanse of Shuswap Lake, the frothing Fraser biting through its canyon — but there was no time now to look at the scenery; as Vancouver grew nearer the rest periods grew shorter. At Kanaka, 149 miles from their goal, Jennie reported gamely that she was in fine trim, "but poor Frank. He has had enough." Frank's feet were bothering him, "but he never complains." Burkman, meanwhile, racing across British Columbia, managed to walk forty-nine miles in one day to reach Kamloops and then pressed on again after only a few hours' rest.

On the morning of June 10, the Behans arrived at Harrison Mills, just sixty-one miles from Vancouver. They were determined to reach the city in one single, magnificent jump. They rested during the day and set off in the early evening in the soft Pacific rain. They walked continuously for twenty-two hours, a remarkable feat of endurance, and arrived in the heart of Vancouver at 2:30 p.m. on Saturday, June 11, to be swallowed up by an immense crowd. The pair were weatherbeaten, tanned and haggard with exhaustion. "It was hard," one reporter wrote, "to determine who was the father and who was the son."

But who had won the race? Jack Behan was confused about the kind of victory they had achieved. They had certainly come in first, but the Dills appeared to be making better time. They had covered eighty-eight miles in two days and were now at Harrison Mills, where they got the news of the Behans' arrival. Jennie was chagrined and again blamed that fatal stopover in Calgary. However, she added, "unless something entirely unexpected happens we will win the race anyway from a time standpoint." She did not congratulate the Behans.

At North Bend, on June 12, Burkman wired his own thoughts: "I know I'm beaten in the great trans-Canada hike, but I'm going to finish it out and believe me I'll make better time in the home stretch than any of the other hikers." And so he did, walking from Field to Vancouver in just twelve days. The Behans had taken fourteen; the Dills took sixteen.

Jennie and her husband reached Vancouver on Tuesday, June 14, at 5:30 p.m. Mrs. Dill, it was reported, "looked more as if she had been on a picnic." She was fifteen pounds lighter than when she had left Halifax, a lean, hard-muscled 113 pounds. The Halifax *Herald* immediately declared that she and Frank were the winners; they had taken 134 days to cross the continent, four days fewer than their rivals, whom Jennie accused of cheating by sneaking aboard a train on the last few miles of their trip in order not to be defeated by a woman. It is a charge for which there is no substantiation.

Burkman was only a few days behind the Dills and he, too, received a warm welcome. He had taken 150 days to cross the country, two months shorter than the hike he had originally planned. During that period, other events of greater significance had occupied the headlines. In Boston, two anarchists, Nicola Sacco, a fish pedlar, and Bartolomeo Vanzetti, a shoemaker, were arrested for murder; their trial would become a political *cause célèbre*. Elsewhere, Marie Stopes was organizing the Birth Control League of America. And in May, in a barn near Guelph, Ontario, the Communist Party of Canada held its charter meeting.

A reception for all five followed and a group portrait was taken to commemorate the event. In the coarse-screened photograph the four men looked remarkably

40

alike in their straw hats and cloth caps: clean-shaven, square-jawed Canadians, a little on the rustic side, totally unremarkable. Only Jennie stands out, standing a little forward of the others; and on those dark, mannish features there is something very akin to a smirk of triumph.

Once they had stopped walking, the hikers ceased to be newsworthy and all references to them vanished from the papers. None made money from the feat; and there is no evidence that the promises made at the height of the publicity ($500 from Halifax businessmen if Burkman made it in six months; "thousands" from a calendar company if Jack Behan made it in five) were ever fulfilled. In fact, the hike probably cost all the contestants some money. The Dills, for instance, spent five hundred dollars — a substantial sum in those days — and this was only partially defrayed by postcard sales.

Once the hike was over all five vanished into obscurity. Burkman, apparently, remained in Montreal; his name, as far as can be discovered, never again appeared in the newspapers. Frank Dill lived for only a few years after the event; he died in 1928. Jennie remarried and died in Halifax in 1941. The Behans, who outlived the others, moved to Massachusetts, where Jack Behan, aged eighty, was interviewed in 1956. It was he who had the last word on the great cross-Canada hike:

"We came home broke, our families in debt and we couldn't get work," he said. "We had to move to the States to pay our debts."

2

The Pirate of the St. Lawrence

History has an odd way of turning rogues and villains into popular heroes. Blackguards, whose very names were once a stench in the nostrils of upright citizens, become dry-cleaned by the passage of time to emerge, after a century or so, as profiles on bas-reliefs, their exploits honoured by ribbon-cutting aldermen and their reputations scrubbed up by local journalists, brochure-writers, and even historians.

Such has been the fate of William Johnston, a thief, plunderer, vandal, kidnapper and pirate. Pure longevity turned Johnston into an honoured citizen; when he died, respected and even loved at the age of eighty-eight, he had outlived all of his bitterest enemies. Another half-century went by and he was memorialized by the very country he had loathed so much, with the inevitable bronze plaque, unveiled by the inevitable flitch of civic dignitaries.

If, in the words of another Johnson (Samuel), patriotism is the last refuge of the scoundrel, then William was as black a scoundrel as ever mounted a cannon on a longboat; his patriotism seems to have been little more than a front for his own acquisitive interests. He was called every name in the lexicon of villainy: rogue, rascal, traitor, turncoat, rotter and wretch. A renegade

Canadian, he pillaged farms, burned ships, chopped off men's fingers and terrorized the border, all in the name of loyalty to his adopted country, the United States. In return for this loyalty he was able to walk the streets of French Creek, New York, heavily armed with knives and pistols, and to carry out snatch-and-grab raids from his fortress in the Thousand Islands without being apprehended or betrayed. But of his main objective there was little doubt; it was booty, and of that he got his share.

Still, it is difficult not to admire him. After all, my country has produced few, if any, pirates and this particular one was everything a pirate should be. He was tough, bold, colourful and dashing — a swarthy, bullet-headed rapscallion, blessed with the traditional pirate's flair for eluding his clumsier pursuers. Again and again, Bill Johnston was able to evade capture. No jail, it seemed, could hold him.

Moreover, to add a touch of spice to his legend, there is a beautiful daughter lurking offstage. She aids him in his escapes. She watches out for his enemies through a telescope from her home in French Creek. She sends him signals in a specially designed Morse-style code. She secretly dispatches food and provisions when he hides out in the watery labyrinth of the Thousand Islands. Small wonder, then, that the saga of Bill Johnston inspired at least two novels, a stage play and a sheaf of popular folk songs.

Bill Johnston was born a Canadian in 1782 at Three Rivers, Quebec, and raised not far from Kingston, the chief naval base for Lake Ontario and later the capital of Upper Canada. There he went into the freighting business, which meant that he was also up to his ears in the smuggling business. Most border freighters in those times were also smugglers, a fairly honourable profession then as it may be still. Protective tariffs on both sides of the border made it profitable. In 1810, Bill Johnston married an American girl, Ann Randolph. According to his later, sardonic account, this caused him to be "looked upon with a jealous eye by the more loyal subjects of His Most Gracious Majesty, George III, and my acts . . . closely watched by the slaves of the despot. . . ."

That's as may be. It is certainly true that after war broke out between Great Britain and the United States in June 1812, he *was* watched carefully by Canadian authorities who felt, not without evidence, that he was more than a little sympathetic to the Yankee cause. He was, after all, consorting with Americans, albeit American smugglers. In November, he was arrested on suspicion, held for twelve hours, and then released for lack of evidence.

The following June, he was clapped in jail again. He had taken an interest in bailing out men who had "rendered themselves obnoxious to the police by their intercourse and conversations with the damned Yankees." In those days, the Yankees were hated by the Canadians as much as the Germans were in two world wars that followed. Johnston's motives here are subject to interpretation. He may well have been a Yankee-lover — he certainly became one; or he may have been a humanitarian, distressed by the conditions in the Kingston prison — conditions so bad that one man, captured with frozen feet, received so little attention that he was later forced to have them amputated.

Johnston was told that he would be held in jail for the duration of the hostilities. Almost immediately he engineered the first of his many jail breaks. In those days, Kingston was encompassed not by fertile farms but by heavy brush, a perfect hiding place for a fugitive. Here Johnston found many like himself, mostly Americans who wanted to get back to their own country and avoid internment. Half a dozen of them came across an old birchbark canoe. In this flimsy craft Johnston determined to escape across Lake Ontario to the American shore. It was a daring and hazardous plan. None was an experienced canoeman and they faced thirty-six miles of open, choppy waters. Fortunately they encountered an American warship, which picked them up and took them to Sackets Harbor, New York.

Bill Johnston arrived on the American side, harbouring an intense hatred of his former countrymen and owning nothing but the clothes he was wearing. He had lost everything — his property was confiscated, his family beggared and his subsequent pleas for reparation ignored. The British government might perhaps have saved itself endless trouble and cost if it had made some restitution to Bill Johnston; it did not do so.

Johnston wanted revenge and he got it; for the duration of the War of 1812, he served as a spy for the Americans. In a fast, six-oared barge, he and his gang darted about the familiar waters of the Thousand Islands, attacking small craft, pillaging farms and intercepting messages. On one occasion, he robbed the mail coach between Kingston and Gananoque, stripping the unfortunate passengers of their clothing and tying the coachman to a tree; he passed the captured military messages on to the American authorities. Another time, he captured a dragoon carrying official papers, shot his horse and drove the man away on foot to wander through the bush. He was far too slippery to be trapped. Once, when he was driven ashore by a gale, his entire crew was apprehended; but Johnston managed to get away and flee across the lake, again by birchbark canoe.

After these depredations, it was not possible for him to return to his native land. He settled down in French Creek (which was to become Clayton, New York), a smugglers' haven directly across the lake from Gananoque. It is likely that in this little lakeside hamlet — it had scarcely more than two streets — every man, woman and child benefitted in some way from smuggling. Certainly Johnston did. At that time, the Thousand Islands were still covered with dense forests and thick underbrush, forming a maze of narrow wriggling channels, tiny hidden coves, protected tree-shaded bays and rocky promontories. No more secure retreat for freebooters could be imagined. By 1838, after the collapse of the Upper Canada Rebellion, the larger islands were inhabited by lawless bands of semi-brigands, their numbers augmented by as many as a thousand rebel refugees. It was said that this group could muster a hundred boats, the swiftest being Johnston's own, so lightly built it could be carried on men's backs across the islands, many of which served as his personal fiefs.

Johnston had one hideout on Wells Island, now known as Wellesley, another on Abel Island and, on the Canadian side, a personal redoubt which he called Fort Wallace on an island now known as Fort Wallace Island.

His daughter Kate became known as the Queen of the Thousand Islands. Still in her teens, she could handle a boat and a rifle as well as any man. As the years went by, her story became romanticized. She was generally referred to as "beautiful" or "handsome," words that journalists tend to apply to any woman under the age of sixty. Perhaps she was at sixteen; but in her later pictures she has the profile of a drill sergeant.

That was the situation on the St. Lawrence in 1838, the year following the abortive attempt by that difficult if dedicated Toronto editor, William Lyon Mackenzie, to overthrow the colonial government of Upper Canada. After Mackenzie's defeat, some of his followers who escaped capture lit out for Navy Island on the

Niagara River, just above the Falls, and there helped set up his so-called Provisional Government of Upper Canada. From this island the nucleus of the Patriot Movement, as it was known, was formed in the states adjacent to the Canadian border.

This fascinating underground venture was really a loose group of various secret societies with such names as "Hunters and Chasers on the Eastern Frontier" and "Lodges of Patriotic Masons." The total membership of the Hunters, to use a general appellation, has been variously estimated at anywhere from fifteen thousand to two hundred thousand persons — expatriate Canadians, rebels, Americans who wanted to free Canada from the British yoke, vagabonds, renegades and self-serving adventurers whose main objective was loot.

The Patriots had a flag with two stars, representing Upper and Lower Canada, and they also had an army and navy of sorts; but they lacked any strong unified control. The military commander was a curious American blueblood, Rensselaer Van Rensselaer, described by a contemporary as "a degenerate scion of an old Dutch family . . . a young man of more ambition than brains." Among other things, he was a drunkard. The naval commander, who bore the title of Commodore of the Patriot Army of the East, was made of sterner stuff; he was none other than Bill Johnston, described as a "gentleman of intelligence, equal to fifty ordinary men" who could raise "two hundred bold volunteers as ever drew a trigger."

It soon became clear that if the Patriot Army was going to fight a war it would have to be fought in Bill Johnston's territory. Early in 1838, the British drove the rebels out of their base on Navy Island and the scene shifted to the Thousand Islands. It was from this jumping-off place that Van Rensselaer and Johnston, with their ragtag-and-bobtail crew, set about giving expression to an ambition that seems, at least in retrospect, to have been as harebrained as it was desperate. They planned nothing less than the invasion, capture and subjugation of Upper Canada. They would free it from British rule and transform it into a republic.

The strategy was sound enough, even though the subsequent execution was abominable. The main point of the attack would be Kingston, the key to Upper Canada, and specifically its citadel, Fort Henry, built on a promontory overlooking the river. Apparently impregnable, the great fortress had one weak point: in wintertime it could be attacked from the south by the ice bridge which forms across the St. Lawrence. The tactics called for the Patriots to launch their invasion from nearby Hickory Island, feinting at Gananoque to draw the militia out of Kingston, and then to attack the unguarded Upper Canadian city. Key objectives would include the citadel and the penitentiary, whose prisoners (especially the political ones), it was assumed, would join the revolt on the side of their liberators.

In addition, the Patriots had devised a remarkably modern ploy. A century before the word was coined, they determined that a fifth column of "traders" and "tourists" would enter Kingston in the days before the attack. When the Patriot Army arrived, these strangers would rise up and capture the town.

It is just possible that this plan might have succeeded, at least initially, and that Kingston could have come under rebel rule. Certainly, the Patriots were well armed. On February 19, they broke into the American armoury at Watertown, New York, and seized four hundred weapons. This was followed by successful attacks on two other state armouries. But there was one fatal flaw in the enterprise. To succeed, such an attack must be planned and executed in the utmost secrecy —

and of that there was none. A child of ten, seeking his father in any one of the numberless border taverns, would know in the first buzz of overheard conversation that February 22, 1838, was the date planned for the capture of Kingston.

Every man, woman and child along the American side of the St. Lawrence apparently knew it, including a young school teacher named Elizabeth Barnett who acted upon the knowledge immediately — thus introducing into an otherwise mediocre affair a dash of genuine romance. Miss Barnett was an American who lived and worked in Kingston. On February 20, while visiting relatives in French Creek she heard the rebels openly discussing the forthcoming adventure. Miss Barnett had no wish to see her Canadian friends murdered in their beds. Accordingly, she cut short her visit, crossed the ice of the St. Lawrence — a remarkable feat of courage and endurance — aroused the community and got word to the military command.

Terror and even panic followed. The militiamen were called up immediately from all neighbouring counties and hastily drilled. Fort Henry, which had been going a little to seed, was spruced up. Arms were polished, ammunition ordered, guns scoured, ovens put into working order. A parade of fearful citizens shortly appeared bearing silver plate and valuable papers for safekeeping. A watch was placed on all suspected traitors. Holes were punched in the ice near Wolfe Island to prevent sleighs from crossing the river. Barricades were erected on country roads. Mohawk Indians were engaged as scouts. Signal rockets were readied. Then, on the fateful night of February 22, the little community waited for the worst: "Never was such a night known in Kingston. Not a soul slept; fire and sword were momentarily looked for."

Nothing whatsoever happened. On Hickory Island, the mustering point for the great Patriot Army, an ill-clad, ill-disciplined and ill-led shamble of men stood with chattering teeth, answering their names to the roll call. On the first call, only eighty-five answered; on the second, seventy-one; on the third, a mere thirty-five. It was just too cold to fight; besides, General Van Rensselaer was clearly drunk. The troops who had crossed the ice on foot and by sleigh melted away in the dark. When a British cavalry patrol gingerly began to investigate the island early next morning, it found only a few shivering stragglers and several large bags of scrap iron intended for use as shot.

Miss Barnett's warning had been timely and accurate but, because of rebel bungling, totally unnecessary. It is pleasant to report that she met and fell in love with one of the militiamen who had swiftly donned uniforms to repel the attack. Subsequently she married him and presumably lived happily ever after until her death in 1906, in Gananoque, at the age of ninety-two — an unsung Laura Secord.

As for Bill Johnston, he was furious at Van Rensselaer. He swore then and there that he would never again take part in a formal attack but would fight a guerrilla war of raid and ambush based on secrecy and speed. The key to his purpose would be his famous pirate craft, a gaudy creation, with a black hull, a white top, a broad yellow side stripe and a crimson interior. Two strong men could carry this twenty-eight-foot longboat through the underbrush of the Thousand Islands; its twelve oars made it the fastest of its kind on the lakes. Now Bill Johnston was ready to carry on a one-man war against Canadian shipping — a war that was aided by the complacency of the American authorities, who were still passively hostile to the British.

Johnston's plans were nothing if not grandiose. His private war reached its zenith just after midnight on May 30, 1838. He determined to hijack one of the fastest and largest ships then plying the lakes — the new passenger steamer *Sir Robert Peel*. A narrow vessel, 160 feet long, of light draught, she had been launched the previous year at Brockville for service on the St. Lawrence and Lake Ontario. The attack was later memorialized in song and legend:

> It was on a Thursday morning, the thirtieth of May,
> While quietly at anchor the British steamer lay
> Among the Thousand Islands, nearer to the Yankee shore —
> That land of peace and plenty, which free men all adore.
> That morn no breath of air disturbed the waters round the keel
> Of that fine British steamer, the proud *Sir Robert Peel;*
> Within the arms of slumber her passengers were laid,
> Unconscious of their danger while riding o'er the wave . . .

The *Peel* was proceeding upriver from Brockville to Kingston when the attack came. She had some twenty-five first-class passengers on board and forty more in steerage, all sound asleep as the poem says. The night was dark and rainswept, exactly the kind of Gothic evening with which readers of the novels of the day were familiar. The ship docked at Wells Island, the largest of all, to take on wood — a pause of two hours during which time the captain should have been thoroughly alerted to the danger. For one thing, one of the passengers had already received warnings of impending violence — warnings which went unheeded. For another, the man in charge of the woodpile, one Ripley, told the captain that he had seen a longboat filled with men running past the island at two or three different times during the night and that when the steamer first appeared someone in the boat had cried: "There she is!" A megaphoned warning could scarcely have made the situation clearer. But when Ripley urged the captain not to tarry, he replied that "if there were not more than 100 or 150 he did not fear them." There were, as it shortly developed, far fewer than that.

The attack came at two in the morning. A group of men burst from the bush, costumed as Indians, complete with feathers and warpaint, but uttering very un-Indian cries, "Revenge for the *Caroline!*" being the main one — a reference to the American-owned ship which the British had shot to pieces on the Niagara River the previous year when she was attempting to run supplies to the rebels holed up on Navy Island.

How many were there? As usual in such cases, the invaders, in order to make the attack seem all the bolder, minimized the number, while their terrified victims inflated it. One of the passengers thought there were one hundred and fifty. The beleaguered captain put the figure between fifty and seventy. Bill Johnston, who planned the attack, reported a modest thirteen: so much for the reliability of eyewitnesses. A later investigation set the figure at twenty-five.

The pirates were armed with muskets, bayonets, swords and pikestaffs. They addressed each other by code names, such as Tecumseh, Nelson, Admiral Benbow, Judge Lynch and Bolivar, but the unmistakeable growl of Bill Johnston could be heard above the din. They ordered the captain and his passengers ashore. One passenger, Colonel Richard Fraser, was almost murdered: hearing a noise on deck, he thought that a quarrel had broken out among the crew. Then he found his cabin door forced open, his windows smashed and five men — four with bayonets and the leader with a sword — towering over his bed. The swordsman spotted the colonel's military tunic hanging on a nail. "He's a British officer. Run him through!" he shouted. The colonel must have had remarkable powers of persuasion. Choosing discretion over valour he disavowed the uniform; the rebels, either through gullibility or compassion, spared his life, merely knocking him to the floor and kicking him several times.

Men and women, many of them half-naked, were herded brusquely onto the deck and refused permission to return to their cabins for warm clothes, trunks or jewelry. There were insults to the ladies: "their cries were truly distressing," to quote a contemporary account. No officer or gentleman could stand for that; a Captain Bullock, taking his life in his hands, "rushed fearlessly among the ruffians to secure the females from insults." Shivering in night attire, the entire company was shoved off the ship and herded into a little shack on the dock where they stayed, embarrassed and numb with cold, until five a.m. when the steamer *Oneida* picked them up and took them to Kingston.

Johnston's plan, apparently, was to use the captured ship as the nucleus of a navy with which he hoped to ravage Canada. Transformed into a pirate warship, the *Peel* would mount an attack on a second vessel, the *Great Britain.* That scheme came to nothing because Johnston, who was a good man in a longboat, knew very little about larger craft. He set off in the *Peel* from Wells Island but ran her onto a shoal almost immediately. Unable to dislodge her, he and his men proceeded to pillage her and then put her to the torch, before departing for Abel Island in their small boats.

The *Peel* was still burning when the passengers were rescued and her charred hulk was visible at that spot for decades after.

The loss was considerable. Many of the passengers had brought small fortunes in banknotes, jewelry and other valuables — people lugged their silver plate about with them in those days. The estimated personal losses amounted to $75,000, an enormous sum in 1838. In addition, there was another $100,000 intended for the paymasters of the Upper Canadian forces.

This was loot on a grand scale. For many years after, on feast days and special occasions, it was said that members of the Johnston family wore jewelry and gaudy clothing plundered from the *Sir Robert Peel*. Certainly, from that day forward, Bill Johnston carried the ship's colours on his person.

This act of piracy was greeted as a rebel triumph by sympathizers south of the border:

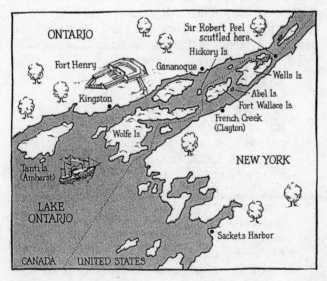

No more upon the waters, will evermore be
    seen
That noble British steamer, Ontario's
    proudest Queen;
Yet oft within their bosoms that gallant
    band shall feel
The pride of righteous justice for burning
    Robert Peel.

In British Canada, however, the sentiment was righteous outrage. Sir George Arthur, the Lieutenant-Governor of Upper Canada, felt it necessary to caution Canadians against any anti-American retaliation; the last thing he wanted was an international incident. Lord Durham, who had just been appointed Governor General, put a price of five thousand dollars on Bill Johnston's head. The Governor of New York, awakened at last to the pirate's lawlessness, added another five hundred to reassure the British that the United States did not condone his actions. None of this bothered Johnston in the slightest. Instead of fleeing, he proceeded to indulge in one of those bold gestures that make men legends in their own time: he issued a public proclamation taking full responsibility for the crime.

To all whom it may concern

I, William Johnston, a natural born citizen of Upper Canada, certify that I hold a commission in the Patriot Service of Upper Canada, as Commander-in-Chief of the naval forces and flotilla. I commanded the expedition that attacked and destroyed the steamer *Sir Robert Peel.* The men under my command in that expedition were nearly all natural born English subjects; the exceptions were volunteers for the expedition.
My headquarters were on an island in the St. Lawrence, without the jurisdiction of the

United States, at a place named by me Fort Wallace. I am well acquainted with the boundary line, and know which of the islands do, and do not, belong to the United States; and in the selection of the island I wished to be positive, and not locate within the jurisdiction of the United States. . . .

I yet hold possession of that station, and we also occupy a station some twenty or more miles from the boundary of the United States, in what was His Majesty's dominions, until it was occupied by us. The object of my movements is the independence of Canada. I am not at war with the commerce or prosperity of citizens of the United States.

Signed, the tenth day of June, 1838

WILLIAM JOHNSTON

In spite of this bold pronouncement, Johnston was neither discovered nor betrayed. From his lair among the Islands, he managed to create such a sense of menace that the Speaker of the Upper Canadian Assembly, Sir Allan MacNab, an old foe of the rebels, passing through Watertown en route to England, thought it prudent to disguise himself as a common labourer. Twelve of Johnston's men were captured eventually, loaded down with booty from the *Peel,* and one of them was tried on six counts of arson. It could not have been much of a trial; the American jury acquitted him and the others were later released. Meanwhile, President Van Buren ordered U.S. federal troops to Sackets Harbor and armed men placed on lake steamers to prevent further attacks.

This did not faze Bill Johnston. With his sixteen-oared boats, all mounted with cannon, and his parties of armed raiders, he kept the frontier in a continual state of agitation. Sorties of sailors were dispatched from Kingston to capture him; they were driven off by fire from an unseen foe. One adjutant, on a secret expedition, discovered a concealed bivouac on an almost inaccessible islet near the northwest part of a channel close to Fidler's Elbow; here he spotted cleverly constructed inclined planes up on which boats could be drawn. Lieutenant-Colonel Sir Richard Bonnycastle, apprised of this, mounted an expedition to capture Johnston and his men but all he found were the smouldering fires of his quarry. The pirate had a spy in the army's midst, who reported every move the British made.

On June 7, Johnston's gang appeared at Tanti (now Amherst) Island, only a few miles from Kingston, and plundered three farmhouses. One settler, trying to defend himself, was shot in the hand, losing three fingers. A week later, Johnston was reported at Ducks Island at the foot of the lake. Shortly after, he struck terror by appearing in the Brockville area. A second attack on a farmhouse on Tanti Island followed. Another farmer lost part of his hand — Johnston had a habit of maiming men in this way with his 12-inch, ivory-handled Bowie knife so they could no longer pull a trigger — and his son died of wounds. By this time, American sympathizers were referring to him as Sir William, a reference to the fact that the British had knighted MacNab, then commander of the Niagara forces, after the destruction of the *Caroline*.

Again and again Johnston eluded capture. On July 4, 1838, a combined British-American force of eighty men had him surrounded. Johnston and most of his gang gave them the slip, vanishing into the dense brush; only two were captured. At Fort Wallace, he maintained a sort of feudal sovereignty aided by sixteen-year-old Kate, who, from her home in French Creek, kept him informed of the whereabouts of his would-be captors.

In November of that year, there was another abortive attempt by a group of Hunters Lodges to invade Canada by way of Prescott. Again Johnston was involved, this time in charge of a vessel called the *Charlotte of Oswego*. Again his poor seamanship caused the ship to run aground, where she was quickly attacked and captured by the British. And again he escaped into the rainswept dark with thirty men and considerable ammunition.

This time he was at large for only five days. American troops, hot on his trail, seized his son and his boat and then flushed him from the woods. Even then he was able to dictate his own surrender terms, insisting that his son and not the soldiers take his weapons; he was carrying a twelve-shot Cochrane rifle, two large pistols, four small pistols and his Bowie knife. In Auburn he was put on trial for his part in the Prescott raid. The proceedings were casual, and Johnston was released for "lack of evidence." This was too much for the U.S. marshal, a man named Garrow, who had been on his trail for months. Garrow immediately arrested Johnston on earlier charges. But to arrest him was one thing, to hold him, another. Before dawn, Johnston had escaped from jail again and was miles away. But this time he was not close enough to his familiar Thousand Islands to elude capture for long. A few days later he was seized again, jailed and tried once more. He was given a year in prison and fined $250, not a very onerous sentence for a man who had killed, maimed, looted and kidnapped.

This time Johnston stayed in jail — not, apparently, because escape was impossible but rather because jail was pleasantly informal. His daughter Kate was allowed to visit him, to look after him and to share his cell. After a few weeks Johnston was to be observed strolling about the streets of Albany, free as the zephyrs that scud over the lakes. On January 23, 1839, there was an even more remarkable incident. A theatrical benefit was held in Johnston's honour. The play itself, *Bill Johnston, The Hero of the Lakes,* was a highly flattering account of his own derring-do. It was announced that Johnston himself would appear as the patron of the drama; and appear he did, with his daughter, seated prominently in the audience, applauding away, and surrounded by friends and well-wishers.

A few months later, with only half of his sentence served, Bill Johnston, tiring of prison, vanished again. As usual, he hid out in the Thousand Islands, to emerge at length from his redoubt with a petition for his pardon signed by scores of adherents. Off the jailbird went to Washington and presented the petition to the White House. President Van Buren did not sign it, but the incoming chief executive, William Henry Harrison, an implacable foe of the British during the War of 1812, was pleased to grant the pirate his unconditional release.

Not only did Johnston get a government pardon; he was also granted a government job as keeper of the Rock Island lighthouse, ironically located on the very spot where he and his gang of marauders had burned the *Peel.* Later on he became a tavernkeeper at French Creek and returned, so it was said, to his old trade of smuggling. And here, some years later, Sir James Alexander, searching for deserters from the British garrison at Kingston, encountered him and left the following description:

"The veritable Bill Johnston . . . now stood before me at the corner of his son's house, which, by the way, contained Bill's very handsome daughter, the Queen of the Thousand Isles, who used intrepidly to row with supplies for her parent, whilst he was dodging the man-of-war's boats.

"Bill, in 1843, was about sixty years of age but he was hale, and straight, and ruddy; his nose was sharp, as were his features generally, and his eyes were keen and piercing; his lips compressed and receding; his height about five feet ten inches; he wore a broad-rimmed black hat, black stock and vest, frock and trousers of dark duffle. His discourse with me was principally about boats; he offered to sell his galley for sixty dollars, "not a cent less." ... He now offered to row or sail against any boat on either side of the St. Lawrence, adding that his galley would not leak a gill, and was altogether 'first rate.' "

It was during this encounter that Sir James was faced with a distressing puzzle: Could all the fooferaw connected with the Johnston nuisance — the border raids, the maimings, the loss of a ship and untold sums in money and goods, the deploying of troops and seamen, the extra guards and posted rewards — could all of that been easily avoided if the British had been less stiff-necked about Johnston at the outset? That was Johnston's contention years after the event. He insisted to Sir James that he could have been bought off early in the game for the sum of fifteen hundred pounds, which was the amount of his claim against the government in 1813, after he fled from Canada.

Did the British, then, pay through their noses for the cavalier treatment of the future pirate? "What has been gained by this rebellion?" someone once asked Johnston with more than a trace of contempt. To which the pirate replied; "Do you call the expenditure of four millions of British cash nothing? That is what our side gained."

A good deal of that, of course, went into Johnston's own pocket, but this only added to the legend that began to flourish during his own lifetime. At least two romantic novels, *The Empress of the Isles* and *The Prisoner of the Border,* were written in the 1850s, based on his exploits. As for the pirate himself, he lived on to the ripe age of eighty-eight, his villainies long forgotten, his offspring respected as "first families." One son, John Johnston, became a prominent banker and New York Assemblyman, with the word "Honorable" in front of his name. Another became the proprietor of the Walton House, then the most popular hostelry in Clayton. Kate, the Queen of the Isles, married the brother-in-law of the Honorable John and had five children of her own. By the time she died, at the age of sixty, Johnston was firmly enshrined as a minor American hero.

The remarkable coda to the story is that in 1958, he became a minor Canadian figure as well. One hundred and twenty years after he burned the *Peel,* the Ontario government put up a plaque to his memory directly across from the site of that malfeasance. Local politicians were delighted to preside at its unveiling.

3

Sailing Alone Around the World

May 6, 1896 — the South Pacific: The sun burnishes the sky and the sea is limitless. In all the vast circle of the ocean, there is only a single moving speck, a sloop barely thirty-six feet long, aptly named the *Spray,* sliding westward on the hot breath of a tropic breeze, like a fly scudding across a polished table. Her decks are empty. There is no one at the helm. Is she, then, a ghost ship conjured up, like a mirage, in the mind of a fever victim? Scarcely; for in all that infinity of water there is none to mark her passage. She is alone in the immensity of the southern sea and she will remain alone and unobserved for seventy-two days — seventy-two days without a stop, from Robinson Crusoe's fertile isle of Juan Fernandez to the coconut palms of Samoa, seven thousand miles as the gull flies. And this is only a small part (one-sixth, to be precise) of a long and remarkable odyssey.

Old Slocum sits hidden in his book-lined cabin aboard the *Spray,* totally alone, as he has been since he departed Yarmouth, Nova Scotia, the previous July. Old? Actually he is fifty-two. It is just that his face is leathered by the sea and the winds — the skin nut brown and crinkled, the chin and ears a little grizzled — that his hands are gnarled and knobby, that his body is all

63

bone and muscle, and that he has already lived a life-time and more. Supple as a bobcat, agile as a monkey, he is the most experienced saltwater man of his age, but also an anachronism — a committed sailor in a world that has done with sail. The days of the clippers have ended. The bustling ports of Saint John, Lunenberg and Halifax have wound down. The big rafts of squared timbers have all but vanished from the Ottawa River and life is beginning to speed up. In Boston, the first American subway has just been completed. In Detroit, the first commercial automobile has just made its appearance. And on the sand dunes of northern Indiana, a man named Octave Chanute is ushering in a new age of flight, with the development of a successful glider. Joshua Slocum, the out-of-work sea captain, cares nothing for this; too old a bird to learn new tricks, he has chosen this moment to do the impossible. He is sailing alone around the world.

He is acutely aware of being alone — alone with the vastness of the horizons, the play of the winds, the wells and currents of the sea, the moving sun and the wheeling stars. The very coral reefs, he will write, keep him company. His living companions are the flying fish that slap onto the glistening deck each night, the whales that cruise majestically past, the sharks, whom he calls "the tigers of the sea," and the birds: the men o'war soaring high above him, the red-billed tropic birds wheeling and arcing in the sky, the gulls and boobies screeching in his wake and settling on his mast.

With the sun rising astern and the Southern Cross abeam every night, he sprawls out in his cabin (for the *Spray* which he has fashioned with his own hands, miraculously steers herself), reading his way through his library (Lamb, Addison, Gibbon, Coleridge, Cervantes, Darwin, Burns, Longfellow and his two greatest favourites, Robert Louis Stevenson and Mark Twain), poking about in his galley (trying his hand at fish stew and hot biscuits to lighten his regular diet of potatoes and salt cod) and occasionally (very occasionally) digging out his sextant to check his latitude.

Carried forward as if on a vast, mysterious stream, he is at one with his surroundings, feeling "the buoyancy of His hand who made all the worlds" — Old Slocum, veteran of a hundred sea adventures, survivor of a dozen murderous encounters, master of the ocean's finest sailing vessels (gone, now, every last one of them, sunk, beached, stove in, ravished, abandoned to the rot); Old Slocum on the greatest adventure of all, an adventure no one else has dared; Old Slocum, owner, master, mate and crew of a cockleshell, sailing all by himself around the world. Forty-six thousand miles. Three full years. Another lifetime.

For what else is there left for Slocum? He has been everywhere, seen everything, done everything — everything but this. He has been around the world five times on more ships than his hands have fingers, shuttling cargoes across the seven seas: he has stacked hay out of Montevideo, salt cod out of Kamchatka, coal from Nagasaki to Vladivostock, gunpowder from Shanghai to Taiwan, natural ice from Hakodati, sugar from the Philippines, timber out of Brazil. He has broken three mutinies (killed one man, maimed another) and survived outbreaks of fever, cholera and smallpox, not to mention storms, typhoons, hidden reefs and the thunderclap explosion of Krakatoa, which killed thirty-six thousand persons in August of 1883, but not Joshua Slocum, who managed to sail the *Northern Light* past the smoking island three days before the eruption that filled the sea around him with floating pumice and buried his decks in hot ash.

He has seen everything, met everybody, from Garfield Hayes, president of the United States, to Bully

Hayes, South Seas pirate and blackbirder. He has made fortunes. His race to catch the crack mail schooner out of Honolulu brought him a five thousand dollar sack of gold. But he has also lost everything. The lovely barque *Aquidneck*, "as close to a yacht as a merchantman can be," with its parquetry floors, its grand piano and its blue and gold staterooms, was battered to pieces off the coast of Brazil with a full cargo of timber, leaving Slocum a pauper.

Since the age of sixteen, Slocum's whole existence has revolved around salt water. All seven of his children were born at sea or in foreign ports and the wife who bore them, the marvellous and beautiful Virginia — who could kill a shark with a single shot from her .32 and who had sailed with him on every voyage — sickened and died at sea, leaving him "like a ship without a rudder." He had married again but it was never the same; Hettie, the new bride, sailed with him and the four surviving children on the most extraordinary voyage of all: fifty-five hundred miles from Brazil to the Carolines in the thirty-five-foot *Liberdade*, a weird cross between a Cape Anne dory and a Japanese sampan. But that was all for Hettie; she never went to sea again. Slocum closed the shutters on what had been a warm and congenial personality and set a solitary course for himself.

So here he is, all alone as he prefers to be — Joshua Slocum, a Bay of Fundy boy from Annapolis County, Nova Scotia, born in 1844 into the age of the clipper ships: a seaman at sixteen, a first mate at eighteen, master of his own ship at twenty-five and at thirty-seven, captain of the *Northern Light,* the finest sailing vessel afloat. Joshua Slocum, master mariner, washed up at fifty, stubbornly refusing to come to any accommodation with steam power or iron hulls, preferring to work as a carpenter in a shipyard but forced out of that, too, for want of a fifty-dollar union fee. Joshua Slocum, picking up odd jobs on Boston harbour boats and hating it, dreaming of the great days of canvas, when he was king of the ocean, dreaming and hating his work until, on one black day, an entire load of coal mixed with dirt ("Cape Horn berries" they call it) half-buries him. In that moment, Slocum, casting his mind back to the *Northern Light* (two thousand tons, three decks, 233 feet long, full-rigged), can stand it no more. He quits his job and determines to return to the sea. He will make the longest possible voyage in the smallest possible craft and he will do it all alone.

Spring, 1893: In a pasture at Fairhaven, not far from New Bedford, Massachusetts, the hulk of an ancient oyster sloop lies rotting in the grass. Slocum can have her; her owner, a retired whaler, is a friend. Like a sculptor gazing on a lump of Carrera marble, Slocum sees a new ship hidden somewhere in the old. He will keep very little of her — only the model, the lines and the name: *Spray.* He cuts a new timber from the woods at Poverty Point and replaces a rotting one, then another and another — new timbers for old until the hull itself is new. He cuts an oak for her keel (she had been a centre-boarder but a drop keel is too likely to ship water at sea). He hauls a spruce trunk from New Hampshire for her mast. He cuts down another oak from the pasture for her stem piece, so tough that months later it will split a coral patch in two at the Keeling Islands without a scratch to itself. People come to watch in astonishment as the new ship takes form from the carcass of the derelict: thirty-six feet, nine inches overall; fourteen feet, two inches, beam; four feet, two inches deep in the hold; nine tons net; rigged as a sloop — a big craft for a lone man to handle. She has no engine, no power windlass, and no navigational aids except for a compass, some charts, a sextant and taffrail logs. But there's a secret to her, which even Slocum doesn't yet know. Later yacht designers, analysing her dimensions, will conclude that he has hit upon a perfectly balanced vessel. Ballasted with cement, she will be almost impossible to capsize. He has worked on her for thirteen months, supporting himself with odd jobs in the intervals, and she has cost him exactly $553.62.

Though the *Spray* claims Boston as her home port, Slocum's voyage will really begin at Yarmouth, Nova Scotia. He has come up to the Bay of Fundy to spend a month in the home town he ran away from, more than a generation before. (His father, a Methodist deacon, came from Loyalist stock; his mother was a Digby lighthouse keeper's daughter.) He must decide now which way to circle the earth: westward, round the Horn, or eastward, through the Mediterranean, the Suez Canal and the Red Sea? He hesitates, chooses, changes his mind; he will go east. He is without a chronometer — he cannot afford the fifteen dollars it will cost to have his old one cleaned and reset. So he buys a tin clock in Yarmouth for a dollar; its face is smashed — no matter.

But he has food. He has two barrels of ship's bread soldered up in tin cans (it must be soaked six hours before he can make bread pudding). He has flour, baking powder, salt, pepper, mustard and curry. He has salt beef, salt pork, ham and dried codfish — real slabs of it, "thick as a board and broad as a side of sole leather." He has condensed milk in tins, butter in brine and muslin, eggs hermetically sealed, potatoes which he will roast in their jackets, sugar and tea, and coffee beans which he will grind himself. He will not need to buy fresh fruit, meat and vegetables: a man attempting such a voyage receives such perishables as gifts at every port he touches.

July 2, 1895: Slocum and the *Spray* clear Yarmouth harbour at a fast eight knots, scurrying to get clear of the track of the ocean liners which might run them down at night. He has designed a self-steering mechanism and discovers that it is successful beyond his wildest dreams. He had expected that the *Spray* would hold her course trimmed close to the wind, but now he finds that she can keep it up with her boom broad in a stiff breeze and a lumpy sea. It is a godsend. He can lash the helm and sleep while the sloop holds her course.

As the fog closes in (the familiar Atlantic fog of his childhood), it seems to Slocum that his past life is running before his eyes like a series of magic lantern slides. A babble of voices chatters in with the wind — all the voices he has heard in all the corners of the earth. The fog lifts, the weather clears, but he cannot shake off the realization that he is totally alone. He begins to shout commands, fearful that in the long days ahead he may lose his ability to speak; then, to keep himself company, he roars out sea chanties. The *Spray* races across the waters, leaving the biggest freighters in her wake, to the astonishment of their captains. Slocum's spirits begin to lift.

He reaches the Azores in just eighteen days. He has some newspaper dispatches to mail (he hopes to pay for the voyage by describing it in the press). He takes on a cargo of various fruits, the gift of the islanders, and sails off again, making a meal of fresh plums and old cheese — a combination that brings on a terrifying attack of stomach cramps. He barely has strength to haul down the mainsail and set the *Spray* on course when he falls to the cabin floor, delirious. For two days and two nights, his mind is wild with visions. The ghost of the pilot of Columbus's *Pinta* stands at the wheel talking to him. The ghost's advice is sound: don't mix plums with cheese. When he recovers, finally, he discovers the

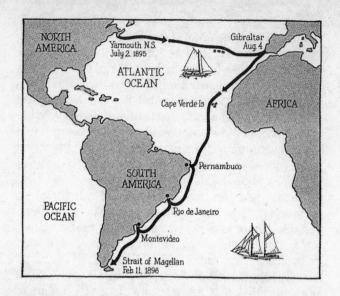

Spray is still on course, and going like a racehorse. He throws the plums overboard and dines on fish hash, stewed onions, pears and coffee. Later that day he harpoons and roasts a turtle, with fried potatoes on the side. When he reaches Gibralter on August 4, he finds that he has crossed the Atlantic in faster time than any vessel except for the big steamers.

And here he learns that he must turn back. The British officers who greet him, fête him, wine, dine and picnic him, urge him to avoid the Suez and the Red Sea. These narrow waterways are infested with pirates to whom a lone man in a small boat will be an easy victim. So Slocum must turn about and set the *Spray's* course westward for Brazil.

Irony of ironies! He is scarcely back in the Atlantic before he encounters pirates. A Spanish felucca is in his wake, manned by a gang of ruffians intent on plunder. He changes course; the felucca follows. He veers; the felucca veers. He puts on sail but the felucca, a swift and slender sailboat, continues to close. Slocum prepares for an unequal fight; and then a monstrous wave strikes both ships, tearing loose the *Spray's* boom. Slocum puts the helm hard down, pulls down the jib, hauls in the mainsail before it is shredded, and snatches up a rifle to ward off his attackers. He turns to fight and finds he has been saved by the elements: the same wave has torn away the felucca's mast.

He is totally used up, too tired even to cook a flying fish that has landed on his deck. Now he realizes, perhaps for the first time, that the voyage will call for "exertions ardent and lasting." In all his life he has never reached such a point of exhaustion. He sets the sloop on course, rolls into his bunk, and sleeps.

He sails with the tradewinds across the Atlantic, the helm lashed for most of the time, the little ship running without his hand. In his snug cabin he reads, writes, mends and cooks. He is still composing accounts of his adventures for the newspapers but there will be few takers. The Boston *Globe* prints three pieces only, then ceases; Slocum takes too long between dispatches. Newspaper readers have been tuned in to the modern journalism of Hearst and Pulitzer. Nelly Bly has already beaten the fictional record of Phineas Fogg by circling the globe in seventy-two days.

It takes Slocum forty days to recross the Atlantic. The voyage is so uneventful he feels himself again possessed by a sense of his isolation: *Leaving the Cape Verde Islands out of sight astern, I found myself once more sailing a lonely sea and in a solitude supreme all around. When I slept I dreamed that I was alone. This feeling never left me; but, sleeping or waking, I seemed always to know the position of the sloop, and I saw my vessel moving across the chart, which became a picture before me.*

Down the coast of South America past Uruguay: The *Spray* runs aground in hard sand. Slocum has fashioned a kind of dory for himself by sawing a proper dory in half and boarding up one end. In this stubby craft he sets out to free his ship. The leaky dory turns turtle. Slocum reaches for the gunwhale as she goes bottom up, for he suddenly realizes that he cannot swim, but remembering all the wiseacres who have predicted he will never return, he determines to survive. He hauls himself back onto the dory, rights her, paddles ashore, and with help frees the sloop.

Down the coast of Patagonia heading for the Horn: The seas are in a fury. A single, towering wave, masthead high, comes roaring down, swamping the *Spray*. She reels under the impact, rights herself and sails on.

Into the Strait of Magellan: Slocum is about to face his greatest ordeal. He has already seen mirages: an albatross sitting on the water looms up large as a ship; two sleeping seals appear as monstrous whales. Now, as he enters the Strait, steering between two great tide races (the wreck of a great steamship looming out of the foam), the mirages become audible. He has scarcely reefed his sails and retired to his cabin when he thinks he hears a warning cry: *"Spray,* ahoy!"

I sprang to the deck, wondering who could be there that knew the Spray so well as to call out her name passing in the dark; for it was now the blackest of nights all around except in the southwest, where the old, familiar white arch, the terror of Cape Horn, rapidly pushed up by a southwest gale. I had only a moment to douse sail and lash all solid when it struck like a shot from a cannon. . . . For thirty hours it kept on blowing hard.

He puts into Punta Arenas, the Strait port, and here an Austrian named Samblich makes him a present of a box of carpet tacks and advises him to strew his decks at night, for brigands haunt these waters, preying on vessels in trouble. The port captain urges him to wait until a gunboat can escort him, but Slocum is impatient to move on. Shoot straight if the savages surround you, the port captain tells him.

February 20, 1896: Slocum's fifty-second birthday. Back in the fury of the Strait again he has encountered the dreaded williwaws, terrible gales that suddenly strike vertically down the mountain slopes — "chunks" of wind, in fact, to use Slocum's word — that can uproot trees or anything else in their paths including any unfortunate vessels that happen to be in the way. He has reached Cape Froward, the southernmost point of the continent of South America; and here he has a dime-novel encounter with a group of native pirates led by one Black Pedro, a renegade Spaniard and notorious as the worst murderer on the bleak island of Tierra del Fuego. They attack the *Spray* in armed canoes, shrieking "Yammerschooner!", a kind of beggar's plea. Slocum must prevent them knowing he is alone. He pops into his cabin, flings off his clothes, dons a new outfit, pops out again, holds up a bowsprit dressed as a sailor and then, as his pursuers try to close, fires a shot across the bow of the nearest canoe. Black Pedro fails to live up to his name; he and his gang turn tail.

The *Spray* clears Cape Pilar and enters the Pacific. But now a violent storm springs up and she is driven southeast down the coast of Tierra del Fuego towards Cape Horn. She runs for four days before the gale, her mainsail in rags. Slocum rigs up a square sail to replace it. The seas are mountainous and in the distance he can hear the deafening roar of tremendous breakers. As dawn lightens the sky he finds that he has entered the dreaded Milky Way of the Sea, a foaming labyrinth of hidden rocks and tiny channels churned into a perpetual fury. Years before, aboard the *Beagle,* Charles

73

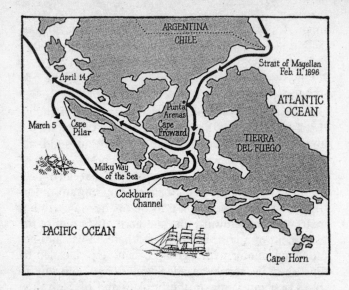

Darwin had written that any landsmen seeing the Milky Way would have nightmares for a week. Writes Slocum: *He might have added "or seaman" as well.* The ordeal that followed he later describes as the greatest sea adventure of his life. Others will compare it with the triumphs of Magellan and Drake and it will be called "in point of pure seamanship, the most remarkable of all."

Somehow he guides the *Spray* through the maze of rock and foam to the comparative safety of some small islands. But his vessel is being blown east into the labyrinth of the Cockburn Channel which leads again to the Strait of Magellan. He has come almost full circle and there is nothing he can do. "Jaded and worn," he contents himself with a meal of venison stew; then, after sprinkling his deck with tacks, he turns in. At midnight he is awakened by a terrifying series of shrieks. A group of natives has boarded the *Spray*, bent on booty and murder; terrified by the tacks and howling like a pack of hounds, they are already leaping into their canoes and fleeing into the night. Slocum goes back to sleep.

Two days later, still trapped in the channels, he salvages a barrel of wine and an entire cargo of tallow from the wreckage of a doomed ship. The tallow comes in eight-hundred-pound casks, which Slocum must winch aboard by hand. But the old sea trader knows its value; later he will make a fancy profit from its sale.

Again he tries to head the *Spray* towards the Pacific. Again he fails. Again he is attacked by Fuegians, who launch a shower of arrows at him, one of which sticks fast in the mainmast. Slocum seizes his old Martini-Henry repeating rifle and drives them off. The land is as cruel as the inhabitants: black, broken cliffs that rise directly from the fury of the sea; sere slopes denuded of trees by the williwaws; dismal, foam-swept islands, half-hidden by the combers.

Day after day he struggles to sail west out of the prison of the Strait. Six times he is driven back by the gales. An Argentine cruiser offers to tow him east to safety; but that would mean giving up and that he will not do. It is almost two months since he cleared Cape Froward. He tries one more time and finally he succeeds. The *Spray* veers so close to the shore that her mast becomes entangled in the branches of the tree. Slocum calls out to his ship "as an impatient farmer might to his horse." *Didn't you know you couldn't climb a tree?* Clearly she has become, to him, a living companion.

April 13, 1896: The *Spray* sails out into the Pacific and a giant roller washes over her as if to cleanse her of the memories of those frustrating weeks. Slocum has been at the helm for thirty hours without rest. But soon the sloop is under full sail, jib full out, main unreefed and, for the first time, the jigger spread from the aft mast, converting her, temporarily, into a yawl. Next stop: Juan Fernandez, the island of Alexander Selkirk, the real-life castaway who was Defoe's model for Robinson Crusoe. They reach it in ten days.

Here, on this "blessed island" (Slocum's phrase) are lovely, wooded hills, fertile valleys and pure bubbling springs. There are no snakes and no wild animals and none of the frustrating trappings of civilization: a total absence of liquor, policemen and lawyers. All forty-five inhabitants glow with health and the children are beautiful. A boatload of natives arrives to greet the mariner who treats them to a breakfast of coffee and doughnuts cooked in the salvaged tallow. They are delighted. He shows them how to make doughnuts and then sells them the tallow; they reward him with a pile of gold coins salvaged from the wreck of a Spanish galleon. There are other rewards; he scampers about the hills with the children, picking wild fruit, including ripe quinces which he will preserve as he sails out again across the empty Pacific on that long seventy-two-day leg to Samoa.

What are his thoughts as the *Spray,* almost unaided, carries him westward? He writes that he is *en rapport* with his surroundings, that he feels the presence of the hand of God, that he has made companions of the birds, the fish, the mammals and the reefs (and, he might have added, the uncannily human *Spray).* Oddly enough, though sailing before the mast is a lonely life for most seamen, Slocum is not used to such loneliness. He has never cottoned to the kind of ersatz marriage which has been the fate of so many ship's captains: brief honeymoons snatched between long periods at sea. His beautiful, part-Indian wife, Virginia, had accompanied him on every voyage, from their first honeymoon trip out of Sydney, Australia, to Cook Inlet, Alaska (which

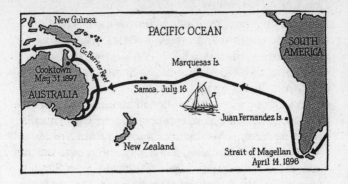

ended in shipwreck) to that last, sad voyage aboard the *Aquidneck*. She had been the ideal shipboard wife, schooling her children, sewing and embroidering, playing the grand piano, all aboard ship. When a mutineer stabbed Slocum's first officer aboard the *Northern Light* in 1882, Virginia had covered her husband, a revolver in each hand, as he subdued the crew. Her death at thirty-four was a terrible blow. In his loneliness he had taken to visiting spiritualists but this could not bring her back. Nor could his twenty-four-year-old cousin, Hettie, whom he married two years later, hope to fill his first wife's shoes. After that one remarkable 5,500-mile voyage on the *Liberdade*, they drifted amicably apart. For the rest of his life, Joshua Slocum will be a loner.

July 16, 1896: The *Spray* casts anchor in Samoa. Three lissome women approach in a canoe. "*Talofa lee*," they carol: *love to you, chief*. They cannot believe he is all alone. *You had other mans, but you eat' em.*

Slocum is far more interested in the widow of his great hero, Robert Louis Stevenson. She comes down to greet him personally and presents him with her husband's four beautiful volumes of sailing directories for the Mediterranean and another for the Indian Ocean.

He takes the books with "reverential awe." He is invited to use her husband's desk to write his letters but he cannot bring himself to sit in that hallowed spot.

He spends an idyllic month in Samoa and then sails off again, this time for Australia where more enthusiastic welcomes await him, not to mention a shower of presents, including a telescope and a new set of sails. Here, he recoups his finances, moving from Sydney to Melbourne to Tasmania, lecturing as he goes to paying audiences. Then he swings north again, past Sydney, Newcastle, Brisbane and Rockhampton, towards the entrance to the Indian Ocean.

May 24, 1897: The *Spray* moves gingerly through the Great Barrier Reef directly opposite New Guinea. Again Slocum has occasion to remark upon her self-steering capacities. From Thursday Island to the Keelings, a run of twenty-three days and 2,700 miles, he spends no more than three hours at the helm. He lashes the wheel and lets the ship scud along on her own; no matter where the wind is, abeam or dead aft, she sails faithfully on course. After leaving the Keeling Islands, Slocum is lost to the world; he has neglected to write home and in New Bedford the newspapers report that he is lost at sea. It is not until he arrives at the island of Mauritius, off the coast of Africa, that the New York *Evening Post* is able to correct the error. The date, by now, is September 21.

Meantime, he has been the chief actor in a comic opera scene on the remote island of Rodriguez, a flyspeck in the Indian Ocean, some thousand miles east of Madagascar. The local abbé has been filling the islanders' heads with terrifying tales of the approaching Antichrist, a piece of sermonizing calculated to keep them on the narrowest of pathways. Suddenly, into the harbour, scudding before a heavy gale, her sails all

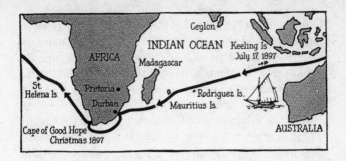

feather-white and her single gaunt occupant holding down the deck like a bearded prophet, comes the *Spray*. Down to the jetty flock the faithful crying that the Antichrist has truly arrived: "May the Lord help us, it is he and he has come in a boat!" One elderly creature makes for the safety of her home, locks herself in, barricades her doors as Slocum advances up the street, and refuses to emerge from her self-imposed prison for the full eight days he spends on the islet. The others soon recover and entertain him royally. The abbé invites him to his convent in the hills for an overnight stay and when finally he prepares to depart, wishes him a safe journey — whatever his religion. Slocum, the free-thinker, cannot resist a slight dig: *My dear abbé, had all religionists been so liberal there would have been less bloodshed in the world.*

Then through the Mozambique channel to Durban, fighting against a hard four-day gale. The *Spray* is famous by now: a signalman on a bluff station reports her progress from fifteen miles off. At eight miles he signals a piece of news that confounds the sceptics: the *Spray* is shortening sail and one man, working alone, has reefed the main in just ten minutes. Three minutes later, the news is rushed to a Durban morning paper and as Slocum reaches port a copy is handed to him.

In Durban, Henry Stanley, the greatest explorer of the age, is brought to meet him. *Mr. Slocum I presume,* or some such greeting. Livingstone's saviour is fascinated that the ship has travelled through treacherous waters without any built-in buoyancy compartments. What would happen, he asks, if the *Spray* should strike a rock? Slocum's answer is succinct: *She must be kept away from the rocks.*

A more bizarre trio of savants awaits his pleasure. Their master "Oom Paul" Kruger, president of the Transvaal, is firmly convinced that the earth is flat. The Word of God has said so and the Word of God cannot be wrong. The three Boers are struggling with a thesis to prove this contention and Slocum is a prize catch. Alas, not such a prize, for he has just girdled the globe and is convinced that it is spherical. The flat-earthers are annoyed; they pore over a Mercator's projection of the world showing the *Spray's* track and point out triumphantly that it looks remarkably flat. Slocum leaves them to their deliberations but the following day encounters one of the fanatics on the street. They engage in pantomime, Slocum bowing and making curves with his hands, the other responding with flat, swimming movements.

Off to Capetown and inland to Pretoria to meet the great flat-earther himself. A prominent jurist introduces Slocum to the President and clumsily mentions that he is on a voyage around the world. The terrible word "round" incenses Kruger: "you don't mean *round!*" cries he. "It is impossible! You mean *in* the world!" He turns away, crying "Impossible! Impossible!", and not one further word does he utter to Slocum or his companion.

March 26, 1898: Slocum sails from South Africa for St. Helena, the island of Napoleon's exile in the mid-Atlantic. The *Spray* moves steadily along until the quack of a booby warns him that land lies dead ahead. He takes a swig from a bottle of port as a toast to his invisible helmsman, the pilot of the *Pinta,* and prepares for the inevitable receptions. He is a celebrity by now. He lectures, dines with the Governor, accepts a fruitcake from the first lady of the island and, unhappily, the gift of a goat from an American friend. The goat is a disaster. Safely ensconced aboard the *Spray,* he begins to eat his way through the ship. No rope can hold him; he devours them all. Then he turns his attention to the charts of the Caribbean and gobbles them up. Finally he munches Slocum's straw hat. Slocum must suffer the presence of the ravenous goat for a thousand miles, until at Ascension Island, in mid-Atlantic, he kicks him ashore.

He crosses the Equator off the coast of Brazil. An American battleship, the *Oregon,* speeds up behind and hoists a puzzling signal; Slocum has difficulty reading it because he has no binoculars. Finally, he makes it out: *Are there any men-of-war about?* He is baffled. No one has been able to tell him that war has broken out between the United States and Spain. *Let us keep together for mutual protection,* he signals back. The *Oregon* ignores this badinage and steams away.

Chartless and cursing his late passenger, the goat, he racks his memory of wind and water as he approaches Tobago and Trinidad. He moves from island to island, packing lecture halls with spirited accounts of his adventures. He is becalmed for eight days in the horse latitudes, the sea so smooth that each evening he can read by candlelight. A three-day gale follows the calm and he begins to weary of the ocean — "tired, tired, tired of baffling squalls and fretful cobble-seas." For more than three years he has lived with the whistling of the wind in the rigging and the slop-slop of the sea against the sloop's sides, music to any seaman after a stint in the doldrums, "but there was so much of it now and it lasted so long!" In the Gulf Stream late that June he is savaged by a terrifying storm, hailstones pelting down on the *Spray* and lightning pouring from the clouds in an almost continual stream.

On June 25, the elements strike again. A tornado has cut a swath through New York City. Slocum sees it coming and receives it with bare poles; even so, the little *Spray* shivers as it hits, heeling over on her beam ends and then, miraculous as always, rights herself and faces out the storm. Slocum is powerless and knows it. *What is man in a storm like this?*

June 26, 1898: Slocum reaches Newport and journey's end. Because of the war, the harbour is mined and he must hug the rocks as he brings his sloop into port. At one the following morning he casts his anchor. He cannot suppress a sense of triumph: he has gained one pound and feels ten years younger; the *Spray* is as sound as a nut and hasn't leaked a drop — since leaving Australia he hasn't even bothered to rig his pump.

But no bands greet him. No children appear with kisses and garlands. No civic dignitaries clamber aboard with plaques and medals. No reporters seek him out. For America is at war; it is the *Maine* that people remember, not the *Spray*. There are some, in fact, who believe that Slocum is a charlatan until he produces his yacht licence, stamped in every port he has visited; that shuts up the sceptics.

Slowly, the extraordinary character of his feat begins to sink in. He gives a lecture in the New Bedford city hall to an audience of old salts. The *Century Illustrated Monthly* asks him to write an account of his voyage. He docks the *Spray* in South Brooklyn and there, in the cabin that has become his true home, he writes, in the spring of 1899, a book-length account of his adventures. The magazine publishes it in nine instalments, and Slocum is charmed to find himself in print next to his hero, Mark Twain. Published later between hard covers, *Sailing Alone Around the World* is translated into six languages and, for the next seventy-five years will be read continuously as one of the great classic stories of the sea.

But for Joshua Slocum, life begins to go slightly sour. There are no more worlds for him to conquer, no more seas to sail. He suffers from that let-down feeling that always comes at the end of a great adventure or a heroic ordeal. Restless and at loose ends, he contemplates a dozen schemes, but they come to nothing. He wants to pilot a ship in the Spanish American War; he wants to start a college for boys aboard a clipper; he wants to take the *Spray* to the Universal Exhibition in Paris; he wants to make a trip to Iceland by submarine: he even wants to learn to fly. There are no takers.

There is one brief interlude. In 1901, reunited with Hettie, he tows the *Spray* up the Hudson and Erie Canal to Buffalo for the six-month-long Pan-American Exposition. Here he and his sloop go on display in competition with hula dancers, Eskimos, Chiquita the Human Doll, the Scenic Railway, the Trip to the Moon, forty-two Indian tribes, the Temple of Music and the U.S. Cavalry's reconstruction of Custer's Last Stand. His visitors' book fills three volumes and includes the signature of President William McKinley, assassinated on these very grounds.

With his profits, he decides to become a landsman. He buys a house and farm at Martha's Vineyard, plants fruit trees, prepares descriptive lectures about his adventures. But this kind of lecture is no longer in vogue: newer and more fascinating entertainments have arrived with the new century. Barnum has just joined Bailey to promote the Greatest Show on Earth. Buffalo Bill's Wild West Show is attracting thousands. Chautauqua has captured the small towns. The birth of the nickelodeon signals a new age. When Slocum left Yarmouth, the bicycle craze was at its height; now the automobile era has begun. There is no place for a man and a sailboat. More than half a century will pass before people begin to think again about sailing alone around the world.

Joshua and Hettie drift apart, again quite amicably. The farm loses its charm. By 1905, Slocum is back again aboard the *Spray,* moored off the Maine coast in the summer and sailing to the West Indies in winter to harvest conch shells and rare orchid plants, which he hopes to present to the new president, Theodore Roosevelt.

Then, in the spring of 1906, the squall of scandal blows over him. At Riverton, New Jersey, a twelve-year-old girl goes aboard the sloop. A few hours later her father claims that she has been attacked. Slocum is charged with rape. There has been no rape — that much is clear; a doctor confirms it and the father agrees, but he calls Slocum "a fiend . . . posing in the limelight of cheap notoriety." Slocum is arrested, jailed, held without bail, the charge reduced to committing indecent assault. At the preliminary hearing he makes an odd statement: if the misdemeanour had occurred, then it must have been during one of the mental lapses to which he is subject. Mental lapses? It is the first and, indeed, the only indication that he suffers from them. He spends forty-two days in jail and then is haled before a judge who reproves him, orders him to pay costs and forbids his return to Riverton — a queer and indecisive ending to a baffling incident.

What actually went on that spring day in the cabin of the *Spray*? Was there a sexual advance? Was it simply the imagination of an impressionable child? Or was it something else — at once more tenuous and more explicable — a desolate old sailor attempting, in his loneliness, to reach out to another human being? No one will ever know. Slocum himself does not contest the charge and apparently it has little effect on his reputation; for he sails immediately to Oyster Bay where he delivers one lone orchid (the others have died during his incarceration) to the President who, in his turn, entertains him royally at his home on Sagamore Hill.

These are pinpoints of excitement in an otherwise dreary half-life. Slocum is running down, like a leaky schooner, his personality increasingly waspish, his appearance more and more slovenly and his sloop, once so trim and shipshape, filthier and filthier. He is withering away, a man born out of his time, an old salt clinging to the past, a caricature in a shapeless felt hat, a collarless shirt and vest, unbuttoned trousers, and old, unpolished felt boots. Old Slocum, closed up tight, impenetrable, a mystery even to his sons.

There must be one more adventure. He is sixty-five years old and more than a little slack, but he is determined to undertake a new voyage — he and the *Spray*. Together they will penetrate the mysteries of that most mysterious of rivers, the Amazon. He will sail his sloop to Venezuela, follow the Orinoco and the Rio Negro to the headwaters of the great river and then set his course downstream into the unknown sponge of the jungle. Slocum has dreams of grandeur; he is confident the natives will mistake him for a god and, if they do, he intends to be ready for them: he will take along one of Mr. Edison's new-fangled gramophones.

November 14, 1909: Once again Joshua Slocum boards the *Spray* on a voyage that no one has made before. He sets sail from Tisbury and drives the *Spray* into the very teeth of a gale blowing in from the east. The little sloop scuds along as always, white sails billowing in the wind until she vanishes beyond the horizon. And that is the last that anyone sees of her. She and her master vanish without a trace. No shred of sail, no splinter of wreckage, not so much as a floating spar or a waterlogged straw hat remain to give a clue to her fate. His ship — his home, his faithful and sole companion, his last, true love — is with him to the end.

4

Samuel Hearne's Epic Trek

In the crowded pantheon of early explorers there are only a few whom I would care to invite to dinner. Cartier and Champlain are admirable historical figures, no doubt, but both were hard cases: the former was a kidnapper, the latter an assassin; in each instance their victims were unsuspecting Indians. Radisson, Groseilliers, Brûlé and their ilk are intriguing forest creatures, viewed from a distance, but all were out-and-out rascals. One would be unwise to trust them with either wife or pocketbook. The Scots — the Simpsons, Mackenzies, Frasers *et al* — are certainly indomitable, but they would make dour companions, I suspect, for they were single-minded men and not a little frightening. Nor can I warm to the Arctic adventurers of the nineteenth century — Franklin, Rae, Belcher and their kind — ambitious certainly, brave, foolhardy and sometimes foolish, but not really engaging company.

Samuel Hearne is an exception. I would dearly love to have spent an evening with that uncommonly sensitive and sensible man, a week or so, say, after the completion of his five-thousand-mile trek across the bleak desert that he named the Barren Ground. *Five thousand miles*, almost all of it on foot, in just two years, seven months and twenty-four days in a land that no white man had ever visited! The mind boggles.

The idea of anybody actually *walking* five thousand miles is almost incomprehensible to us. And we must remember that Hearne did not travel, as the Cross-Canada hikers did in 1921, on well-defined railway embankments. He stumbled in his moccasins over miles of rubbled glacial moraine; he waded through acres of cheerless swamp; he trudged on home-made snowshoes through leagues of drifting snow. In the summer he was beset by swarms of insects that all but blotted out the sun; in the winter he set his face into shrieking gales and raging blizzards. Much of the time he was hungry; often he went without food for three days or even a week. The wonder isn't that he thrived, which he did; it is that he survived at all.

Surely a more unlikely explorer never existed. It was not Hearne's ambition to conquer new worlds as it was Fraser's or Franklin's. He was a seaman, not a landlubber. He had only elementary surveying experience and his arithmetic was abysmal. He hadn't a scrap of geological training, knew scarcely anything about Indians and very little about northern land travel. Yet his masters sent him off without any sensible direction to find a mysterious Indian chief and an equally mysterious treasure of copper somewhere — no one was terribly sure where — on the Arctic's rim. The remarkable thing is that at the third attempt Hearne succeeded, perhaps because, not being a professional explorer, he approached his task without preconceived ideas.

Yet it is not the great feat of discovery that sets Hearne apart from your run-of-the-mill pedlar, voyageur coureur de bois or map-maker. Certainly he demonstrated all the adaptability and common sense of the best of these. His other qualities I find even more engaging and, considering the time and place, more remarkable. His curiosity was boundless. Everything he saw intrigued him: animals, people, customs, food, environment; and he was patient enough and prescient enough to record all his observations in detail. This is not as easy as it sounds. A man who has struggled for twelve hours, heavy-laden, over broken country, wants to put his feet up at the end of the day and swallow a brandy and some hot food before collapsing in his tent. He does not want to scribble endless descriptions in his notebook or make pencil drawings of what he has encountered. But Hearne, scarcely educated and ashamed of his deficient grammar, managed to produce, en route, a journal that has become a literary classic.

There was no side to him and no bigotry; he accepted his Indian companions for what they were and made no attempt to impose upon them or upon his view of them any of the values of Christian Europe. He was remarkably sensitive; his famous account of the massacre at Bloody Falls shows that the incident left him permanently horrified. He was also fastidious; robbed by the Chipewyans of almost everything he possessed in the summer of 1770, he asked, and was allowed to take, as much soap as he felt he would need on the long retreat back to his post. He loved animals. He kept two house-broken beavers as pets and fed them on plum pudding, and he also tamed mink, lemming, foxes, eagles, buntings and horned larks. A self-taught naturalist, he left behind accurate descriptions of creatures no European had ever heard of, much less seen: musk-oxen, wood bison, whooping crane. He was a great reader; Voltaire was a favourite. One night, driven to despair by the failure of an expedition and unable to sleep, he tells us how he repeated "above an hundred times the following beautiful lines of Dr. Young: 'Tired Nature's sweet restorer, balmy sleep. . . .' " All in all an adaptable, agreeable fellow, brave and stubborn as we shall see, but never prey to ego or to the kind of false heroics or foolish impetuosities that characterized so many of his contemporaries.

One might easily wonder why the Hudson's Bay Company would send a seaman like Hearne on a journey which no other white man had attempted, from Fort Prince of Wales (the present site of Churchill, Manitoba) on Hudson Bay to the shores of the western Arctic in search of copper. But one must consider the curious fashion in which that great business enterprise was managed. In 1769, the year in which Hearne was first launched on his expedition, the gap of understanding between the absentee landlords of the Honourable Company and its post managers was at least as wide as the Atlantic. No London official had ever set foot on the shores of the Bay, let alone in the Arctic desert or tundra that stretched off, treeless and forlorn, into the fog of the northwest.

It is true that the London Committee was well supplied with maps and reports on sub-Arctic Canada from their representatives in the field. But it is also true that as late as 1784, long after Hearne had returned from the Arctic, officials in the London office actually dispatched one hundred and fifty copies of *The Country Clergyman's Advice to Parishioners,* to be distributed among the traders and the Indians who, apparently, were held to be panting for this form of salvation. The noble Governors, enjoying the music of Mozart and Haydn, the tabletalk of Samuel Johnson, the plays of Goldsmith and Sheridan, the parliamentary oratory of William Pitt and the iconoclasm of Hearne's favourite, Voltaire, could not comprehend the kind of journey that lay before him.

Nor could they have really understood the strange, terrible creature who was Governor of Fort Prince of Wales. Moses Norton is simply too much: he could scarcely survive as a believable villain in the most macabre melodrama. The half-breed son of a previous governor, brutal and semi-literate, he had had the advantage of nine years in England. But this veneer of civilization peeled off him easily on the shores of Hudson Bay, where he lived like an Oriental potentate and acted like one, abusing all those beneath him, especially his white employees. Although he prevented any European from attempting sexual relations with any Indian woman, he himself kept a veritable harem of them — five or six of the most comely girls that he could select from the available crop. And select he did in the most savage fashion. He kept a box of poison about him to administer to those wretched natives who refused him the pleasure of their wives and daughters. The poisoning was not confined to the menfolk. When two members of his harem were observed to fancy younger men, Moses Norton calmly poisoned *them*.

This was the man who convinced the Governors in England to send Hearne on a voyage of discovery to seek the fabled coppermines of the Arctic. No one had the slightest idea where the mines were. Indians had been bringing copper samples into the post for more than half a century, but none had ever seen the legendary trove. Thus Hearne's instructions from the villainous Norton were vague: to find the "Far Off Metal River" with the help of an Indian Chief in the Athupuscow country, one "Captain" Matonabbee, and trace that river to its mouth. It was Matonabbee who had originally brought some crude maps of the copper country to the fort, but exactly where the river was and where the chief was, and why the Indian would agree to go anywhere without formal instruction or reward — these important pieces of information were never spelled out. In Hearne's description, Moses Norton seems to have been as incompetent as he was unscrupulous. Hearne says he was a notorious smuggler, but adds that he never made any money at it.

At this point, Hearne was twenty-four years old and had been a seaman since the age of eleven, having served at one point under that Captain Samuel Hood who, as Lord Hood, was to merit Nelson's accolade as "the best officer . . . that England has to boast of." He had seen action throughout the Seven Years' War and then, when the war ended, had joined the Hudson's Bay Company, serving for two years as the mate of a sloop and two more as the mate of a brigantine sailing out of Fort Prince of Wales. His ambitions were nautical: he wanted to be captain of his own ship. He applied to the company for such a post. Instead they decided to turn him into an explorer overnight.

In addition to the instruction to find the river of copper, Hearne was given two other tasks. He was to arrange for more tribes to bring in furs to the post and he was to find the North West Passage — that elusive waterway said to lead directly to the jewels and spices of fabled Cathay, and which had captured the imagination of every explorer. There was also a hard political objective to Hearne's journey. On originally receiving its charter, the Hudson's Bay Company had promised to explore and develop the Hudson Bay watershed, an immense area embodying about two-fifths of present-day Canada. It had done nothing of the sort. Company men sat on their rumps on the margin of the Bay while their rivals, the "pedlars" who later formed the Montreal-based North West Company, ranged far into the hinterland. Now, with questions being asked in the British Parliament, the Company finally decided it was time to thrust inland. Samuel Hearne would form the spearhead of that thrust.

"The continent of America is much wider than many people imagine," Hearne was to write. It was the understatement of the century. Clearly, Norton himself, let alone his masters in London, had no idea what their servant was in for. More than half of Canada was then a blank spot on the crude maps of the day. The Rockies had been seen from a distance but no white man had ever set foot in them. The first tentative Spanish discoveries on the Canadian west coast were five years into the future. The gargantuan fresh-water seas of the north — Great Bear, and Great Slave lakes — were as unknown as the Mackenzie River.

The Barrens were a mystery. Hearne could not know that his goal lay a thousand miles to the northwest and that everything between Fort Prince of Wales and that far-off river of metal was treeless desert. To reach it he would be subjected to unknown terrors and unbelievable horrors; he would eat the most exotic of foods (the carcasses of unborn animals, for example) and witness customs no man could imagine. For more than two years he would live a life so far removed from that of the ordinary Englishman that few could give it credence.

Physically, the tundra has scarcely changed since Hearne's day. It rolls on for hundreds of miles, a cold, forsaken land, carpeted by a thin mattress of moss and lichen and scoured by the bulldozer action of the great Keewatin ice sheet, two miles thick, the relics of whose passage may still be seen in the form of vast rubbles of broken rock, and the serpentine embankments called eskers, which are the silted remains of sub-glacial rivers.

The tundra is a canoeist's nightmare. The inexorable glacier disrupted the ancient drainage pattern so that the few remaining rivers run every which-way and the myriad of little lakes (more than one can count in all the rest of the world) are joined only by spasmodic stretches of white water. For an untried traveller the country can, and has, meant terrible death. In the summer, the swarms of mosquitoes and black flies can drive men and animals into imbecility. In the winter, the cold is so savage that, in Hearne's day, it sometimes caused the thin gun barrels to burst apart on being fired.

There is a worse obstacle to sustained travel — one that strangers to the tundra have difficulty in comprehending. In all this empty thousand-mile expanse there is scarcely a sliver of timber: no twigs with which to kindle a fire, no poles with which to erect a shelter, no wood to repair a broken paddle; nothing but caribou moss and sedges and small trailing vines which, in microscopic examination, are seen to be willows and birches, some of them more than half a century old.

This was the desert that Hearne set out to conquer. The marvel is that after two setbacks that could have driven a lesser man into a permanent funk, he actually set out again.

His first expedition began on November 6, 1769. Hearne and his two white companions were given as a guide, a singularly untrustworthy Indian chieftain named Chawchinahaw. His main purpose appears to have been to steal everything Hearne owned and then leave him and his comrades to starve on the Barrens. He very nearly accomplished that purpose. Two hundred miles from his base, the tyro explorer found himself without food, and forced to subsist on his hunting ability and the largesse of some friendly Indians whom he fortunately encountered in his humiliating retreat back to the fort. He reached it on December 11, "to my great mortification."

Undeterred by this setback, Hearne tried again on February 23, 1770. He had already learned one valuable lesson: travel with the Indians only and with no other white companions. Outside the Company factories, the natives' loyalty to one another gave them an advantage over any Englishman. Hearne determined to become like a native: to move with the tribes, allowing them to set the pace and the patterns; to adopt native customs and eat native foods, and to follow, as much as possible, native folkways. This simple acceptance of the natives' superiority in their own environment — it seems so obvious now — tells us a great deal about Samuel Hearne. He was totally unaffected by the egotism and snobbery that was to bedevil some later English explorers. He was perfectly prepared to eat raw whitefish and beavers' wombs, food that would have nauseated most white adventurers. Moreover, he had the patience to follow wherever the Indians led, even when the trail seemed to lead in circles. Franklin's seamen, almost two centuries later, had still not grasped the truths that Hearne absorbed after a month on the tundra. Had they done so, they might have returned safely to the warmth of their English beds.

Hearne had learned a second lesson: to take women along on any expedition. They were needed, he realized, to haul baggage, dress skins, pitch tents and cook food while the men did the hunting — a practical division of labour which the natives had relied on for centuries. But Moses Norton would have none of this, claiming that there would be too many extra mouths to feed. In spite of his Indian blood, Norton showed himself to be remarkably obtuse in his judgment of people, customs and geography. He saddled Hearne with an even more incompetent guide, one Conn-e-quese, who had no real idea of where the Coppermine country was, though he pretended to know. He led the expedition in a desultory fashion through the *taiga*, the thin forest that borders the tundra; then, in springtime, he guided them out onto the Barrens, feasting one day and starving the next and gathering about him an ever-increasing gaggle of hangers-on, until by the end of July the party of six had become an army of six hundred.

Hearne felt himself constantly cheated by these Indians, who made continual demands upon him for ammunition, guns, tobacco, medicine and clothes, "as if I had brought the Company's warehouse with me." Finally on August 12, after his quadrant was broken, he knew that he must return to the fort.

There followed an appalling ordeal. The Indians stole almost everything Hearne owned, including his ammunition and most of his tools. With winter approaching, lacking both warm clothes and a tent, the young explorer fell behind the main party and must surely have frozen or starved to death if, by a stunning stroke of luck, he had not run into the very man he had originally set out to find, Chief Matonabbee.

This handsome, six-foot native, agreeable and modest, had lived for several years at Fort Prince of Wales, as the adopted son of Richard Norton, Moses' father. He was a Northern Indian (Chipewyan) but could speak the dialect of the Southern Indians (Crees) and also a few words of English. He is as important to Hearne's journey, and hence to history, as Hearne himself, for it is quite clear that, without him, the white man would never have accomplished his objective. Thus Matonabbee takes his place with the large and noble band of intelligent native leaders whom history has largely neglected. He was to Hearne what Donnaconna was to Jacques Cartier or the English Chief to Alexander Mackenzie: absolutely essential.

This remarkable Indian immediately took Hearne under his wing, rustled up some food and warm clothes, and offered to guide him on another expedition to the Coppermine. Hearne could have been pardoned if, after all his travail, he had rejected the offer, but, "as I had already experienced every hardship that was likely to accompany any future trial, I was determined to complete the discovery even at the risque of life itself."

First, however, he and his guide had to make their way back to home base. It took them two gruelling months. Hearne had no ammunition to hunt game and had to make do by chopping up his ice chisel into square lumps to use for ball — a dangerous experiment. Pickings were very slim. During one seven-day stretch he lived on a diet of water, burnt bones, cranberries and scraps of leather. The blizzards were so bad that his only dog froze to death and he was obliged to pull his own sledge. He and Matonabbee finally made it back on November 25, having been absent for eight months and twenty-two days on a fruitless journey.

The wonder of it is that he was chafing to return and, indeed, could scarcely contain himself waiting for Norton to give him the go-ahead. Just twelve days later he set off again with Matonabbee, "the most sociable, kind and sensitive Indian I have ever met with." This time they took women with them because, as the chief explained, "women were made for labour." They could carry burdens "as much as two men can do," pitch tents, mend clothing and keep the men warm at night. They were cheap to feed, too, since they could lick enough food off their fingers as they did the cooking to keep themselves alive. They did not eat until the men had eaten, on pain of a beating, and if the men ate everything then they did not eat at all.

Hearne's account of the journey that followed is a chronicle of marvels intermingled with tales of hardship and flashes of horror. His dispirited diary entry, on December 27, 1770, noted that nothing had passed his lips for the previous three days except a pipe of tobacco, and a swallow of snow water. Already his strength was failing, and "I must confess that I never spent so dull a Christmas."

But he and Matonabbee pressed on until they reached the camp of women and children who were

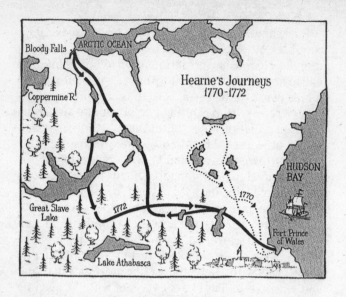

waiting for their chief's return from the fort. Hearne discovered that his guide rejoiced in five wives, seven children and two adopted orphans. These formed part of the entourage that now moved slowly westward through the thin *taiga* forest in the bitter cold of January and February.

"It is impossible to describe the intenseness of the cold we experienced this day," Hearne wrote on February 7 as the party crossed Partridge Lake. It was so cold that one of Matonabbee's wives, who belted her clothes up high for easier walking, froze her thighs and buttocks. "I must acknowledge that I was not in the number who pitied her," Hearne wrote, "as I thought she took too much pains to shew a clean heel and good leg, her garters being always in sight, which, though by no means considered here as bordering on indecency, is by far too airy to withstand the rigorous cold of a severe winter in a high Northern latitude."

Hearne's earlier guides had erred in trying for a direct route to the copper country in the dead of winter. Matonabbee did not make that mistake. The party crept west in the shelter of the *taiga* and it was not until April, when the numbers had been swelled to some seventy persons, that they began to ready themselves for the Barrens, gathering birchbark with which to fashion canoes and cutting tent poles that could be converted into snowshoe frames in the winter. Here Matonabbee bought himself a sixth wife from a party of passing Indians. She was a strapping woman, built like a grenadier, in Hearne's phrase, and a commonsense choice, as he acknowledged, considering the rigours of the impending journey. Hearne had already grasped something of the practicality of Indian existence on the Barrens. If an Indian fell sick (as one was to do with consumption) and could not keep up with the main band, he or she was simply left behind. Hearne himself recognized the necessity of this custom, cruel though it sounds. There was no use everyone sitting down and dying with the invalid.

The party was about to move on but was delayed for two days by a woman in a difficult condition of labour. Once the child was born, however, she set out with the rest carrying the infant on her back. For the first day, some one else pulled her sledge, but after that she was on her own, carrying the baby as well as the heavy load, wading knee-deep in water and snow and moaning all the while. Hearne noted that the Indians gave no help to a woman in labour. Even other women refused to serve as midwives. For four or five weeks she was considered unclean and forced to stay in a tent by herself, the father prohibited from seeing his offspring lest he take a permanent dislike to it, since newborn infants were considered ugly.

That May, two hundred more Indians joined the band and these tried to plunder Hearne's small supply of trade goods. Matonabbee stopped them. Hearne's attitude to his guide and friend was, at this point, a little ambivalent. On the one hand, Matonabbee was his protector; on the other, he behaved atrociously, by European standards, to his women. He had stolen one of his wives from a younger man and when the cuckolded husband ventured to complain, the chief stabbed him three times. The incident, Hearne wrote apologetically, "by no means does honour to Matonabbee."

It was, however, the custom, as Hearne was at pains to explain. The stronger men and the good hunters habitually took the best wives from the weaker men. It was their habit to wrestle for the women, cutting off their own hair and greasing their ears before the struggle so that their opponent would have nothing to grasp. They did not, however, punch or kick each other. The prize was stripped and borne off to the victor's tent, often against her will. It is well to note that these practices were not greatly different from the treatment of women in many parts of the seventeenth-century world, where men were not only predominant but also held the power of life and death over their female chattels. The Indians sometimes beat their wives but rarely killed them, as the Japanese samurai often did in that same era, with a single, unpredictable sword stroke.

Hearne accepted these customs philosophically. To him the Indian was neither a noble savage nor a sub-human. As for Matonabbee, he got his come-uppance, after a fashion, when the man who had sold him his sixth wife returned and demanded further payment for her. Since his opponent was bigger and stronger, the chief had to give in; but he was angered and humiliated and Hearne had great difficulty persuading him to continue the journey north to the copper country.

On May 31, the men left the women and children camped on the edge of the tundra and headed merrily into the north while their families wailed their good-byes. They were soon joined by another band of Indians whose intention was to go to the Coppermine on an Eskimo-murdering expedition. Hearne was horrified by this turn of events, but the Indians scoffed at what they considered his cowardice. Knowing that his life depended on their good humour, the explorer told them that he would not interfere but would help them only if the Eskimos themselves actually attacked. "This declaration was received with great satisfaction, and I never afterwards ventured to interfere with any of their war-plans."

They were now so far removed from civilization that the people they encountered had never seen a white skin. A group of Copper Indians, who had joined the party, circled the explorer with great curiosity, pronouncing him a perfect human being except for the colour of his hair and eyes. The former they likened to the stained hair of a buffalo's tail and the latter, being light, to those of a gull. As for his skin, they thought it looked like meat that had been sodden in water until all the blood was extracted. All the combings from the stranger's hair were carefully collected and hoarded as souvenirs.

And then, just after midnight on July 16, in the gloomiest corner of the Canadian mainland, near a series of cataracts that bear to this day the name of Bloody Falls, there occurred the incident that was to overshadow all of Hearne's other adventures and discoveries.

The Indians lay camped in some scrub brush near the Coppermine River, which was only 180 yards wide at this point and totally unnavigable. Three spies returned from a reconnaissance and reported five tents of Eskimos pitched on the west side. One can imagine the air of expectancy and tension that fell over the party. Hearne's companions painted their faces and picked up wooden shields which they had emblazoned with representations of their guardian spirits. They had all tied up their hair or cut it off and now, to make themselves light for running, they removed their stockings, rolled up or cut off the sleeves of their jackets and, in some cases, stripped down to breechcloths and shoes in spite of the maddening hordes of mosquitoes. Hearne, who refused to stay behind lest he be slaughtered by an escaping Eskimo, took off his own stockings and cap and tied his hair. But he told the Indians that he would not join in the killing except in self-defence.

Then in the bright rays of the midnight sun, the Indians mounted the attack on their defenceless and unsuspecting prey while Hearne stood by and watched in horror. No writer can improve on his own account of what happened in that bloody midnight hour so long ago:

"Men, women and children, in all upward of twenty, ran out of their tents stark naked, and endeavoured to make their escape, but the Indians having possession of all the landside, to no place could they fly for shelter. One alternative only remained, that of jumping into the river; but, as none of them attempted it, they all fell sacrifice to Indian barbarity!

"The shrieks and groans of the poor expiring wretches were truly dreadful; and my horror was much increased at seeing a young girl, seemingly about eighteen years of age, killed so near me, that when the first spear was stuck into her side she fell down at my feet, and twisted round my legs, so that it was with difficulty that I could disengage myself from her dying grasps. As two Indian men pursued this unfortunate victim, I solicited very hard for her life; but the murderers made no reply till they had stuck both their spears through her body, and transfixed her to the ground. They then looked me sternly in the face, and began to ridicule me, by asking if I wanted an Esquimaux wife; and paid not the smallest regard to the shrieks and agony of the poor wretch, who was twining round their spears like an eel! Indeed, after receiving much abusive language from them ... I was at length obliged to desire that they would be more expeditious in dispatching their victim out of her misery. ... One of the Indians hastily drew his spear from the place where it was first lodged, and pierced it through her breast near the heart. The love of life, however, even in this most miserable state, was so predominant, that though this might justly be called the most merciful act that could be done for the poor creature, it seemed to be unwelcome, for though much exhausted by pain and loss of blood, she made several attempts to ward off the friendly blow. My situation and the terror of my mind at beholding this butchery, cannot easily be conceived, much less described; though I summed up all the fortitude I was master of on the occasion, it was with difficulty that I could refrain from tears; ... Even at this hour I cannot reflect on the transactions of that horrid day without shedding tears."

This slaughter was scarcely concluded when the Indians spotted seven more Eskimo tents on the east side of the river. They could not cross, having left their canoes upstream, but opened fire on these new targets. Now an odd thing occurred. As each bullet struck the ground, crowds of curious Eskimos would run forward to see what the Indians were sending them and to examine the pieces of lead that ricocheted off the rocks. Only when one man was shot in the leg did the whole multitude tumble into canoes and flee.

But one old man fell behind while collecting his belongings and twenty Indians speared him until, in Hearne's grisly phrase, "his whole body was like a cullender." And one old woman, so blind and deaf that she was oblivious to danger, was spotted sitting alone by a waterfall, killing salmon. She, too, was butchered in the most hideous fashion, being stabbed first in the eyes and then in the non-vital parts so that she would die slowly in pain. This was savage treatment, certainly, but no more savage than that visited upon the Aztecs of Mexico about the same time by the Christian conquistadores of Spain or upon heretics and witches of Europe who were consumed by slow fires in full public view. Hearne, who missed nothing even in moments of high emotion, noted that the river, which must have been running red with blood, was also clogged with an incredible number of salmon, heading for the spawning grounds.

Now, at last, the young explorer was able to fulfill his mission. He erected a mark and took possession of the bleak coast in the name of the Hudson's Bay Company "for the sake of form," as he put it. After the events of that night and in those dismal surroundings there could be no joy in such an empty gesture. The crooked river, with its banks of solid rock, winding through a dreary region of barren hills and marshes, was of no value as a water highway. And the fabulous mines turned out to be nothing more than a jumble of rock and gravel. Though the Indians had talked about hills of solid copper, Hearne, after four hours' search, found only a single ingot weighing about four pounds. It found its way eventually into the British Museum and is there to this day. Even if there had been copper in quantity, the problems of mining and transporting it south would have been insurmountable.

Hearne's other discoveries were more valuable. It was clear to him by now that the North West Passage, that legendary channel of open water supposedly joining the two great oceans, was a myth; it did not exist in any navigable form. More important were his detailed observations of native customs and habits, which he continued to set down in great detail and in spite of incredible hardships as the party moved south again. His feet and legs were swollen, his toenails had dropped off and all the skin between his toes had been chafed away by the constant sandpaper action of the terrain. "I left the print of my feet in blood almost at every step I took," he recorded.

But when they reached the camp of the women and children these afflictions soon abated and the entire party, reunited, arrived at last at Athapuscow Lake, which we know as Great Slave. Hearne, the first white man to see this immense stretch of slate-grey water, must have been impressed. Lashed by storms as wicked as those on the ocean, the lake is so huge that no shoreline can be seen from its waters. Here, on its margin, Hearne made his sketches and observed and recorded the native rites.

He was particularly intrigued by the rituals of the medicine men, all of them expert conjurers, who pretended to swallow and disgorge knives, hatchets and other tools in an attempt to cure their patients. Specially built conjuring houses were constructed for the sick and in these the naked doctors would suck and blow on the afflicted parts, administering charms, singing and talking to spirits as they worked their legerdemain. Hearne saw one medicine man devour a bayonet in an attempt to succour a sick man and confessed that, although he did not believe the conjurer had actually swallowed it, he could not see how he managed to hide it. The man then feigned great pains in his stomach and eventually appeared to vomit the bayonet out again, "a very nice piece of deception, especially as it was performed by a man quite naked." The patient recovered.

On another occasion, one man fell dangerously ill, his whole side paralysed. The medicine man pretended to swallow a large board and all the men who administered to the invalid fasted for several days until they, too, fell ill. All recovered, including the paralysed man who was able to walk within three weeks and go hunting in six.

What Hearne was observing, no doubt, was a primitive form of psychosomatic medicine. So strong was the faith of the Indians that it was believed, with considerable evidence, that if a medicine man cursed somebody, death was inevitable. Matonabbee believed that Hearne himself had the power to curse his enemies and at one point persuaded him to put a hex on an Indian who had treated him badly. Hearne obligingly drew a rough sketch of two figures representing himself and Matonabbee's enemy. Opposite the figures he drew a pine tree with a large human eye over it and a hand projecting from it. He gave this paper to the chief. When the enemy heard of the curse he sickened and died. Hearne was careful not to repeat this mumbo-jumbo and so preserved his reputation.

He was now eating almost everything the Indians ate and enjoying it. He became so used to eating his food raw that for the rest of his life he preferred his fish undercooked. He was especially fond of a dish made of half-digested food from a deer stomach and mixed with blood and fat first chewed by men and boys and then heated and cooked for several days in the deer's paunch. Wombs and genitals became normal fare and unborn calves, fawns and beavers, taken from their mothers' wombs, he pronounced "the greatest delicacies that can be eaten." The Indians also enjoyed eating the lice that crawled through their long hair and deerskin garments and the warble flies that settled on fresh meat, but these Hearne refused — not through any sense of disgust, he hastens to tell us, but because he did not want to become addicted to delicacies that he would not be able to get when he returned to his own world!

His own world in that winter of 1771-72 must have seemed very far away. James Watt had just invented steam power; the Russians had seized the Crimea from the Turks; and in the American colonies the first rumblings of revolution were being felt — a revolution which would have a glancing effect on Hearne's own future. Hearne knew nothing of these events. The slow progress of the Indians, who moved this way and that, following the game or meeting up with other tribes, might have maddened a less patient man but does not seem to have concerned him. He had reached the Arctic in July of 1771. The following January found him moving even farther to the west, somewhere between Great Slave and Athabasca Lake.

It was in these environs that he had another remarkable encounter, this time with a young Dogrib woman who had been taken prisoner by the Athupuscows eighteen months before. She had escaped and had managed to survive for seven winter months, all alone, in a hut of her own construction, living on game she snared herself and wearing clothing made from rabbit skins. Her attire, Hearne noted "shewed great taste, and exhibited no little variety of ornament." She had never seen iron before but she had found a shank of an arrowhead and a bit of hoop and from these she had made a knife and an awl with which to construct a crude pair of snowshoes. Her fire, which she managed to keep alive for the entire winter, she had first kindled by rubbing two stones together.

This resourceful creature was clearly an uncommon prize for any man and the strongest began to wrestle each other to see who would have her. "The poor girl," Hearne wrote, "was actually won and lost at wrestling by near half a score of different men the same evening." Matonabbee was intent on entering the fray until one of his own women told him, dryly, that he already had more wives than he needed, a remark that so infuriated the sensitive chief that he beat her unmercifully; she died of her injuries.

The party moved on in its wayward fashion. Whenever the Indians encountered a poorer tribe, they fell upon them, plundering their luckless victims of goods and women. On April 14, they robbed a community of strange Indians of all their belongings and gang-raped the younger women. They were heading east again but we cannot be sure of the exact route because Hearne's quadrant had been broken the year before and his watch had also stopped. It was no longer possible for him to measure distances or fix his position.

Finally they encountered another party of Indians who were bound for Fort Prince of Wales with a load of furs. They joined them and on June 30, 1772, Hearne at last reached his home base after an absence of eighteen months and twenty-three days.

What had he accomplished? His chief findings, as we have seen, were negative ones. He was right about the North West Passage but old myths die hard; the Royal Navy, twenty years later, was still instructing Captain George Vancouver to search for one. He was right about the impracticability of mining copper on the Arctic's shore, a judgment confirmed by Franklin in 1821; but such is the optimism of the treasure-seeker that hundreds of claims were filed in the very same region between 1913 and 1954. All were allowed to lapse. Hearne's maps, inaccurate though they were, remained in use for half a century. And nothing approaching his feat of crossing the Barren Ground was attempted until the Geological Survey of Canada sent J.B. Tyrrell there in 1893-94. But Hearne's real contribution was his close and accurate descriptions of the Chipewyan and Dogrib Indians, the flora and fauna of the country through which he travelled, and his willingness to adapt to native ways, which set the pattern of Arctic survival for generations.

Hearne had one more significant feat before him; the establishment of Cumberland House north of The Pas, which marked the first move of the Hudson's Bay Company into the interior in direct competition with the more adventurous Nor'westers. It was here that Hearne, in effect, invented the York boat, the light skiff used for more than a century to convey shipments of furs across the continent.

And now we come to the odd coda to Samuel Hearne's story — one that has caused controversy for two centuries. He was made governor of Fort Prince of Wales in 1776, the year of the outbreak of the American Revolution. The fort itself was a monstrous battlement, constructed of gigantic blocks of granite. It had taken thirty-eight years to complete and was considered to be one of the most impregnable strongholds on the continent. But in 1782, when a French admiral, Le Comte de la Pérouse, sailed into the harbour (the Revolution had once again pitted Britain against France), Hearne calmly surrendered the fort to him without a shot being fired.

Why? Certainly not through cowardice. Hearne's bravery was never in dispute. But as we have seen, he was also a man of prudence and common sense; false bravado was not part of his makeup. Certainly he could have invited a siege and, had he done so, it is quite likely that Fort Prince of Wales would have been memorialized in song and story as an early Alamo, and Hearne and his men hailed as martyr-heroes, of the order of Adam Dollard and Davey Crockett. But Hearne was having none of that. La Pérouse had three ships, mounting a total of 146 guns and he landed four hundred men at arms before the British realized who they were. Hearne, with a mere thirty-nine men, bowed gracefully to the inevitable. Since fortresses were traded back and forth between warring nations as part of armistice documents (Louisburg was a good example), Hearne obviously saw no reason why he should sacrifice a single life for no clear gain. The French could not destroy the fort, only its guns and wooden buildings. Those massive battlements can still be seen, towering above the cold waters of Hudson Bay, a few miles from the modern town of Churchill.

As for Samuel Hearne, he was made a prisoner and taken back to Europe, not to durance vile, but to his native England by the chivalrous La Pérouse, who, having devoured that fascinating journal en route, made Hearne promise that he would have it published. Hearne agreed, but before that was possible the war ended and the Company sent Hearne back again to Hudson Bay, where he built a new fort on the site of modern-day Churchill. He retired in 1787 and it is ironic to report that he quickly frittered away his savings because he did not understand the value of money, having lived for most of his life in a land where it was of no use. Then, in 1792 he sold the manuscript of his northern journey to a publisher for two hundred pounds, a handsome enough sum in those days when you compare it with the eighteen pounds that John Milton got for *Paradise Lost*. Alas, Hearne did not live to witness the birth of his literary progeny; a month after the sale he died of dropsy at what, in those times, was the ripe age of forty-seven.

And Matonabbee, the chief who had befriended him and led him on the greatest journey of his life — what of him? He had prospered after Hearne's return, achieving the leadership of all the Northern Indians and continuing "to render great service to the Company ... by bringing a greater quantity of furs to their Factory at Churchill River, than any other Indian did, or ever will do."

It would be pleasant to report that Matonabbee, having achieved fame and greatness, died in bed surrounded by his many wives. Alas, his end was as tragic as it was remarkable. When he learned in 1783 that Hearne had surrendered to the French without a shot he could not bear the shame. He hanged himself, leaving six of his wives and four of his children to starve to death in the biting cold of the winter that followed.

In death, Matonabbee was unique, as he had been in life. For this is the only record we have of a Northern Indian putting an end to his own existence.

5

Billy Bishop: The Lone Hawk

If you wanted to, you could make out a pretty good case for Billy Bishop as the Canadian Least Likely to Succeed as a World War One flyer. Consider the evidence:

Billy Bishop was a mother's boy. He spoke with a lisp, preferred dancing to the jock sports and was called a sissy by his classmates.

Billy Bishop was a rotten student. He cut classes to play pool. His report cards were terrible. His principal didn't think he'd amount to much.

Billy Bishop was a bust as a military cadet — the worst the Royal Military College had ever known. They would have thrown him out in 1914 for cheating at exams, but the war intervened.

Billy Bishop was a military misfit. His crime sheet carried entries for breaches of discipline and conduct unbecoming an officer. He drank so much champagne, going on leave, that he fell off a gangplank, bashed in his knee and was hospitalized for months. As a pilot he never could manage a decent take-off or landing. On his solo, he pancaked his training plane. The first time he took a Nieuport 17 into the air, he cracked it up.

But . . . when the war to end all wars had ended, Billy Bishop had become the world's greatest living air ace. He had shot down seventy-two enemy planes confirmed and many more which weren't officially counted — more, probably, than the Red Baron himself. He had won the Victoria Cross, two Distinguished

Service Orders, the Military Cross, the Distinguished Flying Cross, the Legion of Honour and the Croix de Guerre with palm. There were no more honours left for him to win. Billy Bishop was a living legend and he was only twenty-four years old.

The schoolmaster who suggested Billy wouldn't amount to much had added a qualification: the one thing he *was* good at was fighting. Anybody who called Billy a sissy got beaten up. The odds against him were sometimes seven to one but that hadn't fazed Billy. Later on, in the air, the odds were often greater. Eddie Rickenbacker once said that Billy Bishop was the only man he ever met who was totally without fear.

On June 2, 1917, the greatest single day of his life, the odds were heavily against Billy. The field was still in darkness when he rose. The rest of the squadron was asleep. Billy was going out on his own, far behind the German lines, without support. He didn't bother to take off his pyjamas, just pulled his flying clothes on over them, trudged off to the mess hall, gulped some hot tea, then headed for the hangar, peering upward into the gloom. The weather wasn't good: heavy clouds at five hundred; light drizzle.

Walter Bourne, his mechanic, had the blue-nosed Nieuport on the field, its engine running. Billy pulled on his oil-stained leather helmet, made one last cockpit check and then was off into the darkness, experiencing "a loneliness such as he had never known before." His stomach felt hollow. It wasn't fear — he knew exactly what he was about to do, had planned it for weeks, prepared for it all the previous day — it was plain hunger; Billy wished he'd had some breakfast.

He was fifteen minutes behind the enemy lines before the Germans realized that a British fighter was over one of their airfields. Billy had no idea where he was, didn't even know the name of the aerodrome below him. (It was Estourmel, near Cambrai.) Coming out of the clouds he could see little black figures running out of the hangars toward their waiting planes.

He raked the field with machine-gun fire. An Albatros began to roll forward for take-off. Billy, two hundred feet above, poured fifteen slugs into it, just at lift off. It tilted; a wing dug in. Billy watched it ground-loop into a mass of wreckage.

A second plane was starting down the field. Billy pulled hard on his stick, gaining altitude for the kill. He fired a burst of thirty bullets but missed. No matter. The German was so unnerved he crashed into a tree.

Two other planes struggled into the air. Billy emptied the rest of his drum into one and watched it crash. The fourth plane attacked, its twin Spandaus flashing. Unarmed for the moment, Billy twisted and dodged, while changing ammunition drums. That done, he emptied the entire new drum — ninety-nine rounds — into the enemy aircraft. The German had no stomach to pursue as Billy streaked for home. As soon as his smoking gun cooled off he tore it from its mount and threw it overboard. He didn't need the dead weight; he needed speed.

The clouds parted. Four enemy scouts appeared above him. Billy kept his plane in the blind spot directly below, matching them manoeuvre for manoeuvre. They never saw him as he broke away, diving to one thousand feet over the German lines. Rifle and machine gun bullets poured up from the trenches. Billy's ears cracked with the sound of shrapnel ripping into fabric. He felt drained, all his early elation gone. He flew in a daze, a queer, sinking feeling in his gut. He felt he was losing his senses. The only thing that mattered was to get home.

When he landed, his comrades were still snoring in their beds; it was scarcely 5:30 a.m. Billy fired off his

Very pistol to wake them and they crowded round: "How many kills?" *Only three; one got away.* Billy was being over-modest. He had damaged several other planes on the ground and wounded the pilot of the fourth Albatros. The raid was, according to the RFC's commander, "the greatest single show of the war." It won the Victoria Cross for Billy. He was the first Canadian airman to wear it — but there would be more.

The Canadians were among the greatest flyers of World War One. Of the twenty-seven super-aces — those who downed more than thirty planes — eleven were Canadians. Of the ten leading aces on the Allied side, five were Canadians. The Canadian flyers among them won 475 decorations, including three VC's.

They came from small, isolated towns, mostly in the west (Billy Bishop, from Owen Sound, Ontario, was an exception) — towns with names like Gladstone, Carberry, Keg River Prairie and Nanaimo. They were all free spirits, rugged individualists impatient with military tradition, reckless of rules and discipline, contemptuous of spit and polish. They took to aerial warfare because there were no military textbooks telling how it should be fought. The Canadians made up their tactics, invented their traditions, as they went along.

They handled their planes like spirited steeds. It was no accident that most of them were superb horsemen. Billy Bishop may have ignored hockey, football and lacrosse, but he learned to ride early and well. Above all they were crack shots. Billy had known how to shoot since his father gave him a .22 as a Christmas present and offered him a quarter for every squirrel he shot. He quickly learned to knock squirrels over with one bullet. In the air he treated Germans as squirrels; often enough he dispatched an enemy plane with a single burst.

The newspapers called him the Lone Hawk. Billy hated the name, but there was truth in it. The Germans

116

hunted in packs but Billy liked to go off by himself between patrols, a solitary killer bursting unexpectedly from the clouds. "I doubt if mankind has ever known a lonelier job than that of the single-seat fighters of World War One," he wrote. The Canadians were used to lonely jobs, empty spaces, vast solitudes. Billy's closest rival among the Canadians, the naval flyer, Raymond Collishaw (sixty kills) had been a seaman on the West Coast and in the Arctic. Don McLaren, the number three Canadian ace (fifty-four kills), was raised in an isolated Indian trading post. Loneliness was in their nature.

It is doubtful if any of them intended to be flyers. Certainly the idea didn't occur to Billy. At the start of World War One, the entire Canadian Aviation Corps consisted of two men and a single airplane that never got off the ground. Billy, the horseman, joined the Mississauga Horse.

When his unit embarked for overseas on October 1, 1914, Billy was left behind, hospitalized by pneumonia and a mysterious allergy. One doctor said the allergy was caused by army food; another said it was caused by horses. Billy thought it was the result of parade-ground dust. The future didn't look too rosy but an old flame consoled him by sending a daily bouquet of flowers to the hospital. Billy, in a panic, turned them over to his sister before his fiancée could find them. There were several old flames in Billy Bishop's life, but all that was in the past. He was engaged to Margaret Burden, Timothy Eaton's granddaughter.

Out of the hospital, Billy transferred to the 7th Canadian Mounted Rifles. At twenty-one, he was the youngest officer in the regiment, and because he was a good shot, they put him in charge of the machine-gun section. The crossing to England was harrowing. The ship was overcrowded; the weather was vile; men and horses

117

were seasick. As they neared the Irish coast, the U-boats moved in for the kill and ships to the port and starboard began to blow up and sink. Billy was petrified — or claimed to be. "I wonder if I shall ever come home to you," he wrote his fiancée.

Billy hated Shorncliffe military camp, one of the muddiest in all of muddy England, "an incredible mass of mud, muck and mire with the special added unpleasantness that only horses in large quantity can contribute." He had not expected the war to be like this. One day, up to his knees in the gumbo of the parade ground, he gazed up into the sky and saw a cleansing sight: a trim little fighter plane zooming out of the clouds. Then and there, Billy Bishop made up his mind to fight the war in the air. Without asking anybody's permission, he applied for a transfer to the Royal Flying Corps. At the War Office he was asked a lot of silly questions: *Do you skate well? Can you ride a motorcycle?* Sure, said Billy; you bet. He wanted to be a fighter pilot but that would mean a six-month wait — in the mud. But they needed observers: "the chap who goes along for the ride," as the War Office interviewer put it. Billy asked for a transfer and was taken on at once.

His first training plane was an Avro two-seater. The aircraft had no guns. It could barely get off the ground. In the air, it gasped and wheezed like an old Ford truck. But Billy was ecstatic: "This flying is the most wonderful invention," he wrote home. "A man ceases to be a human up there. He feels that nothing is impossible"

When Billy began his training, aerial warfare was only one year old and still in a primitive state. There had been some advances: pilots no longer threw bricks at each other or fought with rifles and pistols. The new aircraft were armed with light machine guns, synchronized to fire directly through the propeller. But the planes were often as dangerous as the enemy guns; and, none was so dangerous as the R.E.7, the experimental reconnaissance craft that was Billy's first combat machine when, as a trained observer, he reached France in January 1916.

The R.E.7 rarely reached a top speed of sixty miles an hour. It stalled at about forty-five. In the wind and sleet of northern France, take-offs and landings were nightmarish. In the air, as Billy put it, the R.E.7 was "as manoeuvrable as a ten-ton truck, but by no means as safe." It was supposed to carry four machine guns and a 500-pound bomb, but with that weight it couldn't get off the ground. On their first flight, Billy and his pilot jettisoned two guns and the bomb and just managed to stagger into the air.

Even with two machine guns, the plane was a sitting duck. Billy didn't see how you could fire either one of the guns through the maze of struts and wires that held the wings together. The plane, he said, looked more like a bird cage. Fortunately for Billy Bishop, there were no dogfights that first winter in France.

On the ground it was a different story. Billy, it developed, was accident prone. A series of mishaps kept sending him to hospital. Back in England, following a leave, he was out of action for the best part of a year with a cracked knee and a severely strained heart (the latter ailment blamed variously on brandy, champagne, the tensions of long patrols or a combination of all three.) These misfortunes merely convinced Billy that he wasn't meant to die.

Billy Bishop still wanted to be a pilot. In the summer of 1916 his own squadron had been nearly wiped out in the battles of the Somme. To complicate matters, his records had been lost. Worse, the medicos had declared him unfit for military service. But Billy had charm and Billy had made some powerful friends in England. He pulled strings and got himself accepted at a pilot's training course on Salisbury Plain.

Learning to fly was not the breeze that Billy Bishop, veteran observer, thought it would be. His instructor cursed him for being ham-handed at the controls. In desperation he allowed Billy to solo after only three hours flying time. In the air, without a companion, Billy felt lonelier than he had ever been. Somehow he managed to get the plane onto the ground again "with a spine-jarring 'plonk' " — the first of what were to become known as "Bishop landings."

Billy Bishop went back to France in March of 1917 to the 60th squadron of the RFC at a place called Filescamp Farm. The 60th was the most famous fighter squadron in France, thanks to one of its former members, Albert Ball. Ball, the leading British ace, was Billy's hero; he had attacked as many as forty German planes single-handed, and had shot down twenty-nine. His secret weapon was surprise. He would sneak up on superior formations and launch himself into reckless attack before the enemy could recover from the shock. Billy resolved that that would be his technique too. He had an added advantage: he couldn't miss with a machine gun. He was so deadly accurate he could shoot down enemy pilots before they knew he was behind them. And his eyesight was superb. Like Ball, he did not wear goggles in the air; he felt this interfered with his shooting; and he searched the sky with such intensity, turning and twisting in the cockpit to spot enemy planes, that the back of his neck was often rubbed raw.

The Nieuport 17 was a single-seat fighter with a rotary engine and a Lewis gun fixed on a mount on the top wing. The gun was easily manoeuvrable. It could be fired directly ahead over the arc of the propeller or it could be pulled back into the cockpit to fire straight up at an enemy passing overhead. Billy never allowed anybody but himself to handle his gun; he personally loaded every round into the magazine. He took a great deal more pains with his gun than with his plane (the plane, to him, was merely a flying gun-mount). On his first time out, returning from a patrol, he had crash-landed almost at the feet of the brigade commander who immediately ordered him back to flying school.

Before the order could be put into effect, Billy Bishop experienced, on March 25, 1917, his first aerial dog-fight. It was almost his last. Billy was rear man on a four-plane patrol at nine thousand feet when they ran into a squadron of Albatroses over the German lines. As the enemy planes closed in, the patrol banked to the left in a tight climb. Billy was a little slow. An Albatros, pulling up under the leader's tail, suddenly filled his gunsight. Billy, the one-shot squirrel killer, pressed the firing button and the German went into a dive. Billy figured he might be faking and gave chase. Sure enough, the Albatros pulled out of the dive. As it levelled off, Billy gave it another burst. Once more the plane went into a dive with Billy screaming down behind it at two hundred miles an hour. The Nieuport had one serious fault; pushed beyond normal speeds, the wings tended to break off. Billy Bishop was lucky; the wings stayed on but the motor coughed out. Billy didn't see the Albatros crash to the ground in flames — he was too busy trying to get his nose up and glide over in his own lines. He barely made it; the field into which he landed had just been captured by the Allies. It took several days to get his battered plane back to the squadron, but Billy Bishop had scored his first kill. They told him he didn't have to go back to flying school; he could stay in France and fight.

Billy met the Red Baron — or at least his famous Flying Circus — five days later on March 30, 1917. He was in charge of a patrol when the Baron's pack attacked and shot down two of his men. The following day, far behind the enemy lines, Billy got a partial revenge when he knocked one of the Baron's Albatroses out of the air.

The Red Baron was Manfred von Richthofen, leader of Jagdstaffel II, the deadly "hunting pack," based at Douai. The Baron was a bit like Billy — rugged, sturdy, wiry and short. But the Baron was dark and saturnine while Billy was fair with the features of a Paul Newman and the body of a James Cagney. The Baron had started in the cavalry, too, and got out of the mud and into the air, surviving a dangerous and inglorious apprenticeship as an air observer before becoming a killer pilot. The crimson spinner flying from his wing was his trademark. Billy soon had a trademark as well: a blue spinner on the wing and a blue nose on his Nieuport.

April 1917 went down in history as Bloody April. Squadron 60 and Jagdstaffel II bore the brunt of the fighting, and the Germans were the clear victors. Richthofen alone shot down twenty-two planes to Bishop's twelve. The German Albatros was a faster machine with superior firepower — two machine guns to the Nieuport's single Lewis. And the German pilots were veterans. Number 60 Squadron suffered so many casualties that it had only five experienced men left at the month's end. One of them was Billy Bishop.

Billy learned fast. He got his third Albatros along with an enemy sausage balloon on April 5, five miles behind the enemy lines. Again his engine failed in a dive but Billy now knew what to do: keep pumping the throttle, his mechanic had told him. Billy pumped away as the Nieuport screamed toward the ground: two hundred feet ... one hundred feet ... fifty feet ... thirty feet. At twenty feet the engine caught. Lucky Billy returned to fight another day and to write a letter home in his best Boys' Own Paper prose: "Three more pilots lost today. All good men. Oh, how I hate the Huns. They have done in so many of my best friends. I'll make them pay, I swear."

In 1916, flyers on both sides still operated with a certain amount of medieval chivalry, dropping wreaths over the aerodromes of dead enemies and even toasting captured fighter pilots in the mess. But Billy fought with hate. "I detest the Huns ... I hate them with all my heart," he wrote to Margaret Burden. He experienced a thrill that was almost sadistic in watching a vanquished enemy crash. Like Richthofen, he had the true killer instinct, and not without reason. In 60 Squadron, Billy's friends went to their deaths almost as regularly as they answered mess call.

In the air, Billy Bishop kept his cool. On April 9, 1917 (Easter Monday — the day the Canadians attacked Vimy Ridge), he shot down three planes and came as close to death as any man can. His mechanic couldn't figure out how he'd lived, because his windshield was shattered by a bullet directly in the line of his head. All lucky Billy had was a graze. He kept the shattered windshield for the rest of his life — one of his few wartime souvenirs.

That night in the mess, with the others who had faced death with him, Billy Bishop let off steam. He drank champagne by the bucketfull, sang songs, recited, tap-danced on top of the piano, then poured more champagne on the sounding board to improve the tone. The squadron staggered to bed at three, rose again at dawn and flew off, low over the lines, to give ground support to the attacking troops.

By mid-April, thirteen of 60 Squadron's pilots were dead — men with whom Billy had caroused in the mess and fought beside in the air, men who had become, in a few days, closer to him than the friends of a lifetime. In less than a month Billy Bishop had become a combat veteran, the squadron's leading ace and commander of C-flight. On April 20, after shooting down an enemy observation plane, he returned to find he'd won the Military Cross. There were drinks all round in the mess that night. But then there were drinks all round most nights. No one knew which round might be his last. Wakes and celebrations were indistinguishable.

The squadron lived daily with death but Billy Bishop didn't really believe that he would die. He was far more fearful of being taken prisoner. He found the British discipline oppressive enough; how could he ever stand a German prison camp?

Against that possibility, he kept a fine edge on his shooting with daily target practice. In the air he adopted Ball's tactics of surprise. On April 22, using a comrade as a decoy, he sucked five enemy single-seaters into a trap, swooped out of the clouds, dispatched two of them before the rest of his flight reached the scene, and chased the other three out of sight.

On the way home, Billy came to a decision. There would be no more twisting, turning and manoeuvring in the air; from this point on he would develop the quick, darting attack as the key element of his personal style.

Like a hockey player, Billy was on a winning streak. He made the most of it, for he was a man who liked to win, liked to be the best at whatever he attempted. On the last day of that bloodiest of Aprils, he took part in nine dogfights in two hours. He destroyed one enemy plane and forced down two more that morning. In the afternoon, he ran headlong into the Red Baron himself.

In eight months of combat, the Baron had shot down fifty-two planes. In five weeks, Billy Bishop's score was twelve. The previous day the Baron had scored four kills — an almost unheard-of feat. Now, on the eve of a furlough, he had vowed to equal that record.

Earlier that day, Billy had cheated the Baron out of a sure victory by breaking up his wolf-pack formation with his dive-and-zoom tactics. This time, with the odds five to two in his favour, the Baron was out for blood. As the seven planes (two British, five German), swirled and criss-crossed in the air, the Baron poured a stream of bullets into Billy's Nieuport. One entered the fold of his flying coat, another pierced his instrument panel. It was, Billy would say later (after he had cooled down), "the best shooting I have ever seen." But now, with oil drenching his face, he lost his temper and charged. Black smoke poured from the Baron's Albatros. For one ecstatic moment, Billy thought he had him. But the Baron had merely used an old trick to escape. He dove four thousand feet, flattened out, waggled his wings and was gone. When Billy counted the holes in his plane he found that the Baron had missed him by only six inches. "A miss is as good as a mile," he wrote Margaret. He and the Baron never met again.

April ended; the Baron went on his leave; the air war slackened off; Billy felt let down. He had some leave coming, too, and he needed it. He looked far older than his twenty-three years. He had fought forty battles in forty days, seen close friends plunge to flaming deaths, breathed far too many castor oil fumes from the Nieuport's rotary engine and drunk far too much champagne and brandy in those desperately jovial evenings in the mess.

Billy wanted to bring his score to twenty before he took his leave. On May 2, he fought from dawn to sunset and turned in three combat reports. He engaged twenty-three German aircraft, destroyed two and emerged without a scratch. His only problem came when he landed his plane at the day's end. It wasn't the

Germans who smashed up his undercarriage; it was Billy.

On the day before his leave, Billy's hero, Albert Ball, came over from his squadron at Vert Galand to talk to him. Over brandies, Ball outlined a daring scheme. Why not sneak over the German lines at dawn, just the two of them, and destroy the enemy planes on the ground as they pulled out of the hangars? You bet, said Billy. Soon as I get back from leave. The following day he was whooping it up in London and Albert Ball was dead from enemy gunfire.

Billy Bishop now had the highest score of any surviving British airman; he also had the Distinguished Service Order — next to the VC the highest decoration his monarch could bestow. He was a celebrity and his leave, like all the leaves of that weary war, was a frantic attempt to cram as much living as possible into a fragment of time. He mingled in London society, dined with Princess Marie Louise, hob-nobbed with one famous Canadian, Lord Beaverbrook, and turned down a dinner invitation from another (Lloyd George's house leader, Bonar Law) in order to spend the time with a beautiful young actress. All these various connections, with the possible exception of the actress, would serve Billy well in later years.

Billy went back to France on May 22 and knocked down three more aircraft. But Albert Ball's plan kept nagging at him. Why shouldn't he do it alone? If he could reach the German airfields, unseen, at first light, he might just pull it off. Finally he decided on the day: come rain or shine, he would carry out his scheme on June 2. He spent the first of the month practising his shooting, poring over maps, checking out his plane. The following morning, before dawn, he flew off to win his Victoria Cross.

126

For the next fortnight, Billy Bishop scarcely took a day off. The odds were against him, but surprise was on his side. On June 8 he dove right through a squadron of six enemy scouts, knocking one out of the air, and continued his dive to safety before the other five pilots could gather their wits. His own plane eventually had to be overhauled and fitted with a new skin; there were so many patches on it, the extra weight was slowing him down.

For all his days with the squadron, Billy Bishop was subjected to the conflicting tugs of successive emotions. Elation was followed by frustration, frustration by defiance, defiance by despair, despair by hatred. Frustrated by an inability to find the enemy, Billy led fifteen of the squadron directly over a German aerodrome where they indulged in a full-dress performance of aerial stunting above the astonished audience. "We should have charged the damned Huns admission," said his friend, "Black" Lloyd. The next day Lloyd was killed in a fight with two Albatros scouts and Billy was despondent. "I am thoroughly downcast tonight," he wrote. "Sometimes this awful fighting . . . makes you wonder if you have a right to call yourself human. . . . I am so tired of it all, the killing, the war. . . ."

Billy went on a three-day leave to Amiens, had a fling with a beautiful French girl named Ninette and confessed it all in another letter to Margaret. The affair, he insisted, was more therapeutic than romantic. No doubt it was. When he returned to Filescamp Farm, he shot down five enemy planes in as many days. Billy couldn't seem to miss. He destroyed one with a single burst of ten rounds. He killed another at a distance of a hundred yards.

When the wet weather came at the end of June and flying was rendered impossible, the surviving pilots engaged in manic japery. Domestic animals were seized and painted in assorted hues. The smashing of gramophone records over various heads became endemic. Uniform-tearing contests were a nightly ritual. And the bar never closed.

A French pilot, making a forced landing through the overcast, was given a riotous champagne welcome. Billy inveigled him into a flying contest. Each tried to best the other in a series of wild manoeuvres under a low cloud cover. The Frenchman reached some kind of peak by scraping his wingtip through the grass of the field. Billy outdid him by rolling his wheels on the roof of the mess as he came in for a landing.

New planes — S.E.5s — arrived early in July: they had two guns instead of one and were forty miles an hour faster. Billy was ecstatic; but his euphoria vanished on his first flight: one gun wouldn't work; the other shot holes through the propeller. The squadron went back to the old machines while the new ones were being overhauled.

In his old, patched-up, blue-nosed Nieuport, Billy Bishop fought the highest battle of his career above Vitry at nineteen thousand feet. The single-seater wallowed in the thin air, barely responding to the controls. Billy's hands were numb with cold, his senses dizzy from lack of oxygen, his timing off. Twice he had the enemy in his sights at ten yards but each time his shots went wild. The second time his plane stalled and went into a spin. Billy swore he'd never fight again at that height.

He could hardly wait for the S.E.5s to be overhauled; the Germans in their faster planes were leaving him standing still. When the new planes finally arrived he was so excited that he decided to fight on his day off. That was the day Billy Bishop forgot to be cautious. He chased a pair of two-seaters down to five thousand feet — the ideal anti-aircraft range. The German gunners knocked him out of the air. His flaming S.E.5 crashed into a copse of poplar trees. Lucky Billy, hanging from the cockpit, was pulled out unscratched by some passing soldiers. His nerves shaken, he took two days' rest at Amiens, but on his return to Filescamp he took to the air immediately. Billy had heard too many stories about flyers who had lost their nerve after they crashed. He needn't have worried; his luck still held. On his first patrol he bagged two more of the enemy.

Billy Bishop, now one of the senior living British aces, had become too valuable to be wasted in the daily rough and tumble of aerial combat. With forty-seven official kills to his credit, they sent him to England as an instructor, made him a major, gave him a bar to his DSO, and put his picture in all the papers — the most decorated airman of the war. At Buckingham Palace, King George V pinned medals all over him. Billy was terribly embarrassed; his new boots squeaked audibly.

The hero went off to Canada to help with recruiting. At Montreal, a great, jostling crowd of dignitaries, reporters, photographers and plain citizens roared a greeting. Billy helped launch a Red Cross campaign and then visited his old alma mater, the Royal Military College, which only three years before had been on the verge of kicking him out.

Billy Bishop married his sweetheart, Margaret Burden, in the Memorial Church named for her grandfather. The four blocks between the Burden home on Avenue Road, Toronto, and the church, was dense with people. Billy and his bride went off to the Catskills on a honeymoon and then to the British War Mission in Washington. Billy's job was to help America build an airforce. Back in Canada, Billy made a speech about that: he said the Germans had nothing to fear from the United States' fighting forces; aircraft production was lagging seriously. Consternation! When he got back to

London, early in 1918, he found himself under arrest. The incarceration lasted just ten minutes while Billy wilted under a stiff lecture about his verbal indiscretions.

Billy Bishop was given a new job. He was to form a fighting squadron of his own, the 85th, better known as the Flying Foxes. Training took up most of the late winter and spring. Before leaving for France at the end of May the Flying Foxes in one mammoth binge, managed to consume two hundred bottles of champagne. Their departure was accompanied by a certain relief. "Thank God," a leading actress was heard to mutter, as the curtain rose in a London theatre, "Bishop and his crowd have finally gone to France."

The front was even more hectic than wartime London. The Foxes arrived at the height of the great German spring offensive and were plunged immediately into a "carnival of destruction, which has no parallel in the annals of aviation." By the end of the month the squadron had ten kills to its credit; eight of those were Billy's.

In the mess, the Foxes enjoyed eggs Benedict, chicken livers *en brochette,* ice cream, champagne and Napoleon brandy. They caroused most of the night, flew off each morning on dawn patrol. Billy kept up with them in spite of a mountain of paper work. His favourite time for going out alone after the Huns was the evening, when his administrative duties were done and before the binges began.

The Foxes were soon moved to a permanent aerodrome near St. Omer. Billy was in high spirits: he now had sixty enemy kills confirmed. He took off from the new aerodrome one evening and in eight minutes got two more. Then he received some disheartening news; he was ordered back to London to help form a Canadian flying corps. Billy Bishop was so mad that the following morning he shot down three German planes in half an hour.

His total time with the Flying Foxes in France was just four weeks. In that brief period, with only twelve flying days, he destroyed twenty-five enemy planes, more than Eddie Rickenbacker, the leading American ace, was able to bring down in five months at the front.

On his last day, June 19, 1918, Billy Bishop was invincible. He climbed into a heavy drizzle and headed east toward Ypres, alone. In the clouds he lost his way and came down over Ploegsteert Wood. Just below him were three Pfalz scouts. As Billy swept down on them he spotted two more on his tail. He ignored them and opened up on the three in front from 120 yards. He killed the pilot of the rearmost plane and watched as it went into a vertical dive. The other two, scrambling for cloud cover, locked wings and crashed. Billy pulled up in a steep turn as his two rear attackers slipped past below. He came in at fifty yards and sent the fourth Pfalz crashing. Alone now, his compass broken, his bearings lost, he flew on in the mist, ran into another German two-seater, dispatched it with ten rounds. In fifteen minutes — his last aerial skirmish — Billy Bishop had destroyed five German planes.

The cautious British credited Billy Bishop with seventy-two official kills. The real total undoubtedly exceeded a hundred. As early as 1917, the War Office admitted an additional twenty-three "probable but unconfirmed kills." The RFC was sticky about confirmations. Billy, flying alone, knocked down many of his victims far behind the German lines where no Allied witness could spot the wreckage. Von Richthofen's score, on the other hand, was almost certainly inflated. The Red Baron had eighty kills to his credit when he was shot down in the spring of 1918. At least a dozen of these "victories" were planes that had made forced landings with their pilots alive. Nor did the Red Baron fight alone, as Billy did. Often enough he held himself aloof from battle, let his fellow pilots set up a victim, then swooped at the last moment. His fighting methods, wrote Billy, were "typically German."

When Billy left France, he was the greatest living ace on the Allied side. That record stood until war's end. He had forty productive years left to him but his greatest moments were over. In the dying months of the war there were more medals, more plaudits, more speeches. The inevitable postwar lecture tour followed. It was hugely successful until Billy collapsed on stage from appendicitis. When he returned to the platform a month later, only ten persons showed up. War heroes were passé. The tour was cancelled.

Billy went into partnership with another Canadian ace, Bill Barker, who had won the VC by taking on single-handedly no fewer than sixty enemy planes and knocking down five of them. The two heroes formed a commercial aviation firm. The Canadian National Exhibition hired them to do stunts over Lake Ontario; the contract was cancelled abruptly when Billy dove directly towards the grandstand and looped at the very last minute, causing panic, fainting and (it was claimed) at least one miscarriage. Then Billy, testing a new two-seater, turned it over on landing, squashed his nose, damaged his eyesight and washed himself out of flying. That was it for the Bishop-Barker partnership.

But Billy's luck held. He invented a successful formula for a quick-drying paint and with the proceeds paid off his debts. He became front man for a Canadian firm in Britain. His contacts and celebrity easily opened doors; his native shrewdness at negotiation gave him a formidable reputation. He had, it was said "the face of an angel and the mind of a murderer." He could not stay still, kept taking on new sports and hobbies, always excelling, always trying to be the best. He played polo, learned golf, took up boxing. He became part of the high society of the Twenties. He chummed around with Ernest Hemingway, Scott Fitzgerald and Josephine Baker, mingled with royalty, drank champagne with Hermann Goering and, like so many others, was wiped out financially in the crash of 1929.

Once again, Billy's social connections came to his aid. He was soon on his feet again, vice-president of an oil company. A pillar of Montreal society, Air Vice-Marshal in the peacetime RCAF, Billy Bishop, impeccable in London-tailored clothes, driven to work by his personal chauffeur, was no longer the callow, hell-raising youth from Owen Sound.

Like his friend Winston Churchill, Billy was sure another war was coming. He began to spend more and more of his time trying to persuade the government to train pilots for the future Armageddon. To encourage the trend he himself joined the Montreal Light Aeroplane Club and took to the air again. On his first outing, he landed the plane on its nose. "Haven't lost my touch," said Billy.

In the summer of 1939, Billy Bishop, now Honorary Air Marshal of the RCAF and head of the Air Advisory Committee, figured out a neat way to sneak American planes into Canada without causing an international incident. The planes were landed at border strips, left purposely "unattended" on the American side, lassoed by Canadian airmen and dragged across, without violating the international boundary or American neutrality. That charade seemed to suit everybody.

After war was declared, Billy Bishop was put in charge of recruiting. The job was full time. For the first time since that earlier war, Billy was completely happy, every minute taken up. But he still made time to learn to play the piano and to practise three to four hours a day. Then he learned to play table tennis; not indifferently, but expertly. Billy always had to have a hobby, always had to be the best.

Billy's pace never faltered. He toured airforce bases, stimulating recruiting, travelling, lecturing, inspecting, even playing a role in a Hollywood movie about the airforce, driving himself once again as he had in those months at Filescamp Farm. In November 1942, in the middle of a speech to air cadets, he collapsed. The doctors said he wouldn't survive, but lucky Billy proved them wrong. He rested, recovered, and went back to work. But a lot of the old steam was gone; when he finally hung up his uniform in 1944, Billy Bishop was close to exhaustion.

In semi-retirement after the war, Billy Bishop, still restless, still curious, took up hobby after hobby. He subscribed to a correspondence course in typing; he learned ice carving; he spent hours reading. And then, one by one, the enthusiasms which had kept him alive were abandoned. Illnesses increased. He spent his winters in Florida but on his last winter he was too tired and to ill to come home. In the early morning of September 10, 1956, Billy Bishop died.

Billy Bishop's obituary appeared in the major dailies in most of the countries in the world. In Canada, his funeral was one of the greatest in living memory. Thousands lined the streets to see Billy go to his grave.

That was in 1956. In January 1975, the American men's magazine, *Argosy,* published along article about the leading aces of two World Wars. "While World War I produced numbers of aerial 'aces'," the article said, "two names stand out from all the rest: Baron Manfred von Richthofen and Captain Eddie Rickenbacker." The article had a great deal to say about these two. It devoted three-quarters of a column of eulogy to the Red Baron and even more to Captain Eddie. It described certain other notables of World War One, including Roland Garros of France and the Dutch genius, Anthony Fokker. It even published a list of those it claimed were the greatest aces of World War One, with statistics on their respective victories. But in that list and in that text one name was conspicuous by its absence. Nowhere was there any mention of Billy Bishop. In 1975, the Lone Hawk was forgotten.

6

The Strange Case of The Brother, XII

The limits of human gullibility are infinite. As the British Society for Psychical Research has long known, it is possible to con even the most intelligent people into a firm belief in ghosts with little more than a few yards of gauze, some black velvet and spooky lights. Conjurers, using the oldest principles of misdirection, convince eminent scientists that they have the supernatural power to bend spoons. Cancer quacks flourish; faith healers abound; fake yogis sell mantras for fancy sums. Confirmed atheists, who refuse to accept the principle of Divine intervention, are perfectly prepared to believe that the inanimate planets control our lives. Tens of thousands of otherwise sensible people are suckered into believing that gods from outer space built Stonehenge, that the Great Pyramid sharpens razor blades and that a weird, supra-natural force off Bermuda makes ships vanish.

New messiahs turn up with clockwork regularity to gull the credulous; and for every messiah there are a thousand suckers. But nowhere, it is safe to hazard, are there more messiahs or more suckers than on the west coast of North America. California and British Columbia are hotbeds of off-beat religions. British Israelites, Kabalarians, Rosicrucians, Four Square Gospelers and other cults far kookier, flourish like tropical weeds in the salubrious climate of the Pacific. Of these, there was none so kooky, none so bizarre, none so preposterous — none so downright *evil* — as the Aquarian Foundation, set up in 1927 on Vancouver Island by the man who called himself The Brother, XII.

Half a century later, the mind recoils at the idea of anybody, no matter how imbecilic, taking The Brother, XII seriously for more than ten seconds. His philosophy was a monstrous mishmash, his writings obvious hokum, his rituals pure mumbo jumbo. And yet . . . and yet . . . wasn't it in October 1975, that a mysterious couple, known only as The Two, mesmerized twenty Oregonians with a philosophy called Human Individual Metamorphosis, and talked them into selling all their possessions in order to take a UFO to another planet? The Two, who claimed to be a million years old, could easily be The Brother, XII and his sadistic Madame Zee in reincarnation — that is, if one believed in reincarnation, as The Brother's disciples certainly did.

The Brother's story might have come straight out of *Weird Tales,* the immensely popular monthly magazine of the period. All the names have the incense of the Sunday supplement clinging to them: The House of Mystery . . . The Three Truths . . . The Eleven Masters of Wisdom . . . The City of Refuge. What editor could resist those lures? Few editors, in fact, have. The story of The Brother, XII has served free-lance journalists well for almost half a century.

We have no authentic information on the origins of Edward Arthur Wilson, the man who named himself, variously, The Brother, XII, the God Osiris, Amiel de Valdes, and Julian Skottowe. Most sources agree that he was born sometime in the 1870s, either in England or in India, of an Anglican missionary father and a native or half-caste mother. Characteristically, Wilson claimed that his mother was an Indian princess; he also claimed that he had trained on a Royal Navy windjammer and that he had, at one time, been engaged in trafficking Negro slaves out of Africa. All of these autobiographical notes must be looked on with scepticism. The windjammer tale rings true, however; there is no doubt that Wilson was a superb sailor.

We do know that he was in Canada as early as 1905, in the employ for several years of the Dominion Express Company in Victoria, British Columbia, and that here he indulged his love of the sea, sailing among the rock-bound islands of the Strait of Juan de Fuca and the Gulf of Georgia. He was also deeply involved with occultism. His room at Peggy Reynolds' boarding house was littered with scribblings about the movements of the stars and the planets and with tracts of the Theosophical Society, which had helped to spark a wave of interest in the occult.

Wilson left Victoria some time before World War One. A certain eccentricity accompanied his departure. He did not resign his job; he actively sought dismissal by demanding a salary only slightly less than that paid to the President of the Canadian Pacific Railway. He was then considerably in debt to his landlady, but attempted to placate her by promising to return "as the head of a new religion," a pledge he most certainly kept.

His subsequent movements, until his return to British Columbia, are vague. For much of the time he roamed the world as a seaman. He probably served during the first war with the British merchant marine. Certainly, in his voyages he spent much time studying religious and philosophic mysteries and making contact with various international groups intrigued by the occult. He obviously spent several years in Italy. By his

own account he was converted to the doctrine of reincarnation in Genoa, where he came to believe that
within measurable time the "planet" Aquarius would
collide with the earth and destroy all mankind except a
chosen few. At this time Wilson was engaged in a volu-
minous correspondence with devotees of the occult all
over the world and in these letters he told of his dreams
and visions. Incorporated into book form, they pur-
ported to describe the miracles that called him into
spiritual service. Since large numbers of apparently
sensible people were seduced by this account, it is best
to give it in his own words:

"About 9:30 p.m., October 19, 1924, I was not well
and had gone to bed early. At this time, I wanted to get
some milk to drink, so I lighted the candle which stood
on a small table at the side of my bed. Immediately after
lighting it, I saw the Tau suspended in mid-air just
beyond the end of my bed and at a height of eight or
nine feet. I thought: 'This is strange, it must be some
curious impression upon the retina of my eye which I
get by lighting the candle. I will close my eyes and it will
then stand out more clearly.' I shut my eyes at once, and
there was nothing there. I opened them and saw the Tau
in the same place, but much more distinctly; it was like
soft golden fire, and it glowed with a beautiful radiance.
This time, in addition to the Tau, there was a five-
pointed star very slightly below it and a little to the
right. Again I closed my eyes and there was nothing on
the retina. Again I opened them and the vision was still
there, but now it seemed to radiate fire. I watched it for
some time then it gradually dimmed and faded slowly
from my sight.

"The next day I made note of the matter and recorded my own understanding of it, which was as follows: 'The Tau confirmed the knowledge of the special

path along which I travelled to initiation, i.e., the Egyptian tradition and the Star of Adaptship towards which I have to strive.' Now, today, the Master tells me that that is true but there was also another meaning, hidden from me then, but which he now gives us. The Tau represents the age-old mysteries of Egypt, and the Star of Egypt is about to rise; the mysteries are to be restored, and the preparation for that restoration has been given into our hands. In the great Cycle of the Precession, the Pisces Age has ended, the sign of water and blood has set and AQUARIUS rises — the mighty triangle of Air is once more ascendant and we are to restore the 'Path of Wisdom and the First Path — knowledge.' "

At this point it is necessary to repeat that thousands of people came to believe implicitly in this gobbledygook, possibly because of Wilson's technique of presentation. The specifics of date and time, the confession of early doubt, the revelation that he was partially confused by the meaning of the symbols — these were the trappings of authenticity that lent a certain verisimilitude to his claim that he had been selected to undertake the restoration of the mysteries of Egypt.

Wilson's description of what happened next might easily have been written by that master of pulp fantasy, H. P. Lovecraft:

"A cold wind blew down that enormous aisle of pillars; somewhere in the endless distance lights seemed to move, then from above my head the light flooded me so that the distance and the vistas were dissolved. Then the light faded and I lay still, filled with a sense of wonder and great reverence. . . . The Master bids me say that the voice was the Voice of Dhyanis, of the great Tutelary Deities of Egypt, whom, in the past, we worshipped as 'The Gods.' As I write, further knowledge comes to me. I have to tell that the moment when you meet in this knowledge and for the purpose of discussing it, will be the moment for which forty centuries have waited."

As a result of all this, Wilson said, he was inspired to write a small volume called *The Three Truths*. He claimed divine collaboration — a ghost writer in the truest sense. In the book he told how, during a seance, he had been transported to the world of spirits where he had mingled with the great minds of history. Wilson's spirit world was run efficiently enough by a kind of board of governors, selected over the centuries by the great philosophers and savants. When Wilson turned up, he was promptly recognized as one of the greatest minds of all time and designated as the twelfth man on what had been a sacred council of eleven, "The Eleven Masters of Wisdom." As the twelfth and only earthly brother, he chose to call himself The Brother, XII.

A board meeting was convened immediately to welcome the new brother, who was instructed to return to earth and start a refuge for the chosen few against the oncoming doom. To make themselves worthy of their trust, this select company would have to follow the Three Truths set down in Wilson's little book: Work, Order and Obedience. Obedience meant complete submission to The Brother, XII; and — as the chosen few were to learn — there was to be no swerving from the harsh path of discipline.

Some time after this, Wilson was married. We know very little about his wife except that she was an Englishwoman named Alma and that she was well educated. They lived together in an Italian monastery and it was here (he said) that he received a final message from the Eleven Masters ordering him to return to British Columbia and establish his retreat.

But first he went to England. In June 1926, he was in Southampton, living in a rooming house and hiring a small hall, night after night, in which he harangued the local Theosophists. The Society was, at that time, enjoying a new wave of popularity thanks to the presence in England, on tour, of its president Annie Besant. The Society's philosophy was harmless and not unappealing: its members accepted the Brahmanic doctrines of Karma and reincarnation and believed in the universal brotherhood of man. They were, however, fair game for any charlatan who could subvert the theosophical principles to his own ends.

Members of the Theosophical Society from various points in southern England poured in to hear Wilson speak, lured by the siren appeal of the Three Truths. At his lectures they were transfixed by the man himself — a small, neat, swarthy Eurasian, dressed in a Buddhist's saffron gown with black cabalistic markings, speaking as a delegate of a guru he called the Chela and warning them of the cataclysm to come.

Among the devotees were an elderly retired couple from London named Barley. One would not have expected either of them to have fallen for Wilson's line of gibberish. Alfred H. Barley had his feet rooted firmly in the physical sciences; he had been a chemist all his working life. His wife, Annie, had spent twenty-eight years as a teacher for the London County Council. And yet they both were captivated by The Brother, XII's writings and journeyed at once to Southampton to sit at his feet.

The Barleys were present at a seance when The Brother announced that the other Brothers in the Outer World had a message for him and that he must go into a trance to receive it. He retired behind a black curtain, to emerge after half an hour with his eyes flashing and sweat beading his brow. He had, he claimed, been visiting the other Brothers by "projection." He had come upon them seated on an inner ring of clouds, staring down at what he called the Void. At the bottom of this Void were all the stars and, beneath the stars, the earth and its solar system. Nobody, certainly not Alfred H. Barley, rose to point out that the Brothers had managed to turn the universe topsy-turvy, against all natural laws. They hung on every word as the Twelfth Brother explained how the other eleven had shown him where to build his place of refuge on earth against the collision with Aquarius, an astrological sign which Wilson confused with a planet.

The Brother, XII just happened to have with him an Admiralty chart of the west coast of British Columbia. He placed his pointer on a spot which he said he had never visited but which, in fact, he knew very well. There, on an inlet on the eastern shore of Vancouver Island, he would build his "fortress for the future." He made it clear that those who accompanied him must be uncritical, silent and loyal and also that as equals in a communal society they must renounce all worldly goods. Translated, that meant that they must hand over the proceeds of everything they owned and sold to The Brother, XII.

In the argot of con, an egg once hooked stays hooked. The ease with which Alfred and Annie Barley were hooked by Edward Arthur Wilson is truly astonishing. They lost no time in returning to London and converting everything they owned into cash. They sold their house and the securities into which they had funnelled their life savings and they gave it to The Brother, XII — in all, a small fortune of fourteen thousand dollars. Then, along with The Brother and one or two other disciples, they booked passage for Canada.

In May 1927, the Aquarian Foundation was incorporated under the Societies Act of British Columbia, its power and its funds in the hands of its founder, Wilson. One has to pause and take a deep breath at the revelation that the secretary of this preposterous undertaking was a former United States Treasury agent named Robert England. In his eight years of secret service with the department, England might be supposed to have learned something of the kind of financial chicanery that Wilson was pulling off. His job, after all, had been to search out swindlers who were trying to milk his government. Apparently, however, he was as blind as the others. All that can be said in his favour is that he was among the earliest of the anointed to become disenchanted.

Wilson established his colony at Cedar-by-the-Sea, just south of Nanaimo. From this central headquarters, telegrams, cables and letters began to fly off to the believers, announcing the acquisition of a tract of land for the City of Refuge. Money poured in by return mail. By the summer of 1928, the Foundation claimed a membership of eight thousand persons all over North America, contributing to the upkeep of the colony. A goodly number pulled up stakes and moved to Vancouver Island.

What sort of people were enrolled in this army of disciples? The rational mind has difficulty in accepting the fact that they were not untutored half-wits, scatter-brained spinsters or callow adolescents, but the solidest of citizens, often with good education and considerable means — doctors, lawyers, weavers, carpenters, journalists, chemists and businessmen. A partial list of some of the more distinguished supplicants gives cause for a certain unease about the future of the human race: Will Bevington Comfort, a writer for the *Saturday Evening Post;* Sir Kenneth McKenzie of Tunbridge Wells, England; Mr. A. Laker, editor of a British publication

145

called *The Referee*; Joseph Benner, publisher of a newspaper in Akron, Ohio; Coulson Turnbull, Ph.D., of Philadelphia; James Lippincott of the well-known book publishing family. Many of these people arrived on Wilson's doorstep; others, having read his works, provided financial support. (One man from Topeka, Kansas, who thought the mails too slow, wired ten thousand dollars.) The original tent city of 1927 at Cedar-by-the-Sea gave way by 1928 to a well-established settlement of substantial houses. The neighbours were not terribly curious. As one of them later said, he thought the Foundation had something to do with fish because he confused the name with "aquarium."

At this point the half-tragic, half-comic figure of Mary Connally enters the picture. Mrs. Connally was a widow from Ashville, North Carolina, and ripe for the plucking. Her husband was said to have been a millionaire. She later told a British Columbia provincial police investigator that she was the daughter of a former U.S. ambassador to the Court of Madrid. However that may be, two facts are undeniable: the widow Connally was loaded, and the widow Connally fell totally under the spell of The Brother, XII. She was travelling in the western United States when she first heard of the Aquarian Foundation. Her interest quickened with the arrival of the cult's literature, especially its magazine *The Chalice*. This curious monthly, subtitled "The Herald of the New Age," was crammed with much pure nonsense; among other items, it included some unsavoury ravings against the Jews, the Jesuits and the Bolsheviks, unlikely bedfellows who were seen to be cooperating to secure world domination — a suspicion commonly held by members of the fanatic fringes of that time on both sides of the Atlantic.

Mrs. Connally composed a fan letter to The Brother, XII and included in it a contribution of two thousand dollars, along with a broad hint that there was more where that came from. The Brother was understandably quick to reply. He had a more than nodding acquaintance with the laws of postal fraud and probably for that reason, suggested that he and the widow meet face to face in the Prince George Hotel, Toronto. She agreed. He headed posthaste for the east by way of Seattle, and as the train sped through the mountains he had a complicating but fortuitous encounter with another well-heeled lady.

It is a tribute to Edward Arthur Wilson's considerable powers that he was able to convince Mrs. Myrtle Baumgartner of Clifton Springs, New York, that she was the incarnation of the ancient Egyptian goddess of fertility, Isis. There is little doubt about Wilson's hypnotic talents. In the only photograph extant — an old newspaper cut that, in the late Robert Benchley's phrase, seems to have been engraved on bread — some of this personal magnetism comes through. Beards were not common in the late twenties, especially the Satanic kind of goatee that The Brother, XII sported. This was the kind of get-up affected by the successful stage magicians and illusionists of the period — the Blackstones, Thurstons, Nicolas and Dantés who travelled from Orpheum to Orpheum, sawing ladies in half, producing donkeys out of pocket handkerchiefs and levitating pretty assistants to the plaudits of gasping audiences. Certainly, The Brother, XII looked the part of a sorcerer; and his eyes, which manage to retain a certain demonic glitter behind the blur of a sixty-six line engraver's screen, were part of his pose. Those who remember him have remarked on the delicacy of his hands and the darkness of his features, contrasting sharply with the whiteness of his hair, the seducer's stock in trade.

Mrs. Baumgartner, the respectable wife of a New York State physician, not only came to believe that she was the Goddess Isis, she was also convinced by Wilson that he was the reincarnation of the twin deity Osiris, husband and brother of the goddess. Modern air travel inhibits leisurely seduction, but Wilson had more than three days and a private compartment in which to convince Myrtle that it had been decreed for several millennia that she should play an important part in preparation for what he kept calling the sixth sub-race. Their duty, in their present reincarnation, he said, was to join together in holy union to produce Horus, the ancient Egyptian Sun God, who would be the world's redeemer. Was it religion or romance, faith or illicit sex that intrigued Myrtle Baumgartner? Whatever it was, she was hooked. But Wilson had to keep her on ice in Chicago while he went off to Toronto to keep his tryst with Mary Connally. Myrtle not only agreed to wait for him; she was also prepared to leave her husband, her family and her friends and escape with him to the City of Refuge.

In Toronto, Mrs. Connally was charmed by The Brother and forked over a cheque for $25,850. Mrs. Connally then trotted off to North Carolina to wind up her affairs so that she could become one of the happy few, saved from world catastrophe on Vancouver Island. Osiris returned to Isis in Chicago.

A week later, the twin Egyptian deities were back at the cult's headquarters at Cedar-by-the-Sea. Now it was revealed that Osiris intended to retire with his Isis into the House of Mystery, a kind of *sanctum sanctorum* in the very heart of the City of Refuge. This was too much for Wilson's wife, Alma, who packed up immediately and left the colony, never to be seen or heard of again; in the checkered chronicle of Edward Arthur Wilson, she is no more than a name. The House of Mystery was hidden from the faithful beyond the curve of a winding pathway. A wire strung across the path marked the limits beyond which none could approach. When The Brother, XII prepared to visit the Masters of Wisdom he would retire to his sanctum, encouraging his followers to assist him on his astral travels by standing on the far side of the wire and meditating silently. Sooner or later the silence was broken, first by gossip and now by criticism and grumblings over the defilement of the sanctuary. To the amazement and horror of the grumblers, The Brother, XII appeared and seemed to know every detail of their disloyalty. He had, he said, been conferring in the House of Mystery with the Eleven Masters of Wisdom and they had told him all the details of his subjects' treason. He was even able to quote actual words of criticism and put his finger on the person who had voiced them. The members of his flock were thunderstruck. The man was apparently omniscient — all seeing!

It was some time before Wilson's secret was discovered. A newspaper reporter finally ran into a mechanic for the B.C. Electric Company who recalled travelling by bus to Bellingham and striking up a conversation with an electrician from Spokane. The electrician told his fellow passenger that he was returning from a job "at a strange place near Nanaimo installing the finest microphone system west of the Rockies." He had been forced to work in secret, he explained, hiding a number of microphones behind foliage, stones and tree trunks along the line of a wire crossing a path and leading into a "mysterious little house." The Brother, XII, it turns out, was one of history's first electronic eavesdroppers.

None the less, the carping over the new Isis nettled Wilson. He considered that his relations with Myrtle Baumgartner were nobody's business but his own and decided to remove himself from Cedar-by-the-Sea. He took thirteen thousand dollars of Mrs. Connally's money and bought four hundred acres of property on the heavily wooded Valdes Island in the Strait of Georgia directly across from Cedar. He then announced that he would build a second House of Mystery there and go into seclusion with Isis. Only a select group would go with him to Valdes: the rest must stay at Cedar.

With the establishment of the new colony and a virtual split in the cult, the original serenity of the City of Refuge was shattered. Three of the faithful, shocked by The Brother's doctrine of free love, which he had published in *The Chalice,* began to have serious doubts about his divinity. These were Robert England, the secretary and former treasury agent, E. A. Lucas, a Vancouver lawyer and early adherent and Maurice Van Platon, a Chicago millionaire who had made his fortune building organs.

England didn't fool around; having lost his faith he took precipitate action, laying a charge against Wilson for misuse of the Foundation's funds in purchasing the Valdes property. Wilson was arrested and immediately responded with a counter charge that England had misappropriated twenty-eight hundred dollars from the Aquarian Society in England. England's defence was that this was actually his salary as secretary of the Foundation, but Wilson insisted that none of his people were paid salaries. England, too, was arrested.

The case came up for preliminary hearing in Nanaimo on a hot September day in 1928. The courtroom was jammed, both by the faithful and by those who were beginning to harbour doubts. In the former group was the widow Connally, who had rushed across the continent prepared to testify that her money, which had been used to buy the Valdes property, had been given not to the Foundation but to The Brother, XII as a personal gift.

The hearing was notable for one of those dramatic coincidences that the credulous find significant. Halfway through the defence of his client, Robert England's elderly lawyer, T. P. Morton, suffered, in mid-sentence, a dizzy spell. He simply stopped speaking, then he leaned on the opposing counsel and said: "This is ridiculous but I have completely forgotten what I was saying." The momentary lápse had a profound effect: every Aquarian was convinced that the interruption was the result of The Brother, XII's black Egyptian magic.

The magistrate bound both accused over for trial but before it was called Robert England vanished, never to be heard from again. Was he murdered, as some said? Did he go to work as a British spy, as others whispered? No one knows. Like so many other actors in this singular drama, his trail has long since grown cold. But for Edward Arthur Wilson it was a fortunate turn of events. The case against him was dropped and he was free to expel the malcontents and set about gathering a new and more obedient group of followers.

As for Myrtle Baumgartner, she failed to produce the new messiah. Instead, she suffered a miscarriage and subsequently lost her reason; one suspects that she had been, for some time, on the edge of sanity. Mrs. Connally cared for her for some time in Victoria; later she was sent to a mental hospital, the tragic victim of a gullibility that passes all understanding.

The shabby courtroom proceedings had no effect on the faithful. Money continued to pour in from readers of *The Chalice.* In the spring of 1929, Mrs. Connally returned to Cedar to present Wilson with fifteen hundred dollars with which to buy a new engine for the colony's tugboat and another ten thousand to purchase the three tiny islands in the De Courcey group, which lies between Nanaimo and Valdes. On two of these islands a colony of believers began to build a new City of Refuge. A sawmill was installed; houses were built from cut timber; a huge storehouse stocked with canned and bottled provisions was erected; an entire school-house was built, complete with blackboards and desks and, it was said, a teacher imported from Switzerland. There is no record, however, of any schoolchildren; most of the faithful were beyond the child-bearing age. On these islands in the De Courcey group, the women were apparently separated from the men — one sex to each island. The colonists had not counted on this development but they were afraid to complain. Work on the De Courceys, apparently, was held out as a kind of trial, to sift out the select group who would eventually find refuge on Valdes. The exact mechanics of all this organization is fuzzy; with one exception, no outsider ever set foot on any of the islands during the cult's

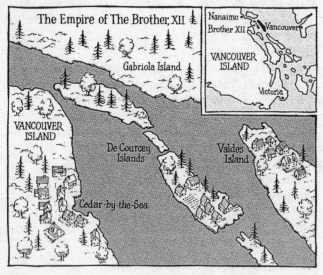

152

existence. But there is no doubt that the cultists worked like virtual slaves, building greenhouses, clearing ten acres for a vegetable garden, planting fruit and nut trees in a model orchard and hauling logs.

Meanwhile, new and prosperous supplicants continued to arrive. The most prominent was Roger Painter, a long-haired and bearded businessman from Florida, known as the "wholesale poultry king," and a firm believer in magic, black or otherwise. He and his wife, who came with him, had already made large contributions to the colony at Cedar. Whenever The Brother, XII wrote for money, Painter would send along five or ten thousand dollars. Remarkably, he kept no record of these donations. Finally, he turned over his business to his brothers and resolved to dedicate his life to the Aquarian Foundation. He brought ninety thousand dollars with him. The Brother got it all.

About the same time, there arrived from Lakeland, Florida, a Bruce Crawford and his wife, proprietors of a cleaning and dyeing business. They, too, had already made generous contributions to the cause. When they arrived in Canada they had eight thousand dollars remaining in cash. The Brother got that, too. He had a horror of banks; when he cashed cheques he asked for bills of one and two-dollar denomination. But mostly, he wanted his money in gold coins, which he treated like preserves. Cult members stuffed them into Mason jars, topped with melted wax; one of the carpenters was instructed to build boxes in which to store the jars. He later testified that there were eventually forty-three of these boxes, each containing ten thousand dollars' worth of gold coins.

To this point, the tale of The Brother, XII has been merely bizarre. With the arrival of the unspeakable Madame Zee, it becomes grotesque. Mrs. Julian Churton Skottowe, to use her legal name, was born Mabel

153

Rowbotham and was variously said to come from Florida and Saskatchewan. Her husband, at least, was a Canadian — a Saskatchewan bank clerk killed in action in the first war. The widow Skottowe was clearly no Myrtle Baumgartner or Mary Connally. She was introduced as the right-hand woman of the cult leader himself. "She is," The Brother, XII told his flock, "my eyes, my ears, my mouth; whatever she says you can take as coming from me." At this point Wilson was engaged in legally changing his name to Amiel de Valdes. Mabel followed suit; she became Zura de Valdes. The faithful dubbed her Madame Zee.

The pulp-fiction name was accompanied by pulp-fiction action. Madame Zee, a dark, gaunt woman of forty, with flaming red hair, flashing black eyes and a harsh, rasping voice, moved into the new House of Mystery with her consort and proceeded to stride about the various island colonies wearing flowered silk pyjamas and carrying a large bull whip, which she used mercilessly on any who questioned her authority. Her temper was vile and her language, to quote one of her victims, "you could hang a shirt on."

Madame Zee entered into her task as a work overseer with a kind of fiendish glee. There is the wretched case of Sarah Tuckett, a 76-year-old retired schoolteacher from the United States, who was so beaten and heartsick from overwork, illness and disillusion that she tried to commit suicide by leaping off the community tug on which the cultists travelled between islands. "Go ahead! Jump overboard!" Madame Zee taunted; and meant it. Roger Painter was later to testify that three of the faithful went insane under this kind of treatment and that it was "a wonder that any of us retained our reason."

154

The case of Bruce Crawford's pretty little wife, Georgina, was even crueller. She was put to work, pulling out stumps by hand until her fingers were cracked and bleeding. Then she was made a goatherd. She fell and hurt her knee, which swelled to melon size; but Madame Zee offered no respite, cursing her and accusing her of laziness. She was later forced to work in the warehouse, hauling hundred-pound sacks of potatoes. Georgina Crawford did her best, hobbling about, struggling with the sacks, but her best was not good enough. She was told she would be banished by boat to another island away from husband and friends. No one was allowed to help her with her baggage. She carried it on her back along a bush trail for several miles, slipping and falling as she went, until she reached the boat and rowed herself to her destination. Her work day, she was to testify later, began at two each morning and continued until ten at night.

A natural question arises: why on earth did Mrs. Crawford submit to these indignities? Eventually, she was asked that question in court. She had two answers, only the first of which was understandable: she did not wish to be separated from her husband, who had been forcibly kept away from her for six weeks. That was one threat that Madame Zee held over her. But, both the Crawfords could have escaped from the community. Why didn't they? Mrs. Crawford eventually supplied the answer: "I did not want my soul destroyed." In spite of all the humiliations — the bullwhip, the foul language, the long hours, the back-breaking toil, the degrading curses and The Brother, XII's own curious behaviour — the Crawfords believed implicitly that The Brother, and he alone, held the key to their spiritual future and could, at a whim, destroy them.

As Roger Painter was later to recall: "He . . . endeavoured to control the mentality, the soul of everybody who came near him. If you raised one little finger — one thing in opposition — implacable hatred was given to you from that time on and, if need be, he would put into operation what I call 'etheric' work, working on the mind and etheric body of a man. He even murdered him."

It was mental murder that Painter was describing and for that The Brother, XII had evolved a ritual. In the presence of Painter and Madame Zee, he would curse and damn *in absentia* the victim of his hatred, making vertical and horizontal strokes of his hands, cutting off the etheric (or "finer") body from the physical body. The idea was that the physical body would become depleted and die. Supposed victims of this mental murder included two British Columbia cabinet ministers for whom The Brother had conceived a hatred. As The Brother's faithful disciple, Painter was ordered to mentally destroy them; both, apparently, successfully resisted the assault.

The disciple who suffered most from Madame Zee was the woman who had done more than any other to aid the community financially, Mary Connally. Mrs. Connally, whose hard cash had purchased the De Courcey island group, was ordered not to set foot upon any of them. Instead she was confined to a shack at Cedar for which she was charged five thousand dollars; it had cost Wilson fifteen hundred. Once Mrs. Connally's money was gone she received short shrift. One winter night in 1929, a wrecking crew arrived at her Cedar home, started moving out the furniture and told her they had orders to send her to Valdes. She was dumped that night on the Valdes beach and left to fend for herself, forced to lug all her possessions up a long hill to her new home a quarter mile distant. This hovel, improperly heated, had been vacant for months. Mrs. Connally, who was given no explanation for the move and who had done no manual labour in her life, was compelled to struggle up from the beach, hour after hour, packing great loads. Roger Painter's wife, Leola, was assigned to guard her and to keep her continuously at work without help.

The widow had scarcely moved her final load of possessions into the house before she was moved again, this time to a hut with gaping holes in the roof and cracks in the walls. Here she was given nothing more than a straw mattress for a bed. Then she was moved a third time and told she must disc, harrow and cultivate a three-acre field. The wretched woman, now sixty-two, found herself toiling from daylight until dark. During this period she lost twenty-eight pounds.

Mrs. Painter, who later corroborated Mrs. Connally's court testimony, explained that Madame Zee had told her that the widow wasn't to have so much as a glass of water.

"I had to make her work. It was terrible to see her lifting those heavy loads. My heart cried out for her and I would gladly have helped her if I could."

But why couldn't she?

"I couldn't," said Leola Painter, "because I was afraid. Zee told me if I did so, I would lose my soul."

Shortly after these episodes, in January 1930, The Brother, XII and Madame Zee left for England, either on a holiday or to raise more money from the faithful. Roger Painter, now a devoted practitioner of The Brother's black magic, was appointed spiritual guide during his absence and given a list of mental murderees to work on. For financial and legal reasons, the title to the original settlement, at Cedar-by-the-Sea, was put in the name of Alfred Barley, one of the original colonists. Then, for some twenty-two months, peace and contentment reigned among the graceful arbutus trees and the grey salal bushes of the Gulf Islands.

In England, Wilson and his consort came into possession of a twenty-five-ton Brixham trawler, owned by an eccentric Englishwoman. The sailing craft, which Wilson renamed *The Lady Royal,* was said to have been a gift of the faithful, though it is possible that he bought it with some of the treasure he had been hoarding since 1927.

Whatever else he was, Wilson was a first-rate seaman. He and Madame Zee sailed the trawler (it had no auxiliary engine) on a daring voyage across the Atlantic, through the Panama Canal and up the west coast to his island refuge. In Panama, he discharged his white crew and took on Indians. He slipped into the Strait of Juan de Fuca in November 1931, apparently skirted Canadian immigration and customs, and ran the craft into one of the San Juan group of islands on the United States' side. He and Madame Zee went to the Aquarian refuge on De Courcey island by small boat and sent the community's tug back to tow in *The Lady Royal.* Then, it is said under Wilson's direction, the Indian crew unloaded a series of mysterious packages, before they were shipped home to Panama.

What was in the packages? Nobody ever found out, if indeed they even existed. The suspicion is that they contained guns and ammunition. Possibly. About the same time, Wilson had purchased fourteen rifles and a thousand rounds of ammunition from an Edmonton mail order house. He also ordered a halt to construction work on the main island of the De Courcey group while gun pits were dug. In addition a stone fort was built, with loopholes for weapons. There was some talk that casual boats trying to put in at the island were warned off by riflemen.

Apparently Wilson was prepared to repel any investigation, for he told the men in the community to man the pits and the women to patrol the intervening area and give notice of the approach of any government launch. Should a skirmish occur, it was his plan to skip across the island to a point where a fast boat was waiting to carry him safely away.

No such confrontation ever took place. In spite of the earlier court case, which had lifted the edge of the curtain on the strange activities at Cedar and Valdes, the government, the provincial police, the newspapers and the local citizenry remained supremely indifferent to the goings-on offshore.

But then the Islanders were used to bizarre cults, strange sects, curious ceremonies and various individual eccentricities. In the letters column of the Victoria *Colonist* (it often ran more than a page) local jingoists, demanding the separation of the Island from the rest of Canada, vied with fervent scriveners who insisted that God's chosen people were not the Jews but the English. On Government Street, retired pukka sahibs trudged about in khaki shorts and pith helmets, jostling Russian emigrés in peaked caps. Ancient ladies traipsed about in floor-length gowns and enormous flowered chapeaux. In Oak Bay, an electric automobile propelled itself at a snail's pace along Windsor Avenue, its veiled occupant only dimly to be seen. Along the Island Highway, at places like Cobble Hill, Maple Bay and Duncan, the longstockings put their military rank on their mailboxes and lived among the splendours of the past in rooms crammed with Zulu assegais, Gurkha kukris, and Bedouin scimitars. They were adept at minding their own business.

The offshore islands were sprinkled with recluses, hermits and beachcombers. On a mountaintop on Saturna, Adam Forness lived alone in a shack, making organ pipes out of local woods. On Morseby, a man named Robertson built a castle with two towers, one it was said for himself, the other for his wife. The Island was fertile ground for off-beat ideas. The church pages of the *Times* and *Colonist* were gaudy with advertisements for curious faiths, many of which proclaimed the imminent end of the world. In his rented temple, Dr. Clem Davies, clad in dazzling white, preached hellfire, while pretty ladies passed the offering baskets. "Boys," Davies told the local press in a refreshing moment of off-the-record candour, "I found there was more money in this God stuff than in anything else."

This was also Edward Arthur Wilson's discovery. It is impossible to say how much of his own hogwash he really believed; perhaps he actually came to think he was divine. However, his technique in handling his disciples is clear enough: attract wealthy suckers, strip them of everything they own, then try to get rid of them. Roger Painter explained it in court: "As I look back on it now the whole scene was to drive you into intense fear and confusion, so that you were glad to go and leave your money and goods behind, regardless of what it might cost you. That was the operation, so that you could get away, and get away from it and leave it forever. He had our money; he had our goods; he had everything we had. We were told that we had to surrender everything. We believed in it. We did it."

When The Brother, XII returned to take command again, there were new murmurings of dissent. The Brother took summary measures: he banished about a dozen of the dissenters, including Mary Connally, the Barleys and the Painters from the colony. No doubt he believed, and not without evidence, that the fear of losing their souls would cause them to keep their mouths shut. But he had forgotten one fact: the tract of land at Cedar-by-the-Sea was legally in Alfred Barley's name and this gave the dissidents a physical base for action. They took it. A prominent Nanaimo lawyer, Victor B. Harrison, was retained and a suit entered against Amiel de Valdes designed to recover some of the money that had been poured into the colony. The case came to trial in April 1933, before Chief Justice Morrison at Nanaimo and for the first time the outside world began to learn of the strange incidents on the innocent-looking islands off the coast.

On the morning of the trial itself, Harrison, the lawyer, was provided with a remarkable example of the power that The Brother, XII still held over the very group that was trying to bring him down. Not one of them, it developed, was willing to enter the witness box to testify against him. Each of them firmly believed that The Brother had thrown a spell around the box and that if any of them stepped into it, he would die.

Fortunately, Harrison that morning had encountered Bruce "Pinky" McKelvie, then the managing editor of the Victoria *Colonist* and an enthusiastic amateur historian. McKelvie heard him out, told him to try to hold the judge for ten minutes, dashed over to his room at the Malaspina Hotel, and rummaged in his dressing case, looking for a double labret — a lip ornament worn at one time by the women of the Queen Charlotte Islands. Back at the courthouse, McKelvie sought out Roger Painter, showed him the artifact and told him it was the greatest charm on the coast.

"It used to belong to one of the most famous of the Haida medicine men," said McKelvie. "As long as you are in association with that, no power under Heaven can hurt you."

Painter, the man who had built up a million-dollar business in Florida, seized the charm like an aborigine taking a mirror from a white man. He and every other witness entered the box gripping the ornament, looked The Brother, XII straight in the eye and told their story.

Some of the tales that followed were hair-raising. Horrors had been going on under the very noses of the

161

press and public that belonged more properly to some Transylvanian mountain castle. The story of Carlin Ruddie of Seattle, as related by Bruce Crawford, was perhaps the most poignant.

Ruddie and his pretty young bride had been invited by The Brother, XII to visit him on De Courcey. When the Brother saw Mrs. Ruddie, he was captivated. He took her aside and told her that the divinities had plans for her: she was to return to Seattle with her husband but once home she was to pick a quarrel with him and return to De Courcey. Again, the head reels: Mrs. Ruddie, a new bride, was perfectly prepared to throw over her husband. She followed The Brother's instructions to the letter.

With his wife missing, the frantic husband, properly suspicious of his former host, decided to return to the colony in search of her. The Gulf Islands in those days were difficult to reach; there was little or no ferry service, even to the largest. Ruddie went to Chemainus on Vancouver Island, hired a boat and rowed the ten miles across the strait. Here the guards in the newly established fortifications immediately captured him. When Ruddie accused Wilson of stealing his wife, Wilson calmly denied it; she was, at that moment, secreted in a closet in his house. Ruddie was held captive overnight, then taken back on the community tug to Yellow Point, near Nanaimo, and dumped there.

Ruddie went at once to the British Columbia provincial police. An officer returned to the colony with him. Wilson swore that Mrs. Ruddie wasn't there and had never been there; his frightened disciples corroborated the story. The policeman was forced to leave with Ruddie.

But Wilson was alarmed at this official visit. That night he had the unfortunate girl transported across the strait and dropped on a lonely beach near Ladysmith.

There, she was finally found, a terrified, lost woman, without possessions or money, trapped in a foreign country.

With that kind of testimony, the court lost little time in finding for the plaintiffs. Mrs. Connally was awarded judgement for twenty-six thousand dollars, together with an additional ten thousand in special damages. She was also given ownership of the De Courcey group of islands and the acreage on Valdes that had been purchased with her money. Alfred Barley was awarded fourteen thousand dollars in addition to his legal title to the community land at Cedar.

These victories, except for the land grants, were hollow. Before the case was completed, The Brother, XII and his consort vanished. On leaving, they did their best to smash and destroy the work of the colony, hacking away at furniture with axes, burning some of the outbuildings and scuttling *The Lady Royal* with a charge of dynamite.

What happened to them? The only published clue to the fate of The Brother, XII came in 1939 in a legal advertisement in the Vancouver *Daily Province* announcing the winding up of the estate of one Julian Skottowe, who had died in Neuchatel, Switzerland on November 7, 1934. Presumably, Wilson had taken the name of Madame Zee's first husband. But what about the gold? Wilson had lived for only eighteen months after the trial. Yet when his estate was settled there was scarcely enough left in it to pay the legal fees. As for Madame Zee, her trail vanishes in Switzerland. Did she take off with all that gold or, indeed, was there any gold left? Would it have been possible for the two of them to have conveyed half a ton of gold from Vancouver Island to Switzerland? For that would be the weight of the forty-three boxes full of coins, to which the witnesses testified in court. To those questions there are no satisfactory answers.

If the gold remained on one of the islands nobody to this day has found it. Mary Connally, who stayed on for several years among the ruins of the colony, didn't find it. Nor did she seem to care. In spite of all that had happened — her own mental seduction, the loss of her money, the false promises, the degradation and the final betrayal — she could not find it in her heart to curse The Brother, XII; quite the opposite. When she finally left British Columbia in 1941, for a nursing home in North Carolina, she made a parting statement to her caretaker, Sam Grunall.

"For the old Brother," said the widow Connally, "I'd do that much again, if I had it to give."

After she left, Grunall himself began to rummage about, seeking a likely hiding place for the gold. Finally, on Valdes Island, hidden beneath an outbuilding, he uncovered a concrete vault sunk into the ground. It was clearly a hiding place of some sort. Grunall found an iron ring attached to the lid and pulled on it. Below him, in the gloom, he saw a bundle. He looked more closely: it was a roll of tarpaper. There was a message scrawled on the tarpaper and Grunall was just able to make it out. The single sentence, in Wilson's hand — a defiant shout from an earlier decade — wrote a kind of *finis* to the odd story of The Brother, XII. It read:

"For fools and traitors, nothing!"

7

The Last of the Red Indians

The story of the Beothuk Indians of Newfoundland is indescribably tragic — and on several levels. It is tragic, of course, because they were wiped out by white furriers and fishermen and Micmac Indians — hunted down like wild geese during a two-hundred-year cycle of haphazard genocide. But it is also tragic in other, subtler ways. There is, for instance, convincing evidence that the blood bath began as the result of an accident; that had it not been for a chance encounter, these Indians might easily have survived as partners in the fur trade. There is also the tragedy of good but failed intentions. There were, in Newfoundland, perfectly sincere and humane people who tried after their fashion to save the Beothuks from extinction; they simply had no sensible idea of how to go about it. Finally, there is the tragedy of a culture lost. Our knowledge of the Beothuks is abysmal because scarcely anybody bothered to find out anything about them until they were all gone. There is something inexpressibly forlorn in the final picture of the lovely Shawnadithit, the last surviving member of her race (her features already sallowed by the ravages of consumption), trying as best she could, through a series of story-maps, to explain how her people lived, hunted and worshipped and how, one by one, they died.

Nobody really knows who the Beothuks were or where they came from. The explorer, William Epps

Cormack, who knew Shawnadithit, thought they might be descended from the Norsemen. William Sweetland, the Bonavista magistrate, who also talked to her, believed they might be descended from a Tartar chieftain, Ogus Khan. More recent and substantial theories suggest one of two possible relations: the Beothuks may be the direct descendants of the prehistoric people known to scientists as "Maritime Archaic" (who go back as far as 3000 B.C.); or they may be related to the Algonkian-speaking peoples, the oldest Indians on the continent. But these are still only theories. We do not even know how the Beothuks pronounced their own name, which means, simply, The People.

Everything we do know about the Beothuks comes from three sources: an anthology of various writings about the Indians published in 1915, much of it hearsay; a manuscript, recently discovered, dating from the late eighteenth century; and some considerable archaeological knowledge derived from modern digs. Most of the drawings of the Beothuks used in illustrations in books and articles are not authentic.

We do know that they were a primitive and migratory people who may have been in Newfoundland for at least four millennia when the first white men arrived. They were, in fact, the original "Red Indians" of North America, so named because they painted their bodies, their clothes, their tents and canoes with red ochre. The pejorative "redskin" derives from the first white encounters with the Beothuks at the end of the fifteenth century.

They had few artifacts — no ceramic pottery and no metal except for copper. They grew no food and had no wheeled vehicles. They were tall by earlier European standards, handsome, fairer than most Indians, with large expressive eyes. They were a shy, unwarlike race, who treated their women with respect, believed in the importance of marriage and were said to reject both adultery and polygamy. They lived in unique conical dwellings made of birch, travelled by canoe, wore garments of hide and fur, and hunted with spear and bow. All their possessions were held in common; the concept of private property was foreign to them; it did not occur to the Beothuks that pilfering from white men's stores would be considered a crime. They were, in short, ripe for killing; a peaceful, innocent people, perfect victims for abuse and exploitation.

The first predators were probably the Micmacs, who crossed to Newfoundland from the mainland much later than the Beothuks and were encouraged by the white men to kill the Red Indians. Once the Micmacs acquired guns from the French, they had no trouble beating their primitively armed enemies in battle. Even before that they had been driving the Beothuks east, so that by the mid-sixteenth century they were in the western heartland of Newfoundland. Nobody knows exactly how many of them there were at that time — perhaps one thousand, perhaps only two hundred. We do know that once driven east their numbers began to deplete. But the real killing began in the seventeenth century.

To the English, Newfoundland was not even a colony — only a gigantic fishing ground. Boats sailed westward from the British Isles each spring and returned in the fall with their holds loaded with cod. Permanent settlement was expressly forbidden by law but that did not stop thousands of Englishmen from calling Newfoundland their home. At St. John's, in the south, a settled community was in the making. On the wild and largely unknown northeast coast, in the land of the Beothuks, a loose kingdom of scattered communities was coming into being, without law, schools, churches or any of the softening influences of civilization. The settlers here were traders and fishermen, many of them indentured seamen who had fled the slavery of shipboard life for the wilder freedom of the northeast coast. Such men could not return to England.

Even if there had been a law against harming Indians it could never have been enforced; in the early days, there were neither courts, judges nor policemen on the northeast coast. But the truth is that until 1769 it was perfectly legal to slaughter the Beothuks. Men set out on shooting parties, as they would for deer or wolves, to bag themselves a few head. Even after the law was changed and it became, on paper at least, a capital crime to kill a Beothuk, the slaughter still went on. Since there were never any witnesses nor any easily available evidence, the law was meaningless. No one was ever punished for killing a Red Indian.

And yet, the first mass slaughter, which was to set the pattern for future massacres, arose out of a tragic misunderstanding. In 1612, one John Guy of Bristol sailed into Trinity Bay, after establishing a colony at the neighbouring Conception Bay. Here he met eight Beothuk Indians. It was a jovial encounter; after some opening shyness, there was feasting, dancing and raillery. Guy was scrupulous in his dealings with them. When the departing Indians left some furs and skins for trade he did not take them all because he did not feel he had enough goods to pay for everything. He selected a beaver skin, a bird skin and a sable skin, and left in return a hatchet, a knife, four needles and thread and a pair of scissors.

Before the shy but friendly Beothuks had departed, Guy, through signs, made them understand that he intended to return the following year to establish trade relations. Had this plan not gone awry, the story of the Beothuks might have been different.

But by a great piece of misfortune, another ship reached Trinity Bay the following spring ahead of John Guy. On the shore several hundred gesticulating natives were preparing a wild welcome for their new white friend. The captain thought the dance of welcome was a war dance and when they paddled out toward his fishing boat he mowed them down with grapeshot. From that moment on, the Beothuks dreaded the whites and their firearms and fled from sight whenever they encountered strangers. Guy and his followers were never able to make contact with them again.

For the next two centuries, visiting fishermen, lawless deserters and Micmac Indians carried out what can only be described as a policy of genocide against the Red Indians. Sometimes the attacks were based on revenge for the pilfering of small objects. Sometimes the object was loot — to steal the Beothuks' venison and furs. But most of the time, the Indians were hunted for pure sport. In 1775, near Trinity Bay, an armed party of whites surprised a group of sleeping Indians and murdered seven of them. One huge man, shot twice, got up and fired an arrow at the whites who retaliated by shooting him through the heart. Because he was seven feet tall, the white men determined to tow his body home behind a boat for exhibition. They were forced to cut the corpse adrift in a storm but when it was washed up at Lance Cove it attracted scores of the curious, who watched it rot away until it was swept out to sea in the autumn.

To kill a Beothuk was considered a matter of pride. Men actually notched their gun butts to tally their kills and boasted of slaughtering women and children (the latter sometimes strangled in cold blood). In 1768, the British government made a desultory attempt to curb the barbarity. In that year, the governor of the colony sent Lieutenant John Cartwright to lead an expedition aboard HMS *Guernsey* up the Exploits River into the heart of Newfoundland to try to open friendly communication with the Beothuks. Cartwright's trip was fruitless; he didn't even *see* an Indian.

He did, however, find plenty of evidence that the Beothuks were gathered in the centre of the island and more evidence of the atrocities committed against them. He found square log houses, caulked with moss, deer pounds, birchbark canoes and bows of sycamore with arrows feathered with goose quills. But whenever he arrived at a settlement, the Indians had already melted away.

Cartwright sympathized with their plight. Secluded from communication with the Europeans, they were also cut off from the society of other natives who were enemies as savage as the white men. They did not even have domestic pets: "To complete their wretched condition, Providence has even denied them the pleasing services and companionship of the faithful dog."

Totally vulnerable without firearms, they were forced to split into small parties in order to forage for food — which made them easy prey for the crew of a single boat. For this reason they tried to avoid the coast. Day and night they kept a wary outlook for strangers, and with good cause. "He that has shot one Indian values himself more upon the fact than had he overcome a bear or a wolf." In Cartwright's words, the English fishermen exhibited "an inhumanity which sinks them far below the level of savages."

Cartwright recorded some horrible examples. A party of fishermen broke into a Beothuk wigwam; the Indians all fled but one woman, who couldn't get away in time and threw herself on their mercy, pointing with entreaty to her pregnant belly. "An instant stab that ripped open her womb, laid her at the feet of those cowardly ruffians, where she expired in great agonies."

Her attackers cut off her hands and took them home as a trophy.

Another fishing party came upon a woman and a baby boy alone and instantly shot the mother through the loins. She dropped her child and began to crawl into the woods, holding her wound and gazing back in anguish as the whites made off with the baby. The boy was sold in St. John's, given the name of John August (after the month in which he was captured) and made a servant. He was one of only two male Beothuks ever captured alive.

Cartwright's sympathetic report was responsible for the change in the law: it became illegal to kill an Indian. But nobody was able to inform the Indians because nobody was able to get within hailing distance of one. The Beothuks, in terror of white men, were hived in the area between Notre Dame Bay (where narrow winding inlets and numberless islands provided some protection from two-legged predators) and the Exploits River as far inland as Red Indian Lake.

Parliamentary committees and various proclamations followed the original Cartwright report, all well-intentioned, all designed to protect the Beothuks. Officialdom was moved by something more powerful than a spirit of Christian humanity: the Red Indians were now seen to be of enormous potential value in the growing fur trade.

The situation was not without paradox. The Indians wanted the white man's trade goods but they were, understandably, afraid to make any kind of approach. Instead they continued to pilfer small articles from white settlements. This caused more massacres by white men seeking revenge. The story of the English attempts to befriend the Red Indians would be comic if it were not so tragic.

In 1807, another governor, John Holloway, began offering substantial rewards in an attempt to establish relations with the elusive Indians. Anybody who would come forward with information about the murder of an Indian would be paid fifty pounds. Anybody who could induce an Indian to come to St. John's, so the governor could explain his new policy, would also be awarded fifty pounds. The reward, later doubled, had an opposite effect to that intended — it encouraged bounty hunters who had no compunctions about kidnapping Indians violently. (All subsequent captives, significantly, were women).

The governor persevered. He decided to commission an enormous oil painting in England, showing a friendly meeting between Indians and Europeans. The painting was duly executed and shipped across the Atlantic. It showed "an officer of the Royal Navy in full dress shaking hands with an Indian chief, and pointing to a party of seamen behind him who were laying some bales of goods at the feet of the chief. Behind the latter were some male and female Indians presenting furs to the officers. Further to the left were seen an European and an Indian mother looking with delight at their respective children of the same size, who were embracing one another. In the opposite corner a British tar was courting, in his way, an Indian beauty."

A Royal Navy officer was duly dispatched with this remarkable work of art to the Bay of Exploits. His instructions were to leave the painting in the woods, along with some trade goods. The idea was that the Indians would gaze upon the Peaceable Kingdom envisaged by the artist, be won over immediately, and start leaving furs in exchange. The navy made two trips to the Bay with the painting; but the Indians didn't bite.

The governor tried a different tack. He approached a fisherman from Fogo, one William Cull, and sent him off to make friends with the Beothuks. The governor's naiveté in this matter is baffling. Had he sent the Devil himself he could scarcely have disturbed the Indians more. Cull's credentials for the job obviously appealed to officialdom but they were not ones which the Beothuks would have considered exemplary. His claim to fame was that he had in 1803 captured a Beothuk woman and brought her to Government House where she had caused a sensation. After being showered with gifts and attention, she was finally returned to the Exploits River the following August in Cull's custody to be freed like an animal released from a zoo. There were many who believed that Cull, who was paid fifty pounds to do the job, simply murdered her and kept the presents and trade goods.

The well-meaning whites in St. John's could not get it through their heads that no Beothuk wanted to be captured in this fashion. Cull, whose later exploits were to

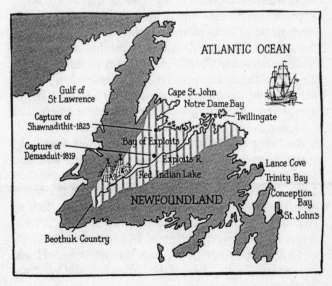

show how little he regarded any Indian's life, made two official expeditions to the Beothuk country in 1809 and 1810. Predictably he found no Beothuks.

Another determined effort was made in 1811, when the armed schooner *Adonis* was sent to the Bay of Exploits with instructions to search the Indians out. The expedition was under the command of Lieutenant David Buchan, a thirty-year-old career officer of considerable ability and no little humanity. Finding no natives in the area of the Bay, he determined on a January expedition into the interior. He took William Cull and two other guides, including a notorious Indian killer, Thomas Taylor, together with eighteen other locals and a dozen of his own marines.

The expedition slugged it out for twelve days, moving steadily into the inhospitable heartland of Newfoundland. On the early morning of the twelfth day, Buchan left half his men behind with the sledges and pushed ahead with the others. A dozen miles into snow-covered forest, they found what they were seeking: a camp of Beothuk wigwams. Buchan's men surrounded the settlement and called out to the Indians, but received no answer. Finally, Buchan ordered his men to fling open the skin doors of the wigwams and there "we beheld groups of men, women and children lying in the utmost consternation; they remained absolutely still for some moments without motion or utterance."

Buchan's first object was to allay their fears. He shook hands with the adults and made a fuss over the children, an action that caused the mothers to embrace him. The Indians then lit a fire and served the naval men venison steaks. Buchan repaid them by offering knives, handkerchiefs and other trade goods. It took him several hours to explain by signs that a dozen sledges loaded with other goods lay twelve miles back on the trail. Finally, four of the Indians offered to return with him. Two marines asked to remain in order to repair their snowshoes and to serve as informal hostages.

The Indians were still timid of white company, as they had every reason to be in the light of the presence of such men as Cull and Taylor, and the other hated furriers and fishermen from Twillingate. Three of them, including the last chief of the band, Nonosabasut, left the party and returned to their own camps. One was persuaded to stay, although greatly frightened at the sight of a dozen armed men waiting to greet him.

Buchan was worried. Would the departing Indians cause the entire camp to flee before he could return? Had the sight of more armed men terrified them? How safe were the hostages? Leaving eight of the party behind he set off in the early morning with the one remaining Indian. When he reached the camp he found his worst fears were realized; it was deserted. The following morning, with the lone Indian as guide, Buchan and his men set off in search of the two hostages. They had not gone far before they came upon a grisly sight. Ahead, on the ice was a human form. Not far away was another. The corpses of the two hostages lay chest down with arrows in their backs. The heads had been removed.

The Indian took to his heels and Buchan did not bother to give chase. He was more concerned that his peace mission would be shattered by his own men, bent on revenge. He hurried the party away from the scene and made haste to rejoin the eight he had left behind. It took the expedition almost two months to make the journey back to the schooner.

Buchan did not blame the Indians for the death of his men. He believed — more or less correctly as it later developed — that the three Beothuks who had panicked and fled back to the camp had alarmed the others and when the hostages panicked in turn and tried to get away, the Indians, in a state of nerves, shot them. It was a sad ending to a promising encounter. "Had it not been for the disastrous fate of the two marines," Buchan wrote, "I would have deemed my journey fortunate beyond all expectations."

Buchan wrote his report in 1811. Eight years went by before any further attempt was made to reach out to the Red Indians. The British had other affairs on their minds: the Canadian border warfare of 1812-13, the struggle against Napoleon, the exploration of the Canadian Arctic and the spread of two great fur companies across the Canadian west. Newfoundland was a true colony, exploited by the merchant princes of St. John's and their British backers. It is not surprising that the renegade settlers and the remnant of a dying native race huddled in their last retreat at Red Indian Lake, were left to their own devices.

Then, in 1819, there was another encounter with the Beothuks, which resulted in the capture of another woman, Chief Nonosabasut's wife, Demasduit. Like most of the other encounters, this one was marred by misunderstanding, bungling, a fair amount of pure savagery on the part of the whites and a tragic finish.

The man who captured Demasduit was John Peyton, Jr., later a magistrate at Twillingate. Peyton Sr. could accurately be described as a dedicated Beothuk hunter. In 1781, he had taken part in a battle of extermination against the Indians, brought on by their revenge in killing one of his friends, a notorious Indian hunter named Thomas Rousell. The senior Peyton and a comrade looted and slaughtered a group of Beothuks, Peyton himself dispatching one wounded native by beating out his brains with a bear trap. The younger Peyton was much more humane.

Twillingate, at that time, was a village of about seven hundred inhabitants. It was their habit to butcher all the Indians they could with any weapon available. Peyton, the future magistrate, did not take quite such precipitate action. When his boat was looted of its cargo he applied for and was given official permission to search for the Indians he believed to be the thieves and, if possible, to capture one of them alive (to gain the substantial reward).

Peyton's party of Indian hunters, which included his bloodthirsty father, carried pistols, muskets, bayonets, hatchets and daggers. Their subsequent meeting with the Indians was bloody and ferocious, though Peyton's own account of it omits much of the gore; another witness, however, supplied the missing details.

The party happened upon a group of Beothuks in their camp at three o'clock one afternoon. The natives fled at once, with Peyton and his men in hot pursuit. As they reached the last of the wigwams, three men and a woman carrying a child burst out in flight. One of the men took the child from the woman's arms but she could not keep up and Peyton was able to overtake her. She fell to her knees and opened her deerskin dress to show her breasts so that he would know she was a woman. There was a pause. The retreating Indians turned about and advanced on the whites. The whites retreated a little and stopped. The Indians also stopped. The whites brandished their guns; the Indians brandished their bows.

Then Chief Nonosabasut stepped forward, a spruce branch in his hand. It was his wife whom Peyton had seized. With his eyes blazing, he made a vehement speech which lasted for ten minutes. Everybody seems to have been transfixed. The chief concluded mildly enough, shook hands all round, then moved to retrieve his wife; but the white men refused to give her up. The

Indian drew an axe from under his deerskin and brandished it. Peyton's men levelled their muskets while two others started to drag the woman away. This was too much for the chief, who sprang forward to seize her.

A terrible scene followed. One of the white men drew his bayonet and buried it in Nonosabasut's back. The wounded Indian whirled and felled his assailant with a blow. He knocked down a second assailant, pulled a dagger from his belt and shook off a third white man. Peyton drew his pistol and fired point blank. The Indian staggered and fell on his face. An agonizing spectacle then took place. The chief, writhing at first in agony, slowly and painfully raised himself inch by inch from the ice, turned about and surveyed the white men with a wild gaze.

"Never shall I forget the figure he exhibited; his hair hanging on each side of his sallow face; his bushy beard clotted with blood that flowed from his mouth and nose; his eyes flashing fire, yet with the glass of death upon them — they fixed on the individual who first stabbed him."

Slowly Nonosabasut raised the dagger that he was still grasping until it was above his head; and then, uttering a scream that made the forest echo, he rushed at the man who first stabbed him. The whites fired as he advanced and the Indian fell forward on his face, struggled for a few moments and then stiffened. Peyton had his captive — but at what a cost! Demasduit "vented her sorrow in the most heartbreaking lamentations." Her husband was dead and her baby, which had been taken by one of the others, would live for only two days. She herself was being spirited away to an unknown fate in a strange world.

Peyton fired over the heads of the fleeing Indians, tied up his captive for the night and the following day headed back with her to civilization. A grand jury in St.

John's found that he and his companions were justified in killing her husband since he had attacked them. No witnesses appeared at that time to dispute Peyton's testimony.

The kidnapped woman was placed in the care of John Leigh, the Anglican missionary at Twillingate, and renamed Mary March. She was about twenty-three, tall, rather stout, with small, delicate limbs and tiny, beautifully formed hands and feet. She tried twice to escape from the Leigh home but was recaptured and after a few weeks appeared to enjoy civilization. She especially liked the new clothes which she preferred to her own deerskin. She pilfered a length of blue cloth and secretly made it into sixteen pairs of moccasins, evidently intending to take them back to her tribe. She hoarded clothes and trinkets given to her, usually dividing them into sixteen shares, apparently for her family.

Clearly, she wished to return to her people and her captors eventually decided to take her back. The plan was to use her as an example to show the Red Indians that the whites wanted to be friends. It was an incredibly naive approach. Why on earth would the Beothuks be disposed to welcome some of the same group that had already slaughtered one of their number and kidnapped his wife? Yet men like Cull and Peyton always insisted, and perhaps believed, that they had the best interests of the Indians at heart. A kind of Christian arrogance was operating here; the members of the white world in Newfoundland were firmly convinced that the Beothuks would be infinitely better off enjoying the benefits of what they were pleased to call civilization.

Two attempts were made in 1819 to return Demasduit to her people. The first was a failure. The second, under David Buchan, now a captain, was successful after a fashion. Buchan, who had just returned from John Franklin's first Arctic expedition, was ordered to take Demasduit north on his ship, *Grasshopper*. He was to winter in Exploits Bay and then take a trading party up the river to where the Indians were thought to make their winter camp.

Demasduit was brought on board on November 25 by John Peyton, Jr., (for whom, inexplicably, she had developed a kind of fondness). She looked ill — so ill in fact that Buchan decided not to take her up the river. Instead, he planned to seek out the Indians and try to persuade them to come and fetch her.

It was obvious that Demasduit was in the final stages of tuberculosis. On January 8, on board ship, while Buchan was waiting for the river to freeze, she began to suffocate and at two that afternoon she expired. Buchan was saddened: "Her mild and gentle manners and great patience under much suffering endeared her to all," he wrote.

He then decided, in his pigheaded way, that he might propitiate the Indians by bringing them Demasduit's body. His blindness to reality is evident in his statement that "a meeting must in its consequence have operated most powerfully toward effecting the desirable object of producing to those poor creatures the blessings arising from civilization." He did not seem to understand that the blessings arising from civilization had just killed his captive.

Demasduit's body was placed in a wooden coffin along with two wooden dolls and some other toys and trinkets. The coffin was marked with a copper plate on which was engraved her name, probable age, date of capture and death — an unnecessary gesture since the legend would be totally indecipherable to the Indians. Then the coffin, together with some two tons of provisions, goods and knick-knacks was dragged up the frozen river to Red Indian Lake by no fewer than fifty marines.

Did they really expect to encounter a welcoming committee of overjoyed Beothuks? The camp, understandably, was deserted when they reached it. The Indians had seen the procession winding its way up the frozen river from afar, and fled. Buchan left trade goods and other presents, had the coffin slung above the ground to protect it from marauding animals, and departed. Once he was gone, the Indians trickled back from the white cover of the forest, found the coffin, broke it open and discarded it, and then placed Demasduit's body in a sepulchre of their own beside the bodies of her dead husband and child.

The white men did not realize it then, but in that year, 1819, there were only thirty-one Beothuk Indians left alive in Newfoundland. Sickness, starvation and the white men's guns and axes had wiped out the rest. After that first tentative encounter with Buchan in 1811, the tribe had scattered and broken into small bands, retreating into the farthest reaches of the northern interior. In the winter of 1813, twenty-two died. The following year more were smitten by hardship and starvation. By 1816, the number was down below seventy. By 1819 that number had been reduced again by half. When William Epps Cormack made his famous trip of exploration across the interior of Newfoundland in 1822 (the first European to do so), he was told that the bloodthirsty Beothuks would butcher him: but he did not find a sign of them.

The final act in the tragedy was played out in the half-dozen years that followed. Once again, William Cull, the trapper-fisherman who had captured an Indian woman in 1803, makes his appearance on a bloody stage. In the spring of 1823, Cull spotted a small party of Beothuks on the ice in an inlet off Notre Dame Bay.

Two of them, a man and his daughter, approached, begging for food; they were literally starving. Cull, the man whom the government had once entrusted with the Indians' welfare, shot them both.

Three women in the party were captured shortly after. Cull brought them in to Peyton, who was now magistrate of the district. Cull and his party were put on trial for the killings but were speedily acquitted for lack of evidence. Freed by the court, the killer then had the gall to claim the one-hundred-pound bounty for delivering captured Indians to the government! There is no evidence, however, that he was paid.

The three women — a mother, Doodebewshet, and two daughters — were given a room in the courthouse in St. John's. A bed was provided for them but they preferred to sleep on deerskins in a corner. The older of the two daughters was already ill with tuberculosis but fought against any form of medication or treatment except that given to her by her mother. Later on Doodebewshet managed to put the girl in a closed wigwam where she heated large stones, produced clouds of steam with cold water and shrieked what the whites believed to be incantations.

The younger daughter, Shawnadithit, was thought to be about twenty-three. Handsome, with beautiful teeth and a swarthy complexion, she was quick to learn. Given a paper and pencil, she proceeded in one flourish to draw a deer perfectly, beginning, surprisingly, at the tip of the tail. The Newfoundlanders renamed her Nancy. Unlike her mother, a violent woman who sat morosely on the floor, looking with loathing on all who entered the courthouse, Shawnadithit was friendly and kissed and shook hands with the visitors. The three women were encouraged to walk freely about the town and they wandered from shop to shop, picking up trinkets, pots, kettles and tools. For these the government paid.

There were those, however, who thought that the trio ought to be returned to their own people and the government eventually gave in to this pressure. Peyton, who was assigned to do the job, took them to the Exploits River and left them there in a small boat. Doodebewshet and her elder daughter were both now suffering from consumption; indeed, they were dying. The trip up the river was clearly going to be too much for them. Shawnadithit indicated by signs that she would go alone to look for her people and bring them back to fetch the other two.

Sadly, she could find no trace of her band. The truth was that there were few, if any, of them left. In the winter of 1822 — 23, before she was captured, there were only about fifteen surviving. Starving, they were forced to separate to hunt for food. By spring there were only eight or nine left to roam the lonely forests of Newfoundland's interior.

The three women stayed on the banks of the Exploits River until their food ran out. Then they walked back to Twillingate, but the mother and daughter died on the way and Shawnadithit stumbled on alone. After she returned, the whites could find no further trace of the Beothuks in the wilderness. By 1825 it became increasingly clear that Shawnadithit was the sole survivor of her race.

The last of the Red Indians became a kind of unpaid servant in the Peyton household. She was bright and she was also artistic, making beautifully carved combs from deer horns, for instance. She was a good worker, washing, scrubbing and cooking for the Peytons. She was vain — she became extremely proud of a pair of silk stockings that Captain Buchan sent her from St. John's.

And she was also subject to fits of melancholy, going off alone into the woods to commune with the spirits of her mother and sister. The Micmac Indians in the community terrified her, sending her running to Peyton whenever she encountered one — and no wonder: her hands, arms and legs bore the marks of gunshot wounds, many of them left by a local Micmac named Noel Boss, who continued to boast that he had killed ninety-nine Beothuks and hoped to make it a hundred.

In 1827, Cormack, the explorer, with some other citizens, helped to form a philanthropic institution dedicated to finding and civilizing the Red Indians of Newfoundland. The Beothuck Institution had everything; a handsome endowment, a slate of officers, a constitution and a secretary. It lacked only Indians to make it a success. Unable to find any in the woods, the Institution concentrated on Shawnadithit. John Stark, the secretary, insisted that the "unfortunate creature" be rescued from her "deplorable and dark situation" and be brought to St. John's, a measure, he wrote Cormack, which "will afford you and me the satisfaction of knowing that we have contributed our mite in the general cause of humanity."

Shawnadithit arrived at St. John's in September 1828, and was billeted with Cormack. Stark suggested that "a stout watch be kept over her morals," a scarcely necessary admonition since she had always held herself aloof and with dignity from the fishermen and trappers of the coast.

The Institution's plan was to educate Shawnadithit in English and in Christianity and then to take her as an emissary to any Beothuks that might still be hiding in the woods — providing, of course, that an expedition could find them.

There was one valuable by-product of all this unctuous meddling. In her halting English and with the

184

help of a remarkable series of drawings, the last of the Red Indians was able to explain to Cormack what had happened to her people and also to tell a little of their culture. She had been a child in her father's wigwam when Buchan first visited Red Indian Lake in 1811. She had watched while the panic-stricken Indians, believing that Buchan had gone back for reinforcements to massacre them, had slain and beheaded the two sailors. She had watched the capture of Demasduit by Peyton's party, and helped to bury her when Buchan had returned with the corpse. In the winter of 1822-23, with only twenty-seven Indians camped on Badger Bay in four wigwams, she had watched the death throes of her people. She described the deaths of her father, her brother, her uncle and her cousin and told how, with others dying of starvation, she had headed for the coast with her mother and sister to look for mussels, only to be captured by Cull. And Cormack wrote: "Here ends all positive knowledge of her tribe, which she never narrates without tears."

In the spring of 1829, Cormack left Newfoundland, taking all his papers and notes which, tragically, have never been found. Shawnadithit was placed in the care of the Attorney General of the colony, James Simms, but she was already in the final stages of tuberculosis. She was moved to the hospital at St. John's and there, on June 6, 1829, she went to her rest — the last of the Red Indians, a tribe that gave its name to all the native peoples of North America and the one we know the least about. Although she died a pagan she was buried in a Church of England graveyard in St. John's. Her grave, however, no longer exists. It was dug up to make way for a new road and so her bones, like those of all her people, are lost forever.

8

The Zeal of Charles Chiniquy

It is given to few men to be venerated as saints and excoriated as devils in their own lifetime but Charles Paschal Telésphor Chiniquy managed it with ease in the last century. His name is scarcely a household word today but there was a time when the Abbé Chiniquy was successively the best-known Roman Catholic priest in the province of Quebec and the best-known Protestant minister in all of Canada. The emotions he stirred were such that tens of thousands hung his lithographed portrait in their parlours; a decade or so later some of these same people became part of the howling mob that tried to tear him to pieces.

A brilliant temperance fighter who was himself a prey to the sins of the flesh, he caused multitudes of supporters to sign the pledge against strong liquor. A spellbinding orator and best-selling author, he was banished and finally excommunicated by his own church, apparently for sexual peccadillos and heresies. A converted Protestant, he managed to seduce more thousands away from the Catholic fold. As a Catholic he was compared regularly to St. Louis-de-Gonzague, one of the most venerated of modern saints. As a Protestant he was hailed as a modern Martin Luther.

It is not easy today to comprehend the emotions that Chiniquy stirred up a century ago; we tend to forget the enormous power and emotional appeal of the temperance movement in nineteenth-century Canada, just as we tend to forget the almost maniacal bitterness of the Catholic-Protestant division. To comprehend the Chiniquy story, it is necessary to understand these twin emotions. Even then it is difficult to really *know* Chiniquy, for his character was anything but simple. It is not easy to like him, for he was clearly a hypocrite, a liar, a sensualist and an egotist. Yet it is hard not to admire him, for he had courage, charisma, passion and a golden tongue. More than most of his contemporaries, he was a product of his time. In these more tolerant and permissive years, I doubt that he could have made much of an impact.

Chiniquy's father was a mean drunk and that has to be borne in mind when one considers his later temperance crusades. He was also a failed student of the priesthood, having switched from a seminary to the law courts. The well-to-do Chiniquys of Kamouraska (the grandfather was the *seigneur*) were certainly religious but there was a kind of maverick streak operating in the family. Charles' uncle, Martin, was a Trappist monk who later gave up Catholicism for Protestantism only to re-embrace his former faith on his deathbed.

Most of what we know about Charles Chiniquy's childhood comes from his own pen and must be scrutinized with care. He can be believed, however, when he indicates that he was born an orator; later events made that obvious: "We were some distance from the church, and the roads, in the rainy days, were very bad. On the Sabbath days the neighbouring farmers, unable to go to church, were accustomed to gather at our house in the evening. Then my parents used to put me up on a large table in the midst of the assembly, and I delivered to those good people the most beautiful parts of the Old and New Testaments. The breathless attention, the applause of our guests, and — may I tell it — often the tears of joy which my mother tried in vain to conceal, supported my strength and gave me the courage I wanted, to speak when so young before so many people."

The elder Chiniquy died when Charles was twelve and the boy's welfare was taken over by his uncle, Amable Dionne, a wealthy Kamouraska merchant who treated him as his own son and subsidized his education at the Seminary of Nicolet. Three years later, however, there was a complete breach: Dionne suddenly announced that he would no longer support the boy. What had happened? Chiniquy in his memoirs glossed over the incident which, he wrote, was a "misunderstanding." But a Dionne grandson, Bishop Henri Têtu, claimed in a memoir that Chiniquy was banished from his foster-father's favour because he tried to tamper with one of Dionne's daughters. In the light of later revelations, Bishop Têtu's story rings true.

Such was young Chiniquy's scholastic ability, however, that two of his teachers offered to pay his fees. The boy repaid the investment by winning prizes for recitation and rhetoric. For the first time, but not the last, his humility caused him to be compared with (and nicknamed for) Saint Louis-de-Gonzague — known, in the Encyclopaedia Britannica's intriguing phrase, for his "intense love of chastity." Not everybody agreed with this assessment. Bishop Têtu later wrote that some thought Chiniquy was "a hypocrite of the first water."

Chiniquy's mother died when he was twenty-one, after eliciting from him the standard nineteenth-century deathbed promise that he would never drink more than two glasses of wine. Three years later, on the occasion of his ordination as a priest, Chiniquy also abjured tobacco, throwing away his pipe and snuff box forever. Some time during the next four years, while serving as a curate and also as a hospital chaplain, he became interested in the problem of alcohol abuse. As is usual in the Chiniquy story, there are two versions of how this came about.

Chiniquy's version goes this way: He asked, he said, for a glass of brandy — for purely medicinal purposes. The Protestant doctor at the hospital, James Douglas, admonished him, explaining that alcohol was a poison. Chiniquy demanded proof; Douglas convinced him by performing an autopsy on an alcoholic. Fascinated, the young priest took up the study, witnessing some two hundred autopsies over the next four years, and was astonished "to view the damage made even in moderate drinkers."

Douglas, in his memoirs, gave a shorter, blunter version, which did not picture Chiniquy as an avid student priest. The doctor wrote that he caught his chaplain drinking brandy and rebuked him severely for setting such a poor example, whereupon the chaplain stalked angrily out of the room. There was no mention of a later interest in autopsies.

Whatever Chiniquy's interest in the curse of alcohol may have been, it lay dormant for some time. He applied to go as a priest to the Red River country but was rebuffed in a letter. The Bishop of St. Boniface mentioned a "blunder" on Chiniquy's part but did not go into detail. Then, in September 1838, when Chiniquy was thirty-one, he was made curé of Beauport, one of the most important parishes in Quebec.

Beauport was renowned for the amount of liquor its parishioners could put away. It was actually cheaper to drink than to eat. A jug of rum cost a mere twenty-five sous — about twenty cents. There were seven saloons in the town exploiting that fact. Chiniquy was shocked to discover that his parishioners did not buy their rum by the jug; they hauled it home by the cask.

For thousands of farmhands and common labourers in both Canadas, liquor provided the only real respite.

Booze was the great lubricant at barn raisings, country bees, sports events and political rallies. Women, banned from the taverns, often sat outside in carts and buggies enduring the freezing cold while their husbands drank themselves into bankruptcy. But the temperance movement, gathering power in Protestant Ontario, sparked by the churches and later by some of these same women, changed all that. By 1831, there were some hundred temperance societies in Upper Canada; thousands, attracted by mass meetings and a snowstorm of anti-liquor pamphlets, were taking the pledge.

Lower Canada was more tolerant. There were only a few temperance societies operating in the early 1830s among the French Canadians — until Chiniquy came along. Almost single-handedly, he changed the Quebecois attitude toward strong drink.

The original spark came from a priest, Pierre Beaumont, in a neighbouring parish, who had been attracted to the fledgling temperance ideal by reading the English-language newspapers. In 1839, he and Chiniquy decided to found twin temperance movements in their two parishes.

Chiniquy began preaching temperance at once. In March, 1840, he founded his Société de Tempérance. No fewer than thirteen hundred of his parishioners took the pledge "to avoid intemperance and never go to cabarets." Then they went on to swear that "I will never use strong drink without an absolute necessity, and if to become temperate I must renounce all kinds of drink, I will so agree; I promise also to do all in my power by my words and my deeds so that my parents and my friends will do as much."

This pledge did not proscribe beer or wine. The following year, however, Chiniquy drew up a new document which demanded total and perfect temperance. More than eight hundred of his flock signed it. The

Catholic Church was never as extreme as Chiniquy; it was more concerned with the general virtues of sobriety. (After all, the serving of wine was part of the Mass.) Chiniquy came to regard this tolerant attitude as a personal attack upon himself and he charged, in his memoirs, that the church had actually opposed temperance, which was certainly not true.

Largely because of his rhetoric, the Abbé Chiniquy became the most prominent priest involved in the temperance movement of Lower Canada. "Everywhere his zeal goes, intemperance flies," Le Canadien reported. His speeches began modestly; frequently he admitted that he had known drunkenness. Then his tone grew feverish as he recounted horrible tales of the downfall of drunks. He was a slight young man, under five and a half feet, with intense, sympathetic eyes and a shock of soft, dark hair. His followers began to call him "le petit père." Sometime later Bishop Bourget of Montreal was to ask, ruefully: "How could such a little man cause such an uproar?"

Chiniquy's initial moment of triumph came in September 1841, when he organized a grand spectacle around the unveiling of a Temperance Column at Beauport. Ten thousand people, accompanied by seven choirs of women and led by two little girls, dressed in white and carrying white flags, marched from the Seminary of Quebec, after Mass, to dedicate the pillar with its gilded Corinthian base and its cross. The Bishop of Nancy, then touring French Canada, also turned up to bless the column, accompanied by twenty-two horsemen.

Chiniquy's star was rising. The Bishop of Montreal, Ignace Bourget, invited him to preach that October at the cathedral where, in Le Canadien's words, he "made a great sensation." His parishioners commissioned one of the province's best portrait artists to render his likeness in oils. He seemed on the verge of greater triumphs when suddenly and without warning, he was gone — flung out of his parish by his bishop and banished to Kamouraska. The bishop acted with so much dispatch that the priest's own parishioners didn't have a chance to bid him goodbye.

What had happened? Clearly, there had been a scandal of some sort. Chiniquy's biographer, Marcel Trudel, mentions a "secret memoire" which describes it, evasively, as "a misadventure which would be comic if the subject were not so lamentable." This titillating remark is reminiscent of Chiniquy's earlier "misunderstanding" in the home of his uncle and the "blunder" to which the Bishop of St. Boniface referred. For all of his years in the Church of Rome, Chiniquy's career followed this topsy-turvy pattern of blinding success followed by "misadventures" hushed up, banishment and then a slow rise to a new pinnacle. The abbé was nothing if not resilient. He bounced from one misadventure to another, blandly dismissing each scandal as a personal and uncalled-for attack visited upon an innocent zealot by dark forces bent upon his destruction.

For the moment Chiniquy was demoted to acting curé of Kamouraska. Some months later, when the ailing priest died, the title was confirmed. Immediately he began to press his temperance campaign.

His attitude to strong drink had hardened. He would have none of the *auberges de tempérance,* which were springing up in Quebec to cater to followers of *la petite tempérance.* These establishments attempted to sell strong drink in a moderate fashion. To Chiniquy they were just as bad as the all-out saloons. By the spring of 1844, when he published his *Manuel de Tempérance,* Chiniquy was accepted as the leading theoretician and preacher of temperance in Quebec. The first edition of four thousand copies sold out quickly. Parish after parish begged to hear him. At St. Gervais, for instance, he persuaded thirteen hundred to take the pledge. His peccadillos, whatever they may have been, were forgotten. And then, once again as he reached for the pinnacle, the weakness of the flesh brought about his downfall.

He had gone to preach in the neighbouring parish of St. Pascal. Here, while he was enrolling abstainers and handing out temperance cards, his eye fell upon a local housewife. Chiniquy started to pay court to her; she tried, not without difficulty, to fend him off. He persisted; at last she fixed a rendezvous. But when the ardent priest arrived at the trysting place it was not a comely woman who came to meet him; it was the local curé. Chiniquy fell to his knees and confessed his sin. Again the scandal was hushed up, but he obviously could not remain in Kamouraska. He asked to enter the novitiate of the Oblate Fathers (an order committed to temperance) at Longueuil near Montreal, and a relieved bishop approved the transfer.

There are always, in the tangled history of Charles Chiniquy, two versions of every one of these intriguing incidents. Years later, when Chiniquy came to write his memoirs, he gave an entirely different account of his sudden switch to the Oblate order. He was so disgusted, he claimed, by the scandals he saw around him among other clergy that he wanted to die. When the head of the Oblates urged him to join, "I fell to my knees and made to God, in the midst of burning tears, the sacrifice of my parish."

En route to the Oblate mission, Chiniquy stopped off at Trois Rivières where he enrolled two thousand persons in total temperance. He had managed by this time to complete a second edition of his *Manuel,* a slicker one than the first, carrying letters of endorsation from four bishops, including one unlikely signator, the Bishop of Walla Walla in the distant territory of Washington. The book, which was published in January 1845, sold ten thousand copies in a few months, became a text in Quebec schools and went into an English-language edition. No book had enjoyed such a success up to that time in French Canada.

As a novice, Chiniquy kept a high profile, continuing to make speeches for temperance and involving himself in the politics of the order to the point where the Superior General called him impertinent. His application for admission was unanimously rejected and Chiniquy, on leaving, wrote to Bishop Bourget of Montreal that "I feel more than ever an invincible repugnance to being an Oblate." Years later, in his memoirs, he took a different tack: "From the first to the last day of my sojourn among the Oblates I was honoured with the esteem and friendship of all, without exception; tears flowed from the eyes of all when I said goodbye." One suspects that, if there were tears, they were tears of relief.

In the spring of 1848, Bishop Bourget assigned Chiniquy to work as a temperance crusader in Montreal. As a result he became more prominent than ever. One religious magazine kept a box score of his converts: by summer it had reached twenty thousand. The mayor and the bishop both turned out to hear him address a crowd of five thousand at the Bonsecours Marketplace in October where Chiniquy made an impassioned speech in favour of drinking water, using himself as a healthy example of total abstinence. The rhetoric made the bishop uneasy. He wrote to Chiniquy suggesting he calm down a bit: "Avoid all kinds of trivialities and unworthy details . . . Guard against self-love, which is so subtle and dangerous above all in the midst of great successes." There is no evidence that Chiniquy took this advice. By the end of the year his converts had reached sixty thousand. Bookstores began to sell lithographs of the painting his former parishioners had commissioned and these became standard adornments in the parlours of French Canada.

The following April, in a monumental crusade, Chiniquy signed up eighteen thousand persons. Then, in a two-week crusade in June, he converted twelve thousand more to total abstinence. In Montreal, at the height of a great temperance fête, he was presented with a gold medal inscribed "in homage to his virtue, his zeal and his patriotism." He would wear it all his life. The third edition of his *Manuel* now contained his portrait along with biographical notes comparing him, once again to Saint Louis-de-Gonzague. In 1850, in recognition of his temperance crusade, the LaFontaine-Baldwin government of the United Canadas presented him with a gift of five hundred pounds, the equivalent of twenty-five hundred dollars, a remarkable sum for those days. There seemed no end to the triumphs of the Abbé Chiniquy; and yet, once again, his downfall was imminent.

Bishop Bourget was clearly aware of Chiniquy's weaknesses. In May 1851, when the abbé went to Illinois to investigate the need for a French-speaking priest to minister to the eleven thousand Quebecois who had settled there, Bourget admonished him to take strict precautions in his relationships with "personnes du sexe." In addition, he reproached Chiniquy for eating meat on Friday. The advice went unheeded. En route to Chicago the priest made amorous overtures to a girl of respectable family. He departed in haste when the Bishop of Detroit started to investigate.

On his return to Quebec he plunged into a new crusade, this one designed to boost French-Canadian immigration to what he felt were the greener pastures of

Illinois. This did not help his deteriorating position with the Bishop of Montreal. The last thing Bourget wanted was a mass exodus of his flock to a foreign land. The bishop knew, of course, about Chiniquy's indiscretions at St. Pascal. Later on he had discovered that there had been three similar incidents at other parishes. On the heels of this knowledge came evidence of still *another* incident.

"We had had proof of M. Chiniquy's guilt for some time," Bourget was to write, "when a certain girl came to give evidence against him, testifying that she would feel repugnance to be confronted by him. . . ."

On September 28, 1851, Chiniquy was relieved of all his priestly functions. He demanded to know the name of his accuser but Bourget refused to give it. Chiniquy, who apparently knew her identity all along, confronted the girl and pressed her to retract. Instead, she repeated her testimony under oath. For Chiniquy this was the end. "I will hide the disgrace of my position in the farthest and most obscure corner of the U.S.," he wrote to Bourget.

The farthest and most obscure corner of the United States turned out to be the twin parishes of Bourbonnais and St. Anne, two relatively new French-Canadian settlements about fifty miles from Chicago, both badly in need of a French-speaking priest. The Bishop of Chicago, James Van De Velde, was in Montreal at the time searching for just such a man and speedily agreed to give Chiniquy a chance. All suggestion of scandal was hushed up; indeed, Bishop Bourget publicly presented his erring servant with a chalice and thanked him for his work, an action that the embattled abbé made much of. Chiniquy's parishioners, who gave him a moving farewell, believed that his departure for the United States was another example of his self-sacrifice. Soon Chiniquy was saying (and perhaps believing) that

Bishop Bourget had offered him a handsome parish to try to prevent him from leaving, but that his resolve had not been shaken.

He was given the parish of St. Anne, a settlement of about a hundred families. And here, Chiniquy threw himself into a new kind of evangelism, and one that brought down anger from his native province. He actively began to persuade immigrants to leave Quebec for the United States. In the summer of 1852, he made a recruiting trip to French Canada and even announced, at Kamouraska, that he would say mass in his old church. But the curé refused him permission and his former neighbours treated him coldly, a considerable rebuke for one who had been raised in the parish.

Back in Illinois, he began to adopt habits that would result in his excommunication. His sexton, Godefroi Lambert, left a memoir, listing some of his transgressions. He ate meat on Friday, for instance, boldly declaring that the Pope would never hear of it. He talked lewdly to women. He even made advances to Lambert's wife and tried to convince her that sexual activities were not forbidden to priests. He consorted with "women of ill repute."

In 1853, a mysterious and disturbing event occurred at the neighbouring parish of Bourbonnais: the chapel, half completed, burned to the ground. There had been a controversy over this edifice. Chiniquy wanted it built of imposing stone; his bishop, Van De Velde, insisted that it be of simpler frame construction. A few days after the bishop visited Bourbonnais and laid down this edict, the wooden chapel was consumed by flames. Oddly, all the consecrated vessels had been removed to the parsonage just before the fire broke out. Suspicion naturally fell on Chiniquy but he claimed that he had actually seen the real arsonist escaping. When his parishioners insisted he name the criminal, Chiniquy backtracked; he had seen him, he explained, but only in his mind's eye. Later on, when he wrote a dramatic appeal to *Le Canadien* for funds to rebuild the chapel, a group of parishioners signed a letter to the paper saying that the donations would be surer of reaching their destination if they were addressed to the bishop and not the priest. Clearly, Chiniquy was on shaky ground; and it was growing shakier.

In 1854 a new bishop, the Irish Anthony O'Regan, replaced Van De Velde. He was not satisfied with the quality of some of the priests in his new charge and determined to weed out the poorest. In the midst of his investigations, which certainly included Chiniquy, the abbé found himself embroiled in a defamation lawsuit brought by a man named Peter Spink with whom Chiniquy had lodged on his first visit to Illinois. The two trials that followed were mainly notable for the fact that Chiniquy was defended by Abraham Lincoln, then a young Illinois lawyer. The first trial ended in a hung jury; during the second Chiniquy backed down completely and apologized. The apology was undoubtedly triggered by the fact that the new bishop had placed him under suspension.

The abbé fought back — and hard. In a letter to his parishioners he denied boldly that he had been suspended. In private letters to the bishop he pleaded for mercy, asked that the interdiction be lifted, and apologized. His public attitude showed no such humility. He told his flock that O'Regan's actions were based on the traditional Irish hatred for French Canadians; as a result the expatriates backed him to a man.

O'Regan's response was excommunication. On September 3, the vicar-general of the diocese arrived at St. Anne with two priests. Their carriage was met by a threatening crowd who hooted when he read the proclamation aloud and fixed it to the door of the church.

Chiniquy blandly announced that the document was not legal: it was nothing more than an unsigned translation of the original. "If you think you can deal with me as a carter with his horse . . . you will soon see your error," he wrote to O'Regan.

He had only just begun to fight. A band of devotees, calling themselves the Société de Tondeurs (Shearers) appeared in the two parishes and began to shear the hair of those whom they suspected of disloyalty to their priest. The French-Canadian press rallied to Chiniquy's side, in the belief that O'Regan wanted to turn his church over to the Irish. When Bishop Bourget entered the fray, challenging Chiniquy to reveal the real reason why he left Canada, the priest retorted that a prostitute had been paid one hundred dollars to perjure herself against him. Bourget then sent two priests to Illinois to persuade Chiniquy to submit. They failed. A second delegation was somewhat more successful. They engineered the defection of the sexton, Lambert, and a good many other parishioners. But some two hundred families remained loyal to Chiniquy.

A year went by. Chiniquy continued to say mass in his church at St. Anne. In September 1857, O'Regan, worn out with worry, returned to Rome. Another year passed; Chiniquy was still in business. Then a new bishop, James Duggan, arrived to take over the Chicago diocese, determined to resolve the Chiniquy question once and for all.

On August 3, 1858, Bishop Duggan arrived in St. Anne accompanied by three priests. The quartet approached the public platform in the village square. There was Chiniquy, standing boldly beside the steps, hand out-stretched in greeting. The bishop ignored him, and ascended to the platform. Chiniquy followed and placed himself on Duggan's right. A stack of books containing press clippings favourable to the abbé, was on the platform. Chiniquy picked one up, opened it and attempted to show it to the bishop. Duggan looked at him coldly. "Leave your books," he said. "If you are not under interdiction I am going to place you under interdiction, and excommunicate you according to the rites."

The bishop then made the sign of the cross and pronounced sentence: "I declare to you in virtue of the authority of the Catholic Church invested in me that Mr. Chiniquy is truly and validly interdicted and excommunicated." The crowd booed lustily.

Duggan wanted no ambiguity. He repeated the sentence: "I again place Mr. Chiniquy under interdiction and excommunicate him so that no person here present will be able to pretend ignorance."

Ignoring the tumult that this caused, the bishop then turned and looked directly at Chiniquy: "Wretch, abandon these people you have deceived, go somewhere to make penance; and then I assure you that you will be pardoned and the church will again receive you in her breast."

By this time the crowd was in a perfect fury. Dozens surged forward to prevent the bishop from leaving the platform — the women "howling like mad dogs" and spitting on him, as the sheriff struggled to help him to his carriage.

The resilient Chiniquy was in no way discomfited by the ritual. In fact he allowed the publicity to work in his favour: as an ex-priest he soon became the object of intense interest to Protestants. In a few weeks he had founded a new sect, *L'église catholique chrétienne* with the same chapel of St. Anne as its headquarters. Chiniquy claimed the move had been divinely inspired — that he had decided to cut his own throat when the hand of God knocked the knife from his grasp and, while he was in a trance that followed, "my Saviour showed himself to my amazed eyes." The seeds of what would be a lifelong anti-Catholic crusade were sown at once; the cross and the statue of Mary were removed from the St. Anne chapel, the confession ritual was ended and the dogmas mocked.

Meanwhile another tempest was brewing. A Canadian Oblate father, Augustine-Alexandre Brunet, who had come to preach in the area, accused Chiniquy in the hearing of others of firing the Bourbonnais chapel. Chiniquy sued Brunet for libel. Brunet, who had returned to Canada, was found guilty *in absentia* and sentenced to pay Chiniquy damages of twenty-five hundred dollars or serve a prison term of seventeen years. Alas for Chiniquy, the verdict backfired on him. Brunet returned to Illinois at once, gave himself up, and announced he would serve the entire prison term before he paid a cent to the apostate. This was a financial blow to Chiniquy because, under the law of that time, he himself would have to contribute three dollars a week to the prisoner's upkeep.

Fortunately for Chiniquy a group of parishioners who had grown to like Brunet decided to free him. They got the sheriff drunk and proceeded to attempt to saw through the bars of the Oblate's cell. It was no easy task. They managed to remove one bar only, and, after much tugging and pulling got the plump Brunet half way through the opening. At that point, the priest stuck fast and it was only with difficulty that he was finally freed and spirited, more than a little bruised and dented, across the Canadian border.

Whatever names one can apply to Chiniquy — hypocrite, publicity seeker, satyr, fanatic — none can deny his personal courage. Who but Chiniquy would have chosen this particular moment in his career to return to Quebec? But return he did, in January 1859, to make a preaching tour funded by Quebec Protestants.

The lions were waiting for their Daniel. He had trouble finding a hotel in Montreal which would accept his custom. No meeting place save one, the Mechanics' Hall, would give him a platform. Bishop Bourget ordered his flock to shun him. Crowds at his meetings chanted: "Go away Judas!" In Quebec City, four hundred angry neighbours surrounded the private home in which he was lodging and forced him to flee by carriage. In St.-Hilaire-de-Rouville his very life was threatened and he had to leave town hurriedly.

All this attention brought invitations to address Protestant gatherings in Boston, Philadelphia, Washington, Pittsburgh, New York, Chicago and Baltimore. Here he told of his battle with the Roman Church and collected money to combat food scarcities, which he claimed were afflicting his parish of St. Anne. The local paper denied there were any shortages but Chiniquy claims to have collected seventy-five thousand dollars and a vast quantity of food anyway. It is unlikely, in the light of later financial discrepancies, that the parish saw all of it.

In February 1860, Chiniquy became, officially, a minister in the Presbyterian Church of the United States. For each new member enrolled, the mother church gave a subsidy of ninety dollars. Chiniquy claimed that he enrolled two thousand members at St. Anne. Considering the size of the community, the figure seems inflated. He was rewarded by a trip to Europe where some saw him as a latter-day Luther. In Scotland, France, Switzerland and Italy, he solicited donations for "the seminary of St. Anne," an imaginary institution which Chiniquy described as having thirty-two dedicated students. He collected ten thousand dollars and returned to the United States where the presbyterian Synod, puzzled by inquiries about the non-existent seminary, called him to account. Chiniquy refused to appear and once again found himself stripped of his ministry.

He turned now to the Presbyterians of Upper Canada, who welcomed him with open arms, formally attaching his parish to the presbytery of London. The Canadians decided that the affair of the ten thousand dollars was all a misunderstanding based on Chiniquy's unfamiliarity with Presbyterian ways. It was not too difficult for them to gloss over his transgressions since he was a very big catch indeed in a country bitterly divided by religious strife. In the battle with the Papists, Chiniquy was seen as a potential general.

The bitterness of the Protestant feeling against the Catholics in the united Canadas is difficult to grasp today. It had its root, of course, in the binational character of the country; but as Confederation approached, feelings grew more extreme as each side feared the other's interference in its own culture. An important factor in exacerbating the issue was the establishment in Upper Canada, achieved largely through the Lower Canadian vote, of separate schools for Roman Catholics. In addition, there was the growing nativist sentiment against the waves of immigrants arriving from Europe; many of these were Roman Catholics.

The focus for this hatred was the Grand Orange Lodge of British North America, founded at Brockville in 1830. In Orange eyes, the Church of Rome was a sinister and secret international conspiracy, bent on controlling the minds of men through the confessional. Papists in Canada were viewed much as Jews were in Hitler's Germany or communists in McCarthy's America. Orange demonstrations on the Twelfth of July were often violent affairs as Catholics and Protestants clashed in the streets. On July 12, 1843, for instance, men were killed in an attack on the Orange Hall in

Kingston. Six years later, on the Twelfth, there were a dozen deaths and countless injuries in street riots in St. John's. The demonstrations on July 12, 1862, just after Chiniquy joined the Canadian Presbyterian Church (he, too, was to become an Orangeman) were said to be the largest on record.

Chiniquy fell enthusiastically in with the church's plan to use him as an effective and energetic weapon against the Romanists. In 1863, he published an inflammatory tract, *The Church of Rome Is the Enemy of the Holy Virgin and Jesus Christ*. In 1864, he married one of his servants, Euphémie Allard; she was to present him with three children. In 1867, he published a brochure attacking the concept of the immaculate conception. In 1869, he mounted a speaking tour of Prince Edward Island on the subject of papal indulgences. The man who had once been the best-known Roman Catholic priest in French Canada was on his way to becoming the best-known Protestant minister in English Canada.

In 1873, the Presbyterian Synod decided to put Chiniquy in charge of a new campaign to undertake the systematic conversion of French Canadians. Before moving to Montreal, the former abbé embarked on a six-month speaking tour of England, collecting twenty-five thousand dollars for himself in fees. Protestantism, he was discovering, was more rewarding — at least financially — than Catholicism.

He moved with his family to Montreal at the beginning of 1875 and began preaching on Craig Street, bringing to his evangelism all the zeal which had once marked his temperance crusades. So much violence accompanied his services that, at the beginning, three hundred men were required to protect him from injury. The same year he published a major work, *The Priest, the Women and the Confessional*. This turned out to be a fairly gamey piece of literature. Chiniquy peppered his polemic with racy accounts of priests who became so aroused by the confessions of their feminine parishioners that they themselves pursued a heady course which brought about their downfall. No doubt Chiniquy was describing his own former condition and, when he said that enforced celibacy contributed to the problem, he was probably right. After his marriage there is no further suggestion that he strayed from the path. As for the book, it was an enormous success, going into fifty editions in two languages by 1892.

The Roman Catholic Church was predictably enraged. Bishop Bourget published a lengthy pastoral letter attacking the author and his work. An anonymous Catholic pamphlet described with relish Chiniquy's future death and even included a deathbed description in which foam issued from the mouth of the dying renegade while a diabolical voice chortled: "Yet another for my kingdom!" But at sixty-six, Chiniquy was very much alive. Between 1875 and 1878 he boasted of having converted seven thousand French Canadians to Protestantism.

In 1878, he began a long series of hugely successful and often tumultuous speaking tours. After a turn around the western United States he travelled to Australia, New Zealand and Tasmania at the invitation of the Orange Society of Australia. His energy was prodigious. He was approaching seventy and yet he managed to give seven hundred speeches over a two-year period and to collect forty thousand dollars. He was nothing if not inflammatory. One town required a full four days of martial law to calm it down after Chiniquy's appearance.

Advancing years did nothing to still those inner fires. Back in Canada, in June 1884, a crowd gathered outside the Protestant church in which he was preaching in

Québec City. Stones began to crash through the windows. Chiniquy escaped by carriage to the railway station. The enraged crowd pursued him, and Chiniquy was forced to hide in a trunk while awaiting the train. The mob tore his carriage to pieces.

Not in the least daunted, the stubborn old man then churned out an eight-hundred-page autobiography, *Fifty Years in the Church of Rome.* It was an enormous bestseller. By 1892 it was in its twentieth edition and had appeared in French, English, Italian, Spanish, Swedish, Czech, Dutch, German and even Chinese. The Protestant world greeted its publication with wild enthusiasm. One leading churchman wrote that "I do not believe there exists in our time a Protestant work more important or more alive with interest."

Chiniquy's own version of his career was not always in accord with the known facts. His treatment of Abraham Lincoln, for instance, suggests how he made free with the truth. Chiniquy implied that the Great Emancipator had sided with him in his struggle with the Catholic Church, writing that Lincoln had acted for him in his victory over Bishop O'Regan. Lincoln, of course, had done nothing of the sort; he had been his lawyer in the two abortive suits involving Spink and there was certainly no victory there.

But this was only the first volume of a longer memoir. At the age of eighty Chiniquy was scribbling away at a second tome, *Forty Years in the Church of Christ,* and continuing to make converts among Quebec Catholics. His most famous convert was Louis-Joseph-Amédée Papineau, the son of the famous rebel of 1837. Papineau insisted that Chiniquy officiate at the conversion ceremony because he considered him "le Luther du Canada."

When this event took place, Chiniquy was eighty-five years old, still energetic, in possession of all his faculties, and, as his photograph shows, remarkably well preserved. (How his religious enemies must have gritted their teeth at this *prima facie* evidence of the fruits of sin!) Eighteen months later he was off on another lecture tour of England. He made eighty-five speeches and would have made more but illness forced a change in his itinerary. Sick or not, however, the old man made a point of visiting Luther's tomb at Wittenburg.

Stubbornly, he refused to die. Returning home he divided his time between his house in Montreal and his country place at St. Louise on the south shore of the St. Lawrence. It was almost three years later, in January 1899, that he fell ill and it became clear that the end was near. Would he, on his deathbed, re-embrace his former faith? There was widespread speculation on that question. The Catholic Church did what it could to encourage a conversion. The Archbishop of Montreal, Paul Bruchési, wrote a letter of encouragement to Chiniquy's son-in-law to which the old man himself replied with unaccustomed gentleness. I am grateful to the archbishop . . . but I have definitely left the church of Rome. I am perfectly happy in the faith of Jesus Christ. . . ."

The détente was temporary. In the final days of his life the old fire returned and Chiniquy dictated a religious testament to be sent to the newspapers and to the archbishop after his death, in which he made one last violent attack on the Catholic Church. Even while he was dying there was a brief, inconclusive struggle for his soul. Two nuns sneaked into the house, apparently in a last-ditch attempt at conversion, but were politely shown the door by his family.

Thus expired the Reverend Charles Chiniquy, at the age of eighty-nine. In death as in life he attracted multitudes. His body was laid out in state in his home and more than ten thousand persons filed past the bier. It was a mixed crowd; for once Catholics and Protestants were united in a common obeisance — or was it curiosity? Certainly, the controversy that swirled around him in life followed him to the grave. The Catholic periodical, *L'Evénement,* reserved no niceties for its editorial comment on the deceased. "Chiniquy," it declared, "leaves to history a soiled name."

He was interred in the Protestant Cimitière de la Montagne. Oral tradition has it that he was buried standing up and that his tombstone was cleft in two by a divine curse. With Chiniquy, anything seems possible: but, like so much that was written by and about the embattled former abbé, this, too, must be taken with more than a grain of salt.

9

The Franklin Mystery

Of all the grim and forlorn corners of the known nine-teenth-century world, the polar regions of Canada were surely the most desolate. Ships which ventured into that maze of serpentine channels and barren islands in the wan light of the brief summers found themselves entrapped, often for years, in the inexorable ice streams that flowed, as slowly as treacle, out of the mists which shrouded the Unknown. In the sullen twilight of the interminable winters it was impossible to tell where the shadowless land ended and the frozen sea began. Maps were of limited value; in mid-century, half the Arctic was still a blank. Certain channels might turn out to be bays; peninsulas could be islands; it was not possible to know which straits lay open, which were dammed by glacial barriers. And no one was sure if there really was any clear passage leading from Atlantic to Pacific through that jigsaw puzzle of gloomy scarps, ice-choked waterways and camel-backed islets.

But if there should be — oh, if there *could* be! — then the will-o'-the-wisp that had intrigued and eluded ex-plorers almost from the moment of the continent's discovery, would no longer be a tantalizing myth. The discovery and navigation of the fabled North West Passage was a prize as glamorous as the secret of the Nile's source. No matter that such a find would be of limited value; no matter that no sensible seaman would be so foolhardy as to use a polar channel as a route to the Orient: since Elizabethan times, the mysterious Passage had been to England's seamen what the Grail had once been to England's errant knights. So important was it held to be, that the Admiralty had a standing offer of ten thousand pounds for the man who would be the first to navigate it.

By the 1840s the English middle classes were hungry for more tales of discovery. British explorers, who were methodically filling in the blank spaces on the map, enjoyed a celebrity akin to that of movie stars in a later era. The Arctic adventurers — Back, Richardson, the two Rosses, Belcher, Beechey, Parry and Franklin — were all household names. Lost to the world for months and even years, they had from time to time emerged from the polar fog with tales of dreadful hardship, high heroism and new lands conquered, to bask in the applause of the nation. The bone-chilling cold, the twin horrors of scurvy and starvation, the back-breaking sledge journeys, the dreadful monotony of the eternal night, the agonizing deaths of close comrades — all these became bearable in the euphoria that attended their return to civilization. Their published narratives became raging bestsellers; their lectures drew overflow crowds and a grateful realm showered them with prizes, medals, awards and knighthoods.

It is necessary to know all this in order to understand why Sir John Franklin, the greatest hero of them all, wanted — indeed, pleaded — to return for the third time to the Arctic. He was almost sixty, balding, paunchy, partly deaf and, as later events would show, not too well. He had already made two hideously demanding Arctic journeys. But none of this was enough. When, in 1845, the British Admiralty under the urgings of its secretary, Sir John Barrow, decided to make one last attempt to find the North West passage, Franklin demanded it as his due.

The First Sea Lord, Haddington, made some slight effort to dissuade him. After all, Franklin with his second, younger wife might easily rest on his laurels as Sir James Ross, also recently married, had decided to do.

"I might find a good excuse for not letting you go, Sir John," said Lord Haddington, "in the tell-tale record that informs me that you are sixty years of age."

Franklin was scandalized. "No, no, my lord," he expostulated. "I am only *fifty-nine*!"

He wanted to prove his mettle once again and the fact is that his wife Jane (a woman of dogged determination, as we shall see) abetted him in his resolve. The Franklins were still smarting under their treatment by the Colonial Office when, as Governor of Van Dieman's Land (Tasmania), the explorer had been dismissed as a result of a political squabble. For years he had been struggling to clear his name, which he fancied was sullied. Now his wife egged him on: "Your credit and reputation are dearer to me than the selfish enjoyment of your society," was the way she put it, in true Victorian style.

Franklin's fellow explorer, Sir Edward Parry, rushed to his defence and urged the First Sea Lord to grant his friend the honour: "If you don't let him go," Parry wrote bluntly, "this man will die of disappointment." Without further ado, Franklin was chosen.

His qualifications to lead the best-equipped polar expedition in British history were impressive. A career naval officer who had served with Nelson at Copenhagen and Trafalgar, he had suffered shipwreck in the South Pacific, been wounded at the battle of New Orleans and was a veteran of Arctic travel. His first expedition to the mouth of the Coppermine River and east along the Arctic coast in 1819 had occupied three years, covered more than five thousand miles and resulted in appalling hardships. Half of his men had succumbed to cold, hunger and exhaustion and the commander himself was reduced to the familiar but desperate expedient of eating his own boots. His second expedition, in 1825, was mounted for the express purpose of scouting the possible route of the North West passage by land. Franklin's first wife was on her death-bed when the project was launched, but — again in true Victorian fashion — she absolutely refused to countenance delay. Her dying days were spent struggling to sew together a flag for her husband to hoist when he first reached the Polar Sea. The standard was successfully planted on Garry Island just as the explorer received the news that she had expired the day after his departure. The crew was euphoric with the joy of discovery and so Franklin maintained the traditional stiff upper lip and "repressed all signs of painful emotion that he might not cloud their triumph." Such was the atmosphere that surrounded the great feats of exploration which Franklin himself, in 1845, intended to outstrip.

No more lavish expedition had ever been mounted to explore the Arctic. Franklin had two vessels, ominously named *Erebus* and *Terror,* and 138 officers and men "as noble fellows as ever trod a plank." For the first time, Arctic sailing ships were specially equipped with auxiliary screws and engines — actually dismantled railway engines, each of twenty horsepower. There were enough provisions on board for three years and these could be stretched to five if necessary. Franklin had no way of knowing until it was too late that seven hundred large tins of preserved meat, taken aboard at Greenland, would prove to be rotten.

Each ship was loaded down with a mountain of para-phernalia that seems extraordinary to modern eyes:

dress uniforms, for example, dress swords, silver buttons, silk handkerchiefs, initialled silver plate, mahogany desks and even a grand piano. However, one must remember those interminable Arctic nights and the twin problems of discipline and morale, when the cold crept into the marrow and even the bottled lime juice failed to stem the ravages of scurvy. Pianos were a necessity; so were theatricals and ship's newspapers, many of the latter exquisitely hand-lettered and illustrated in colour. Officers and men must be smartly turned out to maintain the varnish of civilization which, if it cracked, could lead to dissent and even mutiny. Even the most educated and civilized of men, cooped up for long periods of time, can revert to an animal state. The standards of recruiting in the England of a century ago were not such as to provide the highest calibre of naval rating. If discipline was harsh, if the hierarchy was rigid, if regulations and dress and behaviour were inflexible, there was reason for it. Without the dress swords, the polished buttons and the crisp distinctions of rank, anarchy was almost inevitable.

Franklin was heading into the Arctic at a propitious moment. The northern hemisphere was going through one of it periodic warm-ups, without which the circumnavigation of the polar archipelago would have been considered impossible. Thanks to a change in climate, Baffin Bay was comparatively free of pack ice. The *Erebus* and *Terror* reached it in July, their crews confident that they would be sailing across the Pacific the following year. So certain were some of the officers of success that in their last letters, dispatched from Greenland, they suggested that their wives address future mail to Honolulu or Kamchatka.

Franklin's orders were explicit. From Baffin Bay he was to enter the Arctic archipelago through Lancaster Sound and continue west through Barrow Strait to Cape

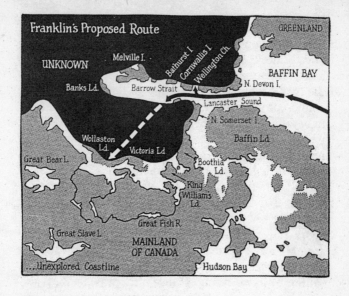

Franklin's Proposed Route

UNKNOWN
Melville I.
Bathurst I.
Cornwallis I.
Wellington Ch.
GREENLAND
Banks Ld.
Barrow Strait
BAFFIN BAY
N. Devon I.
Lancaster Sound
Wollaston Ld.
Victoria Ld.
N. Somerset I.
Baffin Ld.
Great Bear L.
Boothia Ld.
King Williams Ld.
Great Slave L.
Great Fish R.
MAINLAND OF CANADA
Hudson Bay
...Unexplored Coastline

Walker. Beyond that the map was blank. The explorer's orders were to proceed southwest into the unknown "towards Bering strait in as straight a line as is permitted by ice or any unknown land." There was also an alternative plan in case permanent ice should be found to bar the way: Franklin, in that event, was to try to find a passage to the open sea through the channel (later known as Wellington Channel) between Cornwallis and Devon Islands, should that channel be open. The specific nature of these instructions and Franklin's reputation for following orders were to help frustrate the incredible search that followed.

On July 26, 1845, a whaling vessel, sailing through the pack ice of Baffin Bay, spied Franklin's two little yellow ships with their stubby masts, tethered to a drifting iceberg. This was the last view that any white man had of the expedition. Neither Franklin nor any of his men were ever seen alive again. The explorer himself lies in an unknown grave; to this day no one knows how he died. His two ships have never been found.

Two years passed. Mendelssohn died; Edison was born; Wagner composed *Tannhäuser;* the Brontë sisters published *Jane Eyre* and *Wuthering Heights.* There was war in Switzerland and famine in Ireland. The Sikhs revolted in India and the Maoris in New Zealand. The United States annexed New Mexico; the Austrians grabbed Cracow. Carl Zeiss opened his optical factory; Brigham Young led his Mormon followers to Utah. But not a whisper was heard from Sir John Franklin.

At first there was scarcely a ripple of concern. The English public was used to long silences from Arctic explorers. After all, Franklin had told his wife that he might be away for three years. Old Arctic hands professed to be unworried. Sir George Back said he felt no more than ordinary anxiety. Sir James Ross said he didn't have the smallest reason for apprehension. But as the months slipped by, concern began to grow. Sir John Ross (Sir James' uncle), fearing that the ships might be trapped in the ice west of Cape Walker, offered to command a relief ship to seek them out. Dr. Richard King, a former comrade of Franklin's, insisted the ships were icebound near Melville Island and offered to lead an expedition overland to succour them.

Both of these offers were rejected; but a feeling, first of uneasiness and then of dismay, began to creep over England. Where was Franklin? Why hadn't he been heard from? By 1848, with the expedition unreported for three years, the nation was thoroughly aroused and the search was on. There has never been anything quite like it, before or since.

Over the next ten years, thirty-two expeditions were launched to search for the missing Franklin expedition, at a cost of some four million dollars. By 1849, the

British government had offered rewards of twenty thousand pounds to anyone who could rescue Franklin and ten thousand pounds to anyone who could bring back any news of his fate. In 1845 the British pound was worth five dollars, and five dollars was as much as a workingman earned in a week.

Ship after ship set off, year after year, into uncharted waters to search for Sir John Franklin. In 1850, the greatest year of the search, no fewer than fifteen vessels cruised the Arctic with a complement of five hundred men, all seeking the *Erebus* and *Terror*. None of them found a single clue as to their fate.

Where was Franklin? Men painted or chalked gigantic messages on the sides of cliffs in a vain attempt to communicate with the lost expedition. Ships left caches of food and clothing in the hope that the missing seamen might happen upon them. Some imaginative officers even trapped wild foxes and equipped them with collars on which more messages were inscribed, in the unlikely event that one of Franklin's people might shoot them. Balloons were released carrying papers with information about the location of the rescue ships; some of these drifted through the pale Arctic sky for fifty miles. But all this energy and ingenuity produced no answer.

The cost of the search was appalling, not just in expense but also in hardship. Ships were crushed in the ice and abandoned; others sank; men starved and sickened; some were said to have been murdered by Eskimos. One crew was saved by pure accident when it happened upon a thirty-year-old cache of supplies left by an earlier explorer, Parry.

Britons indulged in an orgy of public sympathy. Prayers were offered up in seventy churches by fifty thousand worshippers for the safe return of the expedition. Money poured in to support Lady Franklin's own considerable efforts to find her lost husband; the colony of Van Dieman's Land alone contributed seventeen hundred pounds to finance one of her private expeditions. As one writer put it at the time: "Since the zealous attempts to rescue the Holy Sepulchre in the middle ages, the Christian world has not so unanimously agreed on anything as in the desire to recover Sir John Franklin, dead or alive, from the dread solitude of death into which he has so fearlessly ventured."

Then, in the late summer of 1851, six years after the expedition left England, a few maddening clues turned up. Franklin's first wintering place was found. At Cape Riley a few scraps of rope and rag, some broken bottles and the marks of five tent places were discovered. This led to a further search by several ships. Cape Riley guards the eastern entrance of the Wellington Channel, which was Franklin's alternative objective. Three miles to the west rises the sheer, bold coast of Beechey Island. Here, on the shores of a small bay, were a variety of relics: sledge tracks running inland, a cairn made of tins filled with gravel, the remnants of a garden, an observatory and a shooting gallery, a tent floor paved with small, smooth stones, evidence of an armourer's workshop, several tubs made of the ends of salt meat casks by a frozen stream (indicating a washing place) and, finally, the graves of three of Franklin's men who had died in the early spring of 1846. Here the expedition had whiled away the monotony of the winter of 1845-46.

There was one interesting deduction to be made from these clues: a pair of cashmere gloves was discovered, laid out to dry in the sun and held down by two small stones. These, together with several other items of clothing left lying about, indicated that Franklin's spring departure had been a hurried one. No doubt the ice in the bay had vanished suddenly and he had taken advantage of the good weather and rapidly clearing channel to make a speedy escape from his winter prison.

But where on earth had he gone? Had both his vessels sunk with all hands? That had never happened in all the history of Arctic exploration. Had he somehow changed his route? If so, why hadn't he left cairns, in the naval tradition, to mark his passage? What had happened to the cylinders that he had been instructed to throw overboard after entering Lancaster Sound? None had been recovered. Why not a single clue to his disappearance? In that unexplored wilderness of wriggling channels, uncharted islands and drifting ice, he might be anywhere. Travelling parties, fanning out from Beechey Island and surveying the neighbouring coastline for hundreds of miles, found nothing: not so much as a cairn or a post or a fragment of equipment.

Now every explorer put in his two cents' worth and every part of the Arctic was suggested as requiring the attention of the Admiralty — every part, unfortunately, save for one small square far to the south. The prevailing opinion, held by both Edward Parry and James Ross, was that Franklin was trapped in the ice in the unknown sea somewhere to the east of Cape Walker, his original objective. No one, apparently, considered it possible that he might have been frustrated in his attempt to find a passage by that route and could have attempted a totally different course. And nobody paid any attention to the eccentric theories of Dr. King who, as early as 1847, suggested that Franklin's party, if trapped in the ice, might head for the mainland and the mouth of the Great Fish River. If King's suggestion to the Admiralty for an overland relief expedition had been taken seriously, it is just possible that some of Franklin's men might have been saved.

Blindness and bungling, heroism and happenstance marked the years that followed. A charlatan named

Adam Beck surfaced to announce that Franklin and all his men had been murdered by Eskimos at a place called Ominack; this fairytale was swiftly disproved. Meanwhile, in addition to the myriad of vessels attempting to follow in Franklin's wake, two more — the *Enterprise* and *Investigator* were dispatched around Cape Horn to the Bering Sea with instructions to enter the Canadian Arctic from the west. In all the annals of Arctic exploration there is no more arduous or extended sea voyage than that of Captain Richard Collinson's *Enterprise* and few more harrowing tales than that of his deputy, Robert McClure, commanding the *Investigator*.

Collinson's journey occupied five years and four months. He left Plymouth on January 20, 1850 and

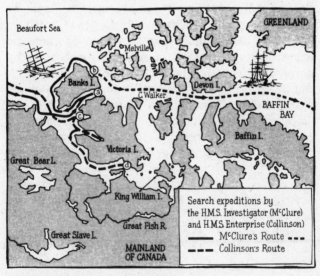

a. Princess Royal Islands. Investigator wintered 1850-51
b. Bay of Mercy. Investigator beset 1851, abandoned 1853.
   Crew joined H.M.Ships Resolute and Intrepid, later H.M.S. North Star.
c. Walker Bay. Enterprise wintered 1851-52
d. Cambridge Bay, Franklin relic found 1853, Enterprise returned to England 1855.

managed to get as far as Cambridge Bay where, in the spring of 1853, he secured from the Eskimos a bolt, probably from a ship's engine, and a fragment of a door hatch. These were certainly pieces of Franklin's ships and had Collinson not been out of touch with civilization he might have caused a sensation with them and won the Admiralty's ten thousand pounds. But it was almost two years before he finally got back to England.

Meanwhile McClure, in the *Investigator,* pushed on ahead to become hopelessly trapped in the ice off the northeast coast of Banks Island in September 1851. McClure and his crew spent two desperate winters in the Arctic. The pressure of the ice was so great against the wooden hull that the caulking between the planks was squeezed out. Men went mad from hunger, loneliness and despondency. There was even a half-hearted attempt at mutiny. Finally, in February 1853, McClure decided to abandon his ship. By uncanny fortune, he and his party of exhausted seamen were discovered by another search expedition under the command of an indifferent seaman, Sir Edward Belcher. The following spring, Belcher panicked and abandoned four of the ships under his command, forcing his men, including McClure's ravaged party, to trudge one hundred and fifty miles farther to a rendezvous with supply ships at Beechey Island.

Six years had now gone by in the search for Franklin. Five naval vessels had been lost. And there was still no real clue as to Franklin's fate. McClure returned to find himself a hero, as much by accident as by design. He had lost his ship and he hadn't found Franklin but, in a blundering sort of fashion, he had discovered the North West Passage. That is to say he had sailed part way through it (though not as far as his superior, the missing Captain Collinson) and had walked part way over frozen channels. It was good enough for the Admiralty:

some kind of triumph was needed in exchange for all that expenditure. McClure received his ten thousand pounds and a knighthood from the Queen.

Sir Edward Belcher returned to face a court martial for his inexplicable retreat. He was acquitted, rather grudgingly and largely because of his ill-health, brought on by his Arctic travail. His reputation, already badly tarnished, was not helped by the fact that one of the abandoned vessels, aptly named *Resolute,* freed herself from the ice without human aid, drifted a thousand miles into Baffin Bay, was salvaged by an American whaler, purchased for forty-thousand dollars, refitted, and then in an unprecedented act of international courtesy, returned to the British Admiralty as a gift.

Surely, it was felt, this generous gesture, an evidence of world concern over the Franklin mystery, would bring renewed vigour to the search. But the Admiralty was weary of the struggle. Belcher's ineptitude hadn't helped. The year was 1854 and the savage war in the Crimea was occupying the nation's attention. The Admiralty gave up the search and pronounced Sir John Franklin and all his men officially dead.

This melancholy intelligence was scarcely made public when the first tantalizing clues to the true fate of the expedition turned up. In October, Dr. John Rae of the Hudson's Bay Company, who had been assigned to an overland search between the Mackenzie country and Hudson Bay, returned from the Boothia Peninsula. Rae reported that he had encountered a party of Eskimos who appeared to have definite evidence of the Franklin party's fate. Several winters before, the natives told him, about forty white men, very thin, had been seen dragging a boat along the north shore of King William's Land. The white men's ships had been crushed in the ice. Later that same season some thirty-five corpses had been found in the vicinity of the mouth of the Great Fish River.

The reports were hearsay. No native appeared who had actually seen the men or the corpses. But it was apparent that these were members of Franklin's party. The artifacts that the Eskimos sold Rae left no doubt of that: silver spoons and forks with officers' crests engraved upon them and Franklin's own silver Order of Merit. That was enough for the Admiralty. Rae was awarded ten thousand pounds for the first news of the expedition's fate (Collinson had not yet returned to England with his evidence) and that was that. The British government had no intention of spending another shilling of public money searching for the late Sir John Franklin.

It was still not clear where the expedition had foundered. It was possible to calculate that sledges of the kind used by Franklin could not have been hauled for more than 150 miles. That fact, coupled with Rae's hearsay evidence and artifacts and Collinson's later report from the same general area, meant that the *Erebus* and *Terror* must have been caught in the ice somewhere off the west coast of King William's Land. The Admiralty had never considered this area. It did not coincide with Franklin's original route and nobody apparently believed the party could have got that far. Obviously, if a new search was mounted, priceless records, highly perishable, could still be found somewhere on King William's Land. Unaccountably, the Admiralty made no attempt to seek them.

Why? Was it for fear of spending more public money? Was it sheer exhaustion after seven years of fruitless struggle? Or was it because the Eskimos may have whispered tales of cannibalism in Rae's ear — tales which the navy was fearful of proving true?

Whatever the reason, the search was officially concluded. But there was one person in Britain who had not the slightest intention of giving up. That person was the redoubtable Lady Franklin, who had already expended half her personal fortune mounting three separate expeditions to find her husband and was now prepared to spend the rest of it — to sell her home, in fact, and to move into rented rooms in one last effort to finance another party.

In an otherwise harrowing drama, marked by tragedy, failure, frustration, bad luck and no little incompetence, Jane Franklin stands out as one who refused to admit defeat. One hesitates to use the word "indomitable" to describe the slender, sloe-eyed woman who simpers winsomely from her youthful portrait. Yet it fits. Jane Franklin was a creature of awesome tenacity. She had already written to the Emperor of France, the Czar of Russia, and the President of the United States begging them to outfit expeditions to rescue the lost men. In Henry Grinnell, the wealthy president of the American Geographical Society, she had found a determined ally. He had mounted two expeditions at a personal cost of one hundred thousand dollars. Now, faced with Admiralty indifference, she spent two years trying to convince the British Prime Minister, Lord Palmerston, that a second-hand account from a group of natives was not good enough. The search must be pressed until bodies and records were discovered. Lady Franklin was now past sixty (she had married at thirty-eight), but she tirelessly traipsed from seaport to seaport, visiting every fishing town in the north of England, questioning old salts as to their opinion of her husband's fate.

To Lord Palmerston she suggested that it would be a national disgrace if the search was left incomplete. But, she added, in her sinewy Victorian prose, should "that decision unfortunately throw upon me the responsibility in the cost of setting out a vessel myself I beg to assure your Lordship that I shall not shrink either from that weighty responsibility or from the sacrifice of my entire available fortune for the purpose, supported as I am in my conviction by such higher authorities as those whose opinions are on record in your Lordship's hands and by the hearty sympathy of much more."

When Palmerston, after much dallying, declined to act, she herself bought a 170-ton yacht, the *Fox,* fitted it out for polar service and set about hiring a captain to take it back into the Arctic.

Her choice fell upon Captain Leopold M'Clintock, a handsome Irishman who had already spent seven years in the icefields in the fruitless search for her husband. She could scarcely have picked a better man. M'Clintock, an amiable and humane explorer, had almost singlehandedly transformed Arctic sledge travel from a laborious and clumsy operation into an efficient method of moving supplies. His innovations were based on observation, experiment and common sense. He devised sledges of lighter construction and he invented equally light and serviceable equipment. These improvements combined with a staging system of back-up teams and regular supply depots made it possible for the first time for groups of men with sledges to travel long distances over the frozen hummocks of the Arctic sea.

The expedition was organized with as much speed as possible and M'Clintock and twenty-five men (seventeen of them Arctic veterans) sailed from England aboard the little *Fox* in July 1857, a dozen years after Franklin's departure. Their goal was King William's Land. It was almost two years before they reached it.

The first year was a total loss. The *Fox* penetrated the heart of the archipelago that summer but was caught in the ice and unable to move for eight months. That was bad enough but the ice itself was moving and the *Fox*, moving with it, found herself forced back for thirteen hundred miles into Baffin Bay; far south of the Arctic Circle. M'Clintock was finally able to escape from the heaving pack and reach the coast of Greenland, where he informed his employer by mail that he was back almost at the point from which he had started.

By February of 1859, eighteen months after he had set out, M'Clintock had managed to reach Bellot Strait at the northern tip of Boothia Peninsula. This was as far as the *Fox* could go; heavy ice barred any further movement south or west. The remainder of the search would have to be carried out by sledge: down the Boothia Peninsula to King William's Land (now recognized as King William Island) and thence on to the Great Fish River on the mainland and back again — a distance of 425 miles. During these sledging trips, across a stark land of rocky, snow-swept terraces and jagged boulders, he and his men found what they were seeking.

They met Eskimos who told them tales of dying men, of a three-masted vessel crushed in the ice, of another that had drifted ashore to be looted by natives, of bodies found near the mouth of the Great Fish River, of white men who dropped in their tracks and died in the snows. They also found a vast scattering of relics, littering the tundra for mile upon mile: massive supplies of sheet lead, watches, silver plate, curtain rods and lightning conductors — in M'Clintock's words "a mere accumulation of dead weight."

They found a skeleton (apparently a ship's steward from the few remaining scraps of clothing) who had fallen face forward and died where he lay. And at Point Victory on the west shore of the island, they came upon a rough pile of stones that contained the first, and indeed the only, documentary evidence of Sir John

Franklin's fate. It was a regular Admiralty form and there were two separate messages scribbled on its margins in cramped handwriting, a year apart. The first, dated May 28, 1847, and signed by Lieutenant G. M. Gore, was cheerful enough. It reported that the two ships had wintered in the ice not far away, a few miles northwest of Cape Felix, that all was well and that the cairn had been erected by a land party of two officers and six men.

The second note, in a different hand, was signed by Franklin's two deputies, Captain James Fitzjames and Captain R. F. M. Crozier. Dated April 25, 1848, it reported that Franklin had died the previous June, that the ships had been trapped in the ice for some nineteen months, that nine officers and fifteen men had also died and that the remainder had abandoned the ships and were trying to reach the Great Fish River.

Another discovery, a few days later, supplied a grisly sequel to this brief narrative. M'Clintock came upon a boat mounted on a sledge containing two skeletons and more than half a ton of clothing and equipment. The distance from the cairn of stones was only about a hundred miles; the fact that the boat was facing north indicated that the party had been returning to the ship, perhaps for more food. The two men left behind to guard the boat had starved at their post; the only food on the sledge consisted of forty pounds of chocolate and a little tea.

With M'Clintock's findings and some later discoveries it is possible to reconstruct with fair accuracy the route that Sir John Franklin took, after he was last seen in Baffin Bay, and the conditions and actions that brought about the expedition's doom:

Franklin, following instructions, sets his course for Lancaster Sound where the webwork of Arctic islands begins. The sun no longer shines for twenty-four hours a day and the two little ships, bobbing about in the heavy seas, crunch through the glasslike bay ice that begins to form each night on the surface of the sea. Ahead lies the imposing entrance to the Sound, whose guardian precipices, streaked with snow look "as if they were formed of steel and inlaid with silver." Speed is now of the essence if Franklin is to make any time before the onset of winter. He does not bother to stop to erect cairns or leave letters; with sails full out he presses confidently on. After all, he expects to be sailing across the north Pacific in less than a year.

The *Erebus* and *Terror* push westward in the lee of the mass of Devon Island. Here the contours have changed. Limestone cliffs, chiselled by the action of frost and storm, tower above them like the battlements of ancient castles. The land is barren, devoid of vegetation, drained of colour. Somewhere ahead looms Cape Walker the last explored point of land. To the southwest lies the Unknown.

But now the way is blocked by heavy floes. Further movement westward becomes impossible. On the western shores of Devon Island, the stretch of water later known as the Wellington Channel lies wide open, sparkling in the sunlight. Following instructions, Franklin chooses this alternate route and sails north into unexplored territory. Is it a strait or a mere bay that he is traversing? The maps cannot tell him.

Northward the two ships sail until the presence of the Grinnell peninsula (as yet unnamed and unexplored), dead ahead, forces them to the northwest. The ships veer off, still flying before the wind, only to find, at the very tip of Grinnell Land, that their passage is blocked by a wall of ice that extends from the head of Wellington Channel for hundreds of miles to the westward.

Franklin is forced to retreat south down a new channel unknown until that time. Now he realizes that he has rounded Cornwallis Land and that it is an island. He enters Barrow Strait, north of Cape Walker, but again his passage west is frustrated: more ice bars his way. Directly to the south he sees another channel. Somewhere beyond that, in the vicinity of King William's Land, he knows the way is clear to the western seas, for he has seen that with his own eyes. Often enough he has pointed to that area on the map and declared: "'If I can get down there my work is done; thence it's plain sailing to the Westward."

But it is too late in the year to make the attempt. He has spent a fortnight in the Wellington Channel and autumn has arrived. Caught up in an avalanche of broken ice floes, the *Erebus* and *Terror* flit to and fro, seeking shelter for the winter. Around them the sea is in a turmoil. The wind pushes the great floes into the teeth of the small islands that dot Barrow Strait, causing them to rip into pieces and pile up into mountainous masses that invade the land itself. Franklin is battling now to reach the safe harbour of Beechey Island, which he examined when he entered Wellington Strait. Fortunately, he achieves it before the pressure of moving ice forces him all the weary way back to Baffin Bay.

He has every reason for confidence. In his voyage up the Wellington Channel and down the newly discovered strait, he has explored three hundred miles of previously unknown water leading to the northwest. From Cape Walker to King William's land, the distance is only two hundred and fifty miles. Surely that will be an easier passage! And then he can enter the familiar waters leading to the west.

It is the first week of November. The sun, its upper edge gleaming for a few minutes over the snow-shrouded shores to the north, vanishes, leaving Franklin and his men to three months of twilight and darkness. The expedition passes its first winter with the usual activities: amateur theatricals, target practice, scientific observations, explorations, the collection of specimens. Only three men die — not an unusual number for an Arctic winter.

At last the sun returns. Then one day, the floes begin to move, the ten-foot-thick ice heaving and cracking with a fearful pressured forcing itself into domes that are often shivered into fragments. Bit by bit the sea is clearing and the two ships are freed at last from the shackles of the bay. Franklin departs without leaving any message. We do not know why; but it is possible that the *Erebus* and *Terror* were driven out involuntarily, along with the ice, in a sudden spring gale.

He sets his course once again for Cape Walker, but does not realize that he is heading directly toward one of the great ice streams that pour down from the Beaufort Sea in an inexorable movement southward. These great frozen rivers, awesome in their power, are composed of masses of ice that break off from the permanent pack — one hundred feet thick in places — and join together in compact, moving masses. Like wriggling tentacles, the ice streams squeeze their way between the bleak islands, seeking warmer waters. Totally impenetrable, unbroken by any lane or channel, they are more like glaciers. No navigator has succeeded in crossing one of them by ship.

Franklin, sailing west from his winter haven, encounters the edge of one of these ice streams. It flows down between Melville and Banks Island, forces itself against the western shores of Prince of Wales Island, curves down the unexplored channel on the east side of Victoria Island (later to be named M'Clintock Channel) and blocks the narrows at King William's Land. Here, the southern edge of the stream encounters the warmer waters flowing northward from the continental rivers

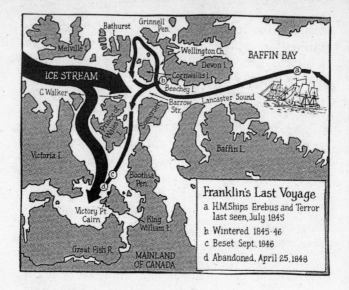

Franklin's Last Voyage
a H.M.Ships Erebus and Terror
  last seen, July 1845
b Wintered 1845-46
c Beset Sept. 1846
d Abandoned, April 25, 1848

and at this point it begins to break apart, leaving the
water to the south relatively clear and easily navigable.

Faced with the presence of this great, slow-moving
mass of ice, Franklin has no choice but to retreat. South
of him, however, lies an open channel, later to be
named Peel's Channel, leading in the direction of King
William's Land. He turns his ships southward, again
into the unknown. But his course seems unimpeded, for
he is protected from the inexorable river of ice by the
east coast of prince of Wales Land.

The scenery here, for those who have the time and
inclination to enjoy it, is magnificent. On his right, the
sandstone ramparts of Prince of Wales Land stand out
starkly against the pale Arctic sky. On his left are the
black cliffs of Somerset, rent by snow-filled chasms and
girdled by an ice ridge forty feet high, made up of
broken floes, which gleam blue and white in the
sunlight.

But Franklin, when he reaches the southern tip of Prince of Wales Land, knows that he must leave the protection of this channel. Ahead of him, just a hundred miles across open water lies the northern tip of King William's Land. But once he emerges from the shield of Prince of Wales Land, he again encounters the ice stream pouring down from the northwest. His ships veer over to the west coast of Boothia Peninsula and cling to it in order to stay clear of the moving ice. But sooner or later Franklin knows he must face it. For the only route to the open ocean that his charts show leads directly down the west coast of King William's Land.

He cannot know that there is another choice, and a safe one. He has no way of knowing that King William's Land is actually an island and not a peninsula. He can escape the ice by cutting around the eastern side of King William Island and slipping through the narrow strait that separates it from the mainland. But no one in his day has explored this corner of the Arctic. And so he turns the noses of his two ships into the ice stream and, just as King William's Land comes into sight and winter closes in, the *Erebus* and *Terror* are beset — imprisoned in that frozen river, which moves south at the maddeningly slow speed of one and a half miles a month. The date is September 12, 1846.

Cooped up in their wooden dungeons, the seamen face a far crueller winter than the previous one at Beechey. Several venture ashore and on Queen Victoria's birthday, 1847, they build a cairn and leave a message that all is well. Less than a month later Franklin dies — of what cause we will never know. Now scurvy begins to take its toll of the rapidly weakening crew. By this time they must have discovered that their entire supply of tinned meat is inedible.

Crozier, Franklin's second-in-command, assumes charge. An explorer of twenty-one years' Arctic experience, he can command his men but not his ships. In that summer of 1847 (no concern yet in England over Franklin's fate) the ice stream pushes the little vessels southward with glacial slowness: ten miles . . . twenty miles . . . thirty miles. Safety and victory lie just ahead — so near and yet so far. There is now only sixty miles between the ships and the safe haven of the open channels off the mainland. But as autumn gives way to winter and new ice forms, the ships cease to move. In the disease-ridden months that followed twenty men perish.

By April 1848, Crozier and Fitzjames know that they must escape from the ships and try to reach the Great Fish River and ascend it to civilization. They realize the odds are against them but they are not aware of the extent to which they have been weakened. The cumbersome sledges are piled with an incredible assortment of gear — ten tons of equipment, most of it totally unnecessary. What weird caprice persuades them that they need button polish, silverware, heavy cookstoves, brass curtain rods and a library of religious books? It takes them three full days to haul this ponderosity of nonessentials fifteen miles. By now, the shivering, diseased seamen realize that they are not equal to the journey. At the cairn at Victory Point they leave behind a mountain of artifacts and here Fitzjames thaws out some ink and scribbles a second note on Gore's Admiralty form of the year before.

The weakened party stumbles southward, strewing the land with unneeded chattels. They have no more than forty days of provisions, perhaps less; that is the most that the best-equipped party can drag on those heavy naval sledges.

Soon the party divides. The weak and disabled can go no further. They must stay behind and wait and hope for help or return to the ships. (Later the Eskimos will find a skeleton on board one vessel.) The others stumble forward, growing weaker day by day. Oblivion swallows them. We see them mistily through the eyes of the natives, telling stories relayed by other natives of gaunt, emaciated men, blundering southward and lying down, one by one, to die. Few could have survived for more than two months; only a handful could have reached the mainland.

Ever since the news of M'Clintock's discoveries burst upon the world a controversy has revolved around the Franklin expedition. Was it really necessary for all these men to die? Could they not have survived, as the Eskimos did? Many old Arctic hands — Vilhjalmur Stefansson has been the most vocal — have found it passing strange that in an age when explorers were so devoted to the scientific method, keenly observing every detail of the flora and fauna around them, making astronomical and geological observations of the most minute kind, they should have ignored the hunting and eating habits of the natives. It is certainly true, as Franklin's defenders have noted, that King William Island is one of the most barren of the Arctic reaches, where game is sparse and fish unplentiful. Yet the facts cannot be ignored: Crozier and his men starved and sickened, watched by natives who survived. The natives carved hooks of bone to catch fish and fashioned harpoons to kill seals. And when they travelled they moved swiftly, dragging light sledges, unencumbered by the trivia of civilization. Why, in all these years of Arctic travel by land and by sea, had the British navy turned a blind eye to the natives? Was it an inability to accept the fact that untutored savages knew more than English officers

Before Franklin expedition, 1845   After M'Clintock expedition, 1859

about Arctic travel and Arctic survival? In India, a similar attitude to the natives (it was, in actuality, a non-attitude) brought on the bloodiest of mutinies. Nobody in the navy seems to have profited from the experience of an earlier seaman, Samuel Hearne.

The contents of the sledges defies rational explanation. Did Crozier and Fitzjames actually believe they could transport heavy iron cookstoves in boats up the Great Fish River? Was it human nature or naval tradition that caused these ravaged sailors to cling so desperately to a mountain of impedimenta? Perhaps it was a bit of both. People fleeing from burning buildings often neglect valuables to emerge with the most outlandish of furnishings: a stuffed moosehead instead of a sack of nuggets for instance, in one memorable Klondike blaze. Old keepsakes take on a value far out of proportion to their real worth. Dress swords, engraved silver cutlery, medals and even bedroom slippers were found as much as a hundred miles from the site of the beset ships. For these, the owners must have felt an attachment that overshadowed common sense.

But there were also the engrained customs and regulations of the Queen's navy. The batman whose skeleton was discovered by M'Clintock's party was carrying brushes and polish as if to keep his officers' uniforms spruce and their buttons shined. It was bad enough that Crozier, the old Arctic hand, still felt he had to haul 1,400-pound boats toward the Great Fish River, when a raft constructed on the spot might have done the job. But to bring along hundreds of pounds of sheet lead, siding and tools just because naval requirements insisted that all ship's boats be kept in good repair — this represents a rigidity of thinking that was equalled only by the Charge of the Light Brigade a few years later.

The Franklin expedition was no triumph, although his supporters, led by his widow, tried to make it sound like one. Jane Franklin insisted, with considerable agreement, that her husband and not McClure should be given credit for discovering the North West Passage. In fact, neither explorer had succeeded in sailing all the way from the Atlantic to the Pacific. That would not happen until, in the years between 1903 and 1905, Roald Amundsen, following in Franklin's and M'Clintock's wake (but nipping round the back of King William's Island), finally succeeded in sailing the entire distance.

That the passage itself had little or no commercial value, at least until the 1970s when the oil tanker *Manhattan* repeated the feat, is beside the point. Franklin did not seek his will-o'-the-wisp for commercial reasons but simply because, like Everest's peak, it was there to be conquered. Like Scott, that other luckless explorer, failure was to bring him greater fame than success. For in less than fifteen years the map of the Arctic was totally transformed by the efforts of those who undertook to find him. Dying with his boots off, abed in his cabin, at the age of sixty-one, he had no inkling of the furore that was to come nor of the immortality that would be the lot of his entire crew because, in the words of his remarkable widow, "they forged the last link of the North West Passage with their lives."

10

Bloody Sunday in Vancouver

There is one photograph that sums up for me all the turmoil and pain of the 1930s. It could have been taken in any number of Canadian cities in almost any one of the years of the great depression: in Regina on Dominion Day, for instance, during the great riot of 1935, or in Queen's Park, Toronto, when the provincial police rode their way through a mass of demonstrators, or in any one of a score of CPR yards when desperate men, riding the rods, came face to face with railway police.

This photograph, stark in its brutality and explicit in its message, was taken in Vancouver at five o'clock on the morning of June 19, 1938, a day that came to be known as Bloody Sunday.

The central figure in the photograph is a young man in a sweater. His face cannot be seen for he is protecting it with his arms and elbows. He is being savagely beaten by a plainclothesman with a rubber hose. He is not armed nor is he resisting. In a second photograph, taken moments later, the young man lies insensible while a horde of police tries to attack him; one uniformed man has suddenly seen the camera and warns them off. All the evidence suggests that the police were doing their best to murder the young man. Only the presence of a photographer saved his life.

The young man's name was Brodie — born Robert, but nicknamed Steve after that sporting Irishman who is said to have leaped off Brooklyn Bridge on a bet — Steve Brodie, on that day the most famous man in Vancouver, and at that moment of public torment, victorious in defeat. At the age of twenty-six he had managed to organize one thousand jobless men and, in a miracle of leadership and planning, to occupy two public buildings, the Vancouver art gallery and the federal post office, for thirty days to dramatize the plight of the unemployed to three reluctant levels of government. Steve Brodie invented the sit-in, long before the word became part of the continental jargon. He planned his operation as carefully as any military manoeuvre and he never deviated from his purpose. Even his opponent, Colonel Cecil Henry Hill of the RCMP, could not contain his admiration for Brodie's tactics. "Excellent staff work," he whispered. And so it was.

Those of us who were in our teens at the time and still in school remember only the sunny moments of that year: three-scoop ice cream cones for a nickel; Benny Goodman's swing music; the radio team of Charlie McCarthy and Edgar Bergen, and the cheerful lunacy of Disney's *Snow White.* We have to struggle to remember what it must have been like for men who could not afford an ice cream cone, let alone a radio: men like Brodie, in their mid-twenties, out of work for almost ten years, shuttling unwanted from city to city and province to province, fleeing from the ruined homesteads of the prairies and the dying factory towns of the East, rejected by politicians, pursued by policemen, never knowing the luxury of a roof over their heads.

Southern British Columbia was their mecca. At least there you didn't need a roof, for it rarely snowed. You could sleep under a bridge or in a boxcar, a park, an empty racetrack stable or even a doorway. In Vancouver, thousands of jobless men did just that.

240

Neither the city nor the province was prepared for this onslaught. Even in 1938, not the worst year of the depression, almost one-third of Vancouver's total work force was unemployed. Of the city's revenue, one dollar out of every four was being spent on relief, but even that wasn't enough. For single transients there was no relief at all. The work camps, where men toiled for twenty cents a day under an unbelievably harsh discipline, had closed. The jobless were reduced to trudging the streets, holding out tin cans, begging for coins.

This was no casual, hit-and-miss affair. The Communist Party, technically illegal but operating underground through a variety of front organizations, welded the transients into highly visible masses of beggars parading regularly through the city. Battles with the police, arrests and injuries, calls for justice, demands for action and political buck-passing between various levels of government kept Vancouver in a ferment all during the thirties. A succession of mayors inserted advertisements in prairie newspapers urging the unemployed not to come west. Prairie and eastern community leaders took similar ads in west-coast papers telling their wandering sons that there was nothing to come home to.

And yet anybody making thirty dollars a week in Vancouver in 1938 lived remarkably well. Steaks were twenty cents a pound, cauliflowers a nickel each and a quart of milk or a loaf of bread could be had for as little as five or six cents. You could buy a quart of rye for around a dollar and a six-room house for about three thousand. But the Communist Party could give its tin-canners (as the unemployed vagrants were called) only thirty cents a day; and to get that they had to turn up at the daily meetings held in the various divisional headquarters of the Relief Project Workers Union. There were four of these divisions operating out of various ethnic and labour halls in the east end of the city. Steve Brodie was the leader of the largest: the youth division.

More than most young men of his era, Steve Brodie was a child of his time. He was born in Edinburgh on June 8, 1912, the son of a Scottish blacksmith and lay preacher. His childhood was spent under the cloud of the Great War. Both his parents died in the terrible influenza epidemic of 1919. The Salvation Army brought him to Canada, as part of a shipload of orphans in 1925. For three years he worked cheaply, like thousands of other immigrants, as a farm boy in eastern Ontario. Then he took one of the harvest excursion trains west to the prairies. Fortunes were being made on paper all over the continent but the west was not burgeoning. At the moment of the great crash Brodie was delivering a load of wheat for a Saskatchewan farmer; there were no more loads.

Drought, plague, dust and depression changed Brodie from an orthodox, God-fearing youth into a radical. His new character was honed on the freight trains of the Rockies and in the winter relief camps of British Columbia, where in bull sessions sponsored by the Communists he learned the techniques of organization and parliamentary procedure. Brodie was in the thick of all the ferment that boiled up in western Canada during the late thirties: the bloody Vancouver longshoreman's riot of 1935 and in the same year the march of the unemployed on Ottawa that ended in an even bloodier riot in Regina. When Brodie returned to Vancouver from Regina he was a committed Communist.

By the spring of 1938, the party was losing its hold on the unemployed. Money was running out, the organization was faltering, the men clearly would not stick together for long unless some new strategy was devised. Brodie tried to puzzle it out. During the day he could be seen talking to himself, mulling over the problem.

"What the hell do we do now?" he kept asking himself. Suddenly it hit him — a way to strike at all three levels of government as well as the private sector: seize the federal post office, the city-owned art gallery and one of the leading hotels in one, sudden stroke.

Before putting the matter to the party's leadership Brodie himself paced off the distance to the three buildings, timing the length of the walk to each target so that they would be invaded almost simultaneously. His private objective was the Hotel Vancouver, but the arrangement of the doors was such that it might be difficult to gain entry; Brodie opted instead for the city's second hotel, the Georgia, just across the street.

On May 19, he called his own division together in one of the ethnic halls and told his followers: "You have been howling for action and I think I have got something now. But first I want a complete vote of confidence in the action committee." That committee, he explained, would be composed of himself, the three other division leaders and nobody else. There were too many police stool pigeons disguised as jobless transients to allow him to reveal his plans. Thus, "if there are any leaks before the action takes place, one of the four of us has to be a stool pigeon."

Brodie got his vote of confidence, the first of many he would enjoy. The men stomped, cheered, clapped and shouted: "Go get 'em, Steve!" These meetings, held on the slightest provocation, were always painstakingly democratic. Parliamentary procedure was followed to the letter, and votes of confidence were the order of the day. In Brodie's memory there was no dissent; the votes were always unanimous.

That night at eleven o'clock Brodie and the three other division leaders met in a small shack on Cambie Street. It was not easy for him to convince his colleagues of the wisdom of his cause. They argued until four in the morning before coming round. Zero hour was set at two the following afternoon.

Brodie had laid the groundwork for his strategy by staging random marches all over the city for several days before the takeover. Vancouver became inured to the spectacle of long lines of men marching this way and that. The men themselves, moving west on May 20 from the union's Cordova Street headquarters, from the Orange Hall and from the more distant Ukrainian and Croatian Halls, believed they were heading for Stanley Park. But when Brodie's division reached the corner of Granville and Hastings, they learned what their real objective was: the federal post office, newly decorated, with its granite façade, its copper dome and its English tower.

Brodie secured the building with seven hundred men at 2:10 p.m. The police reacted exactly as he had expected. The sergeant on the corner — Vancouver's busiest — rushed to a nearby callbox and brought reinforcements from the Granville and Georgia Street corner three blocks away. This left Georgia Street wide open for the two divisions that were marching on the hotel and the art gallery. The hotel was occupied by one hundred and fifty men at 2:15. Three hundred men seized the art gallery at 2:20. A fourth division acting as a decoy continued to march about the city, adding to the confusion and uncertainty and giving Brodie time to consolidate his position.

The post office was closed for five minutes while Brodie held another of his meetings. The men were asked to vote on whether they wished to remain on federal government property until they were arrested or some other action taken. The answer again was a unanimous yes. It never occurred to anybody that the siege would last for thirty days. For all of that time the post office remained open for business, unmolested by the

244

sit-downers under Brodie's iron control. Customers came and went, transacting business at the brass wicket, while the jobless tried to hug the edges of the L-shaped lobby. The brazen quality of Brodie's occupation was illuminated by the fact that the RCMP, in effect, occupied the same building. The north side of the post office touched their headquarters which they staffed, inside and out, night and day, during the sit-in.

At eight that evening, the chief of the city police, Billy Foster, arrived for a conference. Foster, a wartime hero who sympathized with the unemployed, asked and received permission to address the crowd. He congratulated the men on the demonstration, applauded their behaviour, said their discipline was a marvel to behold and their cooperation with the public first-rate. He declared that the whole incident would certainly have

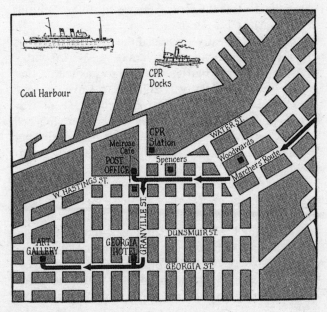

an effect on the authorities. Then he asked everybody to go home.

A chorus of boos greeted this announcement but ceased abruptly on a sign from Brodie.

"I'd like to remind the Police Chief he suggested we go home," he told his followers, "but if we had homes we would not be here. If we had a place where we could be housed and fed we would not be here."

Then Brodie turned to the chief and put to him the challenge that he would continue to use throughout the sit-in: "If we are breaking any law whatsoever, we now — each and every one of us — submit to arrest and it is now your job to see that we are housed and fed, pending our hearing before a magistrate."

This statement was greeted with a unanimous howl of approval. The discomfited chief left, saying only that he would call the Attorney General for instructions. But before he departed, Foster arranged for toilet facilities at the nearby CPR depot.

Brodie had already organized the men into sections of ten with group leaders. Each man was issued with a division card for his group and told to stay within that group. Only one man was allowed to leave any one group at a time to visit the washrooms. In this way Brodie prevented the infiltration of his seven hundred followers by police spies. Nor had he neglected other problems: a first-aid squad, easily identifiable by prominent armbands, ministered to the sick; pickets, in groups of three, patrolled the building around the clock.

That night the men slept on the hard marble floors of the post office and art gallery or the more comfortable carpets of the Georgia. The following day there was a cry of protest to Ottawa from a variety of provincial and civic leaders. But British Columbia's Minister of Labour, G. S. Pearson, announced flatly that there would be no retreat from the stated policy of no aid to single unemployed men who had arrived from other parts of Canada; the protest, he said, was the work of a few agitators. In Ottawa, the federal Minister of Labour, Norman Rogers, echoed Pearson. The government would take no action.

At the Georgia Hotel, where the men were careful to leave the passageway free for the movement of guests, the manager refused to call for police assistance. The last thing he wanted was violence that might cause thousands of dollars' worth of damage. At the art gallery, where the men carefully obeyed the No Smoking signs, a similar situation prevailed. The building was closed to the public who were thus barred from the incongruous spectacle of shabbily dressed men, with their toes protruding from their socks, snoring in the shadow of marble busts and painted landscapes. In the post office, the clerks continued to transact business throughout the sit-in as if nothing untoward was happening. Brodie's guards kept the doors and wickets clear.

Chief Foster announced that unless there was a breach of the peace or the owners of the buildings demanded police action, there would be no attempt at eviction. He praised Brodie's organization: "They have co-operated with us in every way as far as seeing that no fire hazard was created by their occupancy. . . . Every order we have given them in this regard was quickly obeyed." The chief added that if the demonstration didn't do something to solve the perennial problem of unemployment, "it will still be with us and we will be called upon to face other tense situations."

The public was on the side of the unemployed. The Communist Party, the CCF and the trade union movement rallied with cases of tinned beans and coffee on the first night of the sit-in. Five thousand people gathered outside the three buildings, forcing money into tin cans, buying the men cigarettes, and donating armfuls of sandwiches and tins of tomatoes. Across the street from the post office, employees in the Melrose Café kept a constant supply of coffee hot for Brodie's night pickets; the staff paid for it out of their own pockets. The newspaper stories were also sympathetic. Brodie's coup vied with Hitler's on the front pages: the German dictator was making a bid for power in Czechoslovakia. "Tension Rising," one newspaper subhead read. It could have applied equally to Vancouver or Prague.

The sit-in at the Georgia Hotel did not last long. On May 21, the men voted to leave after the city aldermen, in the absence of the mayor, George Miller, collected five hundred dollars of their own money for the strikers. Much to Brodie's disgust, the hotel was evacuated. The mayor, who had left for his summer cottage on Bowen Island (he seems to have been there at every moment of the crisis) returned to berate his colleagues for their action, which he described as "weakness." In the end, however, the city put up the money.

The worst problem Brodie had to contend with in the post office was boredom. There was not much for the men to do during that hottest of Vancouver springs, except sleep. Years later he was to recall the scene in the lobby after darkness fell: ". . . hundreds of men sleeping in various poses, some with blankets, some without, coats on some, others without, coats under their heads, shoes parked along side of them hanging over the Canadian coat of arms above the letter wicket. . . . The place stunk to high heaven from seven hundred pairs of socks and shoes. . . ."

On May 23, Brodie conceived the idea of holding a sports day inside the post office to match the Victoria Day holiday festivities on the outside. He invited the mayor, all members of the provincial legislature and other guests to attend. Only two politicians turned up: Harold Winch and Dr. Lyle Telford, both members of the CCF. The sports consisted of events such as peanut races, that could be held in a small space. The manager of the Georgia Hotel appeared to present prizes and was lustily cheered. But ex-sit-downers from the Georgia had to stay outside; the post office was jammed.

In the days that followed more gifts arrived from sympathetic citizens: bedrolls and blankets, even the odd iron bed; hot meals from local women's groups; free towels from a linen company. Small groups of men were allowed out to enjoy the free meals offered by local restaurants and to attend services at churches, which made a point of inviting them. Dr. Clem Davies, the revivalist, was prescient enough to offer Brodie his rented pulpit at the Auditorium to make his case for the unemployed.

And still the gifts kept coming: bread from a bakery; radios from a music store; five hundred pairs of socks from a department store; tobacco from ordinary citizens. Impromptu concerts were held with banjo, mouth organ and accordion, helped out by volunteers from the musical community. In the art gallery some men took up painting. Brodie, who gave regular press conferences, launched a weekly newspaper, *The Sitdowners' Gazette;* it was sold on a donation basis for as much as five dollars a copy. He himself had become a celebrity, easily identified by an orange sweater, which he purposely wore to make himself conspicuous.

The newspaper editorials remained sympathetic. The general feeling was that Ottawa, which had disinherited the transient unemployed, was responsible for the situation. When Mayor Miller, speaking at a local church hall, tried to justify his own intransigent stand against the men, he was roundly booed and hissed.

Rarely had an act of civil disobedience enjoyed such a measure of public support.

It could not last, of course. Brodie had never expected it to go on for thirty days. Eventually he knew there would have to be a showdown. On three occasions the police approached him quietly and each time got the same answer: "We'll submit to arrest if we're breaking the law."

The city fathers were caught in a dilemma. Sooner or later it was obvious the men would be evicted. But the city had no intention of putting them in jail; that would be tantamount to giving them relief — something everybody had refused to do. It would also make them martyrs. Brodie's maddening tactics were frustrating the authorities. How could they empty two public buildings without arresting everybody and without causing a political backlash?

The solution was provided by Vancouver's chief sanitary inspector, who was growing more and more concerned over the possibility of an epidemic. He feared (or said he feared) an outbreak of spinal meningitis and warned that a case of smallpox, diphtheria or scarlet fever would cause both buildings to be quarantined.

That gave everybody an out and they took it. As the Prime Minister, Mackenzie King, put it, the authorities had acted with patience and forbearance but now the men were becoming a menace to public health and something had to be done. Although King and Premier T. Dufferin Pattullo both took credit for the action that followed, the initiative clearly came from Ottawa.

The authorities determined to make their move at first light on Sunday, June 19 — Father's Day — a time when it was hoped a minimum number of the public would be present to witness the eviction. Every member of the Royal Canadian Mounted Police in Vancouver (there were close to fifty) was ordered to assemble at about three that morning at the Fairmount Barracks. When the men were drawn up, their superintendent, Colonel Cecil Henry Hill, MC, a big man with a bristling mustache who had once trained the famous Musical Ride, told them that he had instructions to clear the post office. The entire division set off in trucks and on horseback for the corner of Granville and Hastings. It was the city's task to clear the art gallery.

Brodie had forewarning of what was to happen. At three that morning he was shaken awake from his mattress on the post office floor and told he was wanted on the phone of the Melrose Café. He ran over and picked up the receiver. "Is that you, Steve?" a voice asked. "Yeah," grunted Brodie. "This is it," the voice said. "Any hour now." And with that there was a click on the line. Brodie never learned who his informant was.

He returned to the post office, informed the pickets of the warning and told them to wake him at the first sign of anything unusual. Ninety minutes passed. Brodie, cat-napping on the floor, was awakened again:

"It's getting pretty busy," one of the pickets told him. "There are cops on every corner. Half of them are drunk."

Brodie walked out into the half-light and saw members of the city police force "laughing and talking and passing around mickeys." Their billies were in their hands, unslung.

Then Brodie heard something else: the measured *clip-clop-clip-clop* of horses, approaching from the west. The Mounted Police were coming on very slowly, and Brodie knew that meant business.

He herded the pickets inside and had them wake the group leaders, who in turn woke their sections. The inevitable mass meeting followed. Brodie told them to prepare for the worst and then asked for and received the usual vote of confidence.

"I want you to listen quietly to whatever they have to say and I will make our usual offer," he said.

Squatting on the floor, half-dressed, rubbing sleep from their eyes, rolling cigarettes, the men nodded approval. One or two asked questions: What would they do if the police used tear gas? Brodie, seated on a window sill, pointed to a small cloud in the morning sky, touched now with the pink of dawn.

"See that little cloud up there?" he said. "Between the outside of that window and that little cloud there is an estimated four hundred miles of fresh air. The best antidote for tear gas is fresh air." Everybody laughed.

"There is no necessity for violence," Brodie was saying. As he spoke, he saw, out of the corner of one eye, a high-ranking Mounted Police officer accompanied by two or three other men enter quietly by the side door on Hastings Street. The officer was Colonel Hill. Brodie repeated his remark for the benefit of the newcomers: "There is no necessity for violence. I hope it will not come to that."

Walking beside Colonel Hill and a post office official was the other major actor in the drama that was about to be enacted: Detective Sergeant Robert S. S. Wilson, an expert in counterfeit money and drugs and the only member of the Vancouver detachment of the RCMP trained in the use of tear gas. Wilson was carrying a white haversack containing three small regulation tear gas bombs and four or five bigger ones of a brand-new design, known as Lake Erie Jumpers. The small bombs, Wilson knew, would not be effective because they could be picked up by the men and tossed back at the police. But the Jumpers, which had perforations in the top, were far too hot to handle. They were timed to go off consecutively, exploding and jumping ten feet into the air half a dozen times before their gas supply was exhausted.

Outside the building, the Mounted Police had been divided into two groups of twenty, one group at the north-end door and the other at the west door off Hastings. Hill ordered his corporal and a post office employee to open both doors. That done, he and Wilson climbed onto a counter and Hill addressed the men:

"We are a federal police force and we have our instructions from Ottawa. After a month of vacillating the federal government has instructed us to put you out. We cannot argue the right and wrong of this. . . . We would not put you out if we were not ordered to do so. But we have no alternative. We have opened the doors and you can go out peacefully. Bear this in mind: this is a police force, when we are told to do something, we will do it. If you resist, someone will get hurt."

Brodie walked up to Hill and was introduced by a postal official.

"This is hardly the time for a social visit," Brodie told him. "I am the men's spokesman and I say to you now, Colonel, that we will submit to arrest if we have broken any law. If we are an unlawful assembly, we are now your prisoners. We await your orders."

"Oh," Hill replied. "I have no instructions on arrest."

"You're only a policeman and doubtless don't know much about the law," Brodie replied, brashly. "The law in Canada is that magistrates and judges punish; policemen arrest. I suggest to you now that you do your duty."

Brodie returned to his men and convened yet another meeting. He told them that if anyone wanted to leave without submitting to arrest he was free to do so. Nobody moved.

"You have six hundred prisoners," Brodie shouted to Hill. "What are your instructions?"

A brief conversation followed between Hill and Wilson. Hill then returned to the men.

"You men are being stupid and ill-advised," he told them. "I think you should over-ride the decision of your leader because in a further five minutes force will be used."

This speech was greeted by catcalls. Meanwhile, Brodie was at the door talking to an inspector of the city police:

"Do I have your word that if the men step out orderly on the sidewalk that you'll arrest them and march them wherever they will be held until they can see a magistrate or judge?"

"I have no instructions about arrest," the inspector told him. "I'm here to see that you keep moving when you hit the street."

Hill had given the men five minutes. Now Wilson stood up on the counter alone, with a Lake Erie Jumper in his hand. He held it up for the crowd to see and from his perch noted that the men were already reaching for various articles to use as weapons. Mounted Police reinforcements were already inside the post office building. Now there were a few moments of deathly quiet. Everyone seemed frozen into position and Wilson couldn't help thinking that the scene looked remarkably like a still picture taken from a movie. The only sound came from the drip-drip of men urinating into their handkerchiefs to cover their faces when the attack came. To Wilson the interval seemed more like hours.

At last he leaned over and whispered to Hill: "Shall I throw it, sir?"

"Yes."

Wilson had never thrown a gas bomb at human beings before but he had had plenty of training at the Regina police school after the 1935 riot. He pulled the safety pin, counted to three, and tossed the bomb at the feet of the crowd.

The instant the first explosion occurred, in Wilson's words, "all hell broke loose." There was one single reverberating crash as every window in the post office was shattered. The men had torn bars from the wickets to use as clubs and even heaved two old iron bedsteads through the windows. Objects of every kind were flying through the air: glass shards, iron bolts, rocks. It was exactly 5 a.m. Bloody Sunday had begun.

The glass came down in sheets and, according to Brodie's later account, "the whips were slashing at us from two directions." The Mounted Police had formed a double row, ten abreast across the lobby, hazing the men out of the building. A second gauntlet of city police waited outside. Although the police were to deny that they used excessive force, the photographs taken outside the post office that morning (no member of the press was allowed inside) support Brodie's contention that riot whips were used with deadly effect, whips "designed to smash heads and burst them open." The press reported that thirty-three men were injured in the resulting mêlée and that five were kept in hospital; none of these was a policeman. The estimate was probably low. A visiting Cleveland physician, Dr. Zoltan Wirshafter, returning from a convention of the American Medical Association in San Francisco, was awakened by the sounds of the riot and immediately volunteered his services. For four hours, at the Ukrainian Labour Temple, he dressed bruised heads, bandaged wounded men and rendered first aid to scores more.

One of the hospitalized men was a sergeant in the non-permanent militia named Arthur Redseth. A devout Anglican, who got a pass from Brodie every Sunday to attend Holy Communion, he had one ambition

255

— to be a soldier. Unfortunately, he slipped to the floor at the western end of the lobby and a fight took place over his body between the attacking police and the sit-downers. Brodie's version of the story is that the police kicked him while he was prostrate and that when his friends tried to help him to his feet they were whipped.

At this point Redseth's friend, Little Mike, entered the picture. Little Mike was the son of a Serbian immigrant who had been killed in a British Columbia mine explosion. When Little Mike reached seventeen, the allowance that his widowed mother received for him was cut off, reducing the family's total monthly income to $10.50. Little Mike left home, wound up in Vancouver and joined the union of unemployed. Because his last name was unpronounceable he was called Little Mike to distinguish himself from a Big Mike, a larger man with an equally unpronounceable surname.

Little Mike managed to drag his friend Arthur Redseth out of the door and through the gauntlet of club-swinging city policemen. Redseth was terribly injured about the face: one eye had slid out of its socket. Little Mike called to a policeman standing in the middle of Hastings Street and asked for an ambulance. In reply, he got a billy across his own face. He half-carried, half-dragged his friend for nine blocks to Main Street, where a passing car stopped and took the injured men to hospital. Little Mike needed five stitches in his jaw. Redseth lost his eye and his chance to become a soldier. He never recovered from Bloody Sunday. When the war came and the army turned him down, he tried the merchant marine and again was refused because of his injury. He became despondent and in 1942 he shot himself. Little Mike was killed that same year in the raid on Dieppe. He was twenty-three years old.

All these events took place in less time than it takes to tell it. The entire evacuation of the post office occupied about ten minutes. Brodie was one of the last three men to be driven from the building. Easily identifiable in his orange sweater, he was the main target of the police attack. He kept his head protected but the whips and billies continued to land on his body until he became numb. Unable to see, because his head was down, he finally blundered to the west door and felt the city police outside seize him and pull him bodily by the heels, his head banging on the stone steps. Thirty-five years later he recalled those moments:

"They got me out in the gutter and it got to the point that there were so many doing it they couldn't all hit my head so they hit me where they could. There comes a time when you don't feel it anymore. It seemed to me that I was watching somebody else. I was almost casually waiting for them to finish it. I was out, and then back, and then passed out again and then back. The same feeling you get when you smoke grass except that's not painful. I was simply numb. . . ."

Brodie was convinced that the police intended to beat him to death. The Vancouver *Sun's* reporter on the spot, James Dyer, felt much the same way. He had heard policemen talking: "Where is that bastard Brodie?" As Dyer put it, "They were laying for him." The police had not forgotten the longshoremen's riot of 1935, when thirty of their number were badly mauled.

The Vancouver *Province's* photograph of Brodie being beaten supports his statement. The presence of that photographer probably saved his life. "If that picture had not been taken I would have been beaten to death and they would have justified it. Of that, I am absolutely certain. I never had any doubt they intended to murder me right there."

Three or four of Brodie's followers, seeing him lying insensible on the pavement, ran the gauntlet of police clubs, picked up their leader and carried him across the street to one of their own first aid men.

"Ambulance!" one of them cried, to a group of police. "Get an ambulance for Brodie."

"Get your own ambulance," came the reply.

A private car pulled up beside the injured man and the driver leaned out and shouted: "Here, put him in — I'll take him to the hospital."

"Don't take a chance, fellow," Brodie moaned.

But the driver took a chance and Brodie was hoisted in. As his friends watched the car pull away, a police sergeant and constable approached: "Get out of here," the sergeant said, "before I cut your heads off."

In planning an early Sunday eviction, the authorities had not counted on the presence of a large crowd. But onlookers had been gathering by the hundreds from the very moment the police took up their positions. They were enraged by what they saw — hundreds of shabbily dressed men, blinded by gas, frantic and screaming as they erupted from the post office into the hail of swinging clubs and whips. Across the street, in the Melrose Café, waitresses were in tears as they watched the police actively pursue and beat men who had become their friends. Members of the crowd screamed encouragement to the unemployed; others became actively involved and were themselves injured. Innocent bystanders were not spared. Margaret Rickett, a visitor from Victoria, had left her suitcase in a nearby drugstore while she bought a return boat ticket at the CPR dock. When she attempted to cross the street to retrieve it, she received a stinging blow across the shoulder from a mounted policeman's whip.

The entire intersection was packed with a struggling mass of humanity — policemen, unemployed and bystanders. The crowd followed the fleeing men down Cordova Street where two big department stores,

Spencer's and Woodwards, were located. An orgy of destruction now took place as the enraged men began to vent their fury on the stores' plate-glass windows. They heaved stones, bottles and any object that came to hand, knocking out twenty-six windows at Spencer's and eighty more at Woodwards. The mob moved on to Cambie and split into two groups, one sweeping east on Hastings, smashing all the windows on the north side and other moving south to attack the Imperial Bank, the B.C. Chamber of Mines and other buildings. In the space of a few minutes, thirty thousand dollars' worth of damage was done.

The evacuation of the art gallery by city policemen, which took place simultaneously with that of the post office, was carried out with no violence except for the use of tear gas. This was due to the actions of Harold Winch, a prominent CCF member of the legislature from East Vancouver, who had once before, in 1935, acted as a liaison man between the city and disgruntled men. Early on Bloody Sunday, Winch was, in effect, kidnapped by the chief of police, Foster, and driven aimlessly around town in a squad car until zero hour. His job was to prevent the destruction of priceless paintings and sculpture at the gallery.

Winch did his job. Once the tear gas bombs were released the men emerged quietly, some of them carrying the paintings they had worked on during their stay. Some of Foster's city policemen helped the sit-downers. There were no beatings. Just as the last man was evicted from the gallery, Mayor Miller arrived on the scene, late as usual, from his summer cottage on Bowen Island.

Brodie's reaction to all this was one of contempt. To him, Harold Winch, soon to be the leader of his party in British Columbia, was nothing more than an "assistant chief of police." Brodie declared that if he had been in charge at the gallery he would have smashed everything in it. "That was the point of the gallery," he said. "A million bucks in paintings and we were worth nothing."

The three hundred men from the gallery, still red-eyed from the tear gas, now began a long march in orderly ranks, four abreast, down Georgia Street to Granville, then down Granville to the post office and east on Hastings. Hundreds of other jobless men rushed to join them; ordinary citizens who had seen the riot followed; scores of cars took up the rear until the march became a long parade of protest.

That afternoon, ten thousand people squeezed themselves into the Powell Street grounds in East Vancouver for a rally to support the cause of the unemployed. The crowd cheered as speakers called for the resignation of Premier Pattullo. Thousands then began a march on the police station, apparently intending further violence; but again Harold Winch, climbing a telephone pole, managed to calm them down. That night thousands more gathered at the CPR docks to cheer a delegation of one hundred who took the midnight boat to Victoria to bring their case to the legislature.

The following day, the press echoed the general indignation of the public. The *Sun,* in a front page editorial, demanded that the federal government act to end unemployment. Other newspapers across Canada echoed that sentiment. But nothing really happened, except for some token jobs. The Legislative buildings were closed to the Victoria delegation. In Vancouver, Pattullo, who had ridden to victory in 1933 with the election slogan "work and wages," bluntly told a delegation of clergymen and unemployed that no further relief projects would be created. Nor would there be emergency food for the single transients. Said he: "There comes a time when too much sympathy can be shown the men. That time has come in Vancouver." The unemployed, said

Pattullo, would just have to find jobs. But there were no jobs; the men went back to tin canning (in spite of the mayor's attempt to make it illegal) and Vancouver simmered down. No one was ever arrested for taking part in the sit-in but twenty-two were charged with wilful damage in the destruction that followed; seven were found guilty and given small sentences.

The Vancouver sit-in, in essence, was a failure. It was not the government that solved the great depression, it was the advent of a new world war. Brodie, released from hospital with a permanent eye injury, was one of the first to apply for active service when war was declared. In the long line-ups at the recruiting office, he spotted many of his old comrades. But the army rejected him because of his eye condition. The unkindest cut came when the Communist Party rejected him, too: he had served his purpose and was now too hot to handle. Eventually, Brodie joined the merchant marine.

A superb organizer and a brilliant leader, Robert "Steve" Brodie might, in other circumstances, have made a different kind of name for himself. But he never again had the opportunity, or perhaps the inclination, to use his talents. When the war ended, he drifted from job to job and when these words were written, in 1976, he was "retired" — out of work again — living in Victoria on a small pension, a burned-out symbol of a vanished era. One can only mourn the waste.

11

Ned Hanlan and the Golden Age of Sculling

Was there ever a world champion like Ned Hanlan? I doubt it. He was one of those athletic paragons who, like meteors, dazzling in their brilliance, flash across the sky only to flare out as suddenly as they burst forth. Hanlan of Toronto — the fastest sculler in the world, almost certainly the fastest sculler in history (all but one of his records still stand after a century) — is it possible that he achieved it all in just ten years? Consider his history: champion of Burlington Bay at nineteen; champion of Canada at twenty-two; champion of America at twenty-three; champion of England at twenty-four; champion of the world at twenty-five; beaten four years later at an age when most men are still clambering slowly toward the crest of their careers. Hanlan was finished as a world champion before he reached thirty; but what a champion he was!

He was to sculling what Roger Bannister was to the mile run. His triumphant decade, 1874-84, was one of those glorious accidents when the accomplishment of an athlete and the popularity of a sport coincide and enhance one another. Hanlan *made* sculling; it might also be said that he unmade it, for he was the de Gaulle of oarsmen. None who followed had his flair. Sculling is not the world's most exciting sport; it lacks the speed of skiing, the danger of sports-car racing, the drama of the greater spectator sports. But Hanlan had the showmanship, the theatre, the pure *pizazz* to turn it into a spectacle.

When Hanlan rowed, the world turned out to watch. In Canada, crowds of ten or twenty thousand came to see him row — more than turned up for Grey Cup matches in a later century when the country was five times as large. He outclassed his opponents; could and did run rings around them. But not for him the long lead, the dull finish. Better to counterfeit collapse, draw a gasp from the crowd, or make it laugh, circle back from the finish line, stage any number of bravado gestures to bring applause from the spectators and groans from his rivals — anything to juice up the audience. Better to row just hard enough to make it *look* like a race. Only once in his ten-year string of victories did Hanlan need to go all out for speed, and that was on the remarkable day when he rowed alone after his opponent's shell had been mysteriously sabotaged. To prove that he had had nothing to do with the crime, to show that he could beat any man alive on the water, Ned Hanlan rowed a five-mile course at a speed that had never before been attained and that has never since been surpassed.

Hanlan's style and showmanship brought him an adulation that has rarely been equalled. He was remarkably good-looking, with the regular features and curly hair so fashionable in the engraved advertisements of the day: "The handsomest gentleman I or anyone has ever seen," to quote the words of a contemporary. In all the accounts of the period of Hanlan and his victories, there was scarcely a snide word written about him; he was undeniably likeable, a man apparently without enemies, the perfect sports hero.

Of the private Hanlan we know very little, except that he was happily married (in 1877) and the father of eight children. The glimpses we have of him are the public ones, and they are all remarkably serene. In all his appearances he seems to be a man without neuroses or observable weaknesses (unless one counts his propensity to clown during a race). His private life must have been equally untroubled, since nobody apparently thought it worth writing about.

He was small for an oarsman, a shade under five foot nine and weighing a mere hundred and fifty pounds. Many of the scullers he vanquished were his physical superiors; but what Hanlan lacked in strength he made up in style. He rowed without apparent fatigue. Often his opponents, straining every muscle, found they were working twice as hard as Hanlan but not travelling as fast. His single-seat shell, someone remarked, seemed to have been drawn along the waters as if by an invisible string.

Hanlan's effortless style grew out of his mastery of sculling techniques. His long stroke was developed because he thoroughly understood some of the technical innovations of the day: the extended rowlocks, for example, and the sliding seat. Hanlan did not invent these new devices, which came into use about the time he began to row in earnest, but he mastered them to such an extent that he revolutionized rowing. In former days, scullers used to gain extra leverage by sliding back and forth on buffalo skins. Hanlan, who became known as the Father of the Sliding Seat (he was the first to adapt it to the single-seat shell), perfected an odd kind of crouch which, together with his acute sense of pacing, made him unbeatable. He used the seat and the rowlocks to extend his arms so that his stroke was always longer than that of his opponents. In his ten-year

265

heyday, he took part in some three hundred and fifty races. He lost no more than half a dozen.

The rise of rowing as a spectator sport in eastern Canada coincided with the decline of the pioneer era after Confederation. The adventure and the excitement had moved westward. Gold had been discovered in British Columbia; the North West Mounted Police were being formed; the Pacific Railway enterprise had just been launched. But in the settled areas, barn raisings and stump blasting bees were giving way to roller skating, snowshoeing, tobogganing and, above all else, to boating. Basketball had not yet been invented. Baseball was in its infancy; the big leagues had scarcely been formed. Ice hockey was a minority game confined to amateurs. There was no Stanley Cup, no World Series. Rugby, football and soccer had scarcely reached the embryo stage. Lacrosse, of course, was highly popular; but rowing was *the* international sport and in no country in the world was it more popular than in Canada.

The increase in leisure time helped. On Sundays and holidays everybody seemed to be out on the water. Toronto and Hamilton harbours vibrated with craft of every shape and description. When a four-oar crew from Saint John, New Brunswick, went to Paris in 1867 and defeated crews from England, France, Germany and the United States, there was no holding the rowing enthusiasts back home. Hanlan was just twelve years old in 1867, living on Toronto Island (where his father ran a store), rowing three-quarters of a mile every day to school and working as a fisherman in his spare time. He was raised, as they say, with a pair of oars in his hands. The Hanlans were poor shanty Irish and young Ned could not even afford a proper shell. His first boat was a home-made contraption, fashioned out of a two-inch plank, sharpened at both ends, with a seat and an outrigger mounted upon it. Hanlan was probably the first

Canadian sports hero to break through the barrier of class: the boating world, after all, had social connotations and the yacht clubs catered to the topmost crust of society. But the day would come when members of the Royal Canadian Yacht Club would be pleased to escort Ned Hanlan home in style and welcome him as one of their own.

He was sixteen when, as a member of a three-man crew of fishermen, he rowed his first race. Two years later he switched to single-seat sculling. By May of 1876, he had acquired such a local reputation that a group of backers made the daring decision to enter him in the International Centennial Regatta in Philadelphia. The wiseacres scoffed; imagine sending a callow youth, unknown outside his own community, to compete with some of the world's most seasoned professionals!

Hanlan almost missed the big time. Just before leaving Toronto he learned that the police were after him for bootlegging liquor on the island. He hid out in a friend's house overnight, but the police caught up with him at the Toronto Rowing Club. Hanlan slipped away to the boathouse float, jumped into a skiff, and skimmed away across the harbour. It makes an apt little tableau: the frustrated bluecoats fuming at the dock while the future world's champion makes the best possible use of his technique to evade them. Far out in the lake a pleasure steamer, crammed with roistering members of the German Club of Toronto out on their annual picnic, was chugging off for Lewiston, New York. Hanlan with his long, fluid strokes easily overtook the sidewheeler and was soon happily ensconced among the *lederhosen* and meerschaums, out of reach of the Canadian law.

He was joined in Philadelphia by the man he had recently bested for the Ontario championship, Billy McKen. They trained quietly each morning. In the evenings, while Hanlan caught up on his sleep, the convivial McKen made the rounds of local taverns, placing bets on Hanlan for his Toronto backers. Hanlan astonished and nettled the big New York gamblers by winning the first two heats against American favourites. That would never do; the decision was made to put him out of the race. Fortunately for Hanlan, but unhappily for McKen, they confused the two men. Somebody poisoned McKen's beer; the following morning his legs buckled under him and he was shipped back to Toronto on a stretcher. To the astonishment of all, the pink-cheeked, curly-haired 21-year-old nobody went on to win the final heat — and in the fastest time on record. He returned in triumph, the summons forgotten, the scoffers confounded. A vast crowd was on hand at the bayside to greet him on his return as, atop a hook and ladder wagon, he led a torchlight parade to a welcoming banquet at the Queen's Hotel. In a single race, Ned Hanlan had become one of the international demi-gods of sport.

In those days champion scullers were owned by syndicates in much the same way as boxers were owned in a later era. Hanlan was backed by the Hanlan Club — no social institution but a hardheaded business enterprise, organized for profit. (One of its members was the local American consul, Colonel Albert Shaw.) Though regattas were drawing thousands, it was the matched races that held the most appeal because, like prizefights, they featured only two men — challenger and champion. In such races, the backers put up prize money and fenced off the course for paying customers. The real profit, however, lay in the side bets placed before the race. The same scullers would meet again and again, as racehorses do, on different courses. Skulduggery of various kinds was not uncommon: Billy McKen was not the only man to succumb to poison before a contest.

Gamesmanship was also used to neutralize opponents. One famous sculler indulged in a series of false starts to exhaust his rival. Another purposely picked a fight with his adversary just as the race began; the angered sculler found he was still arguing at the starting line while his tormentor shot two lengths into the lead.

In 1877, Hanlan's career appeared briefly to falter. He had broken an outrigger in one regatta and lost a second race at Boston when he was disqualified for fouling an opponent. When Wallace Ross of Saint John, then the Canadian champion, challenged him to a five-mile race with a purse of one thousand dollars a side, his backers started to hedge their bets. Ross, having just set a new record for four miles, was the heavy favourite. Hanlan's backers began putting some of their money on the other man. In spite of this lack of support Hanlan remained calm, worked out regularly, ate heartily, slept peacefully. In fact he took a siesta on the day of the race and had to be wakened to go out onto the course. The odds were eight to one on Ross, but Hanlan, pulling at a steady sweep of thirty-two strokes a minute, was a length ahead at the half-mile mark and had doubled his lead, without effort, by the time the first mile was passed. Ross, pulling at thirty-seven strokes a minute, kept forcing himself to the utmost; one observer felt that he was wrenching himself apart. Suddenly, at the mile-and-a-quarter mark, he dug his sculls too deep and was seen to plummet headlong into the water. Hanlan was awarded the Canadian championship.

Hanlan's imperturbable sculling style, the ease with which he managed to skim across the water without perceptible effort, was psychologically devastating. Again and again one finds his opponents coming to physical grief as a result of tension, over-exertion and, perhaps, frustration. One of Hanlan's tactics was to set such a searing pace in the first few hundred yards that rival scullers tended to give up. Not long after he beat Ross, Hanlan won the American championship against Evan "Eph" Morris, a noted oarsman from Pittsburgh who, according to a contemporary account, "made such a terrible effort to retrieve his fortunes that it is very doubtful if he has ever been the same man since." Hanlan literally drove some of his opponents out of professional competition.

One of these was Charles Courtney, a carpenter from Union Springs, New York, who had won the amateur championship at Philadelphia in 1876 when Hanlan won the professional. Courtney was a big man, well over six feet, heavier than Hanlan and fifteen years older. Between 1878 and 1880, he and Hanlan took part in three match races, which were the most peculiar and most questionable of the Toronto sculler's career.

The first match took place at Lachine, Quebec, on October 3, 1878. The match was for twenty-five hundred dollars a side, but the citizens of Montreal were so enthusiastic that they added an additional six thousand dollars to the already substantial stake. Multitudes poured in from all parts of the United States and Canada to watch the contest. Courtney started out as the betting favourite but the odds suddenly changed at the last moment. When Sheriff Harding of Saint John shouted "Go!" the money was on Hanlan, one hundred dollars to sixty.

To the onlookers it appeared to be a seesaw race, but the experts soon knew that Courtney was hopelessly outclassed. At two miles Hanlan was in the lead. After the turn, at the four-mile point, Courtney almost caught him and began forcing Hanlan off the course. Hanlan warned him to straighten out and as he did so, the Toronto sculler pulled ahead and won. That night there was an ovation for the two men in Montreal's Windsor Hotel and a grand reception the following night at the

Victoria skating rink, but those who had seen the race were not satisfied. Some claimed Hanlan had only won because Courtney had intruded on his lane. Others whispered darker suspicions: that Courtney had agreed in advance to lose the first race and that Hanlan's backers had obligated him to throw the second. These suspicions weren't dispelled by the curious events that took place during the later matches. But before that, Ned Hanlan had an appointment overseas.

His backers had matched him against John Hawdon, then considered to be the coming champion oarsman of England. The two men would compete on the three-and-a-half-mile championship course on the River Tyne. English boating experts laughed at the idea of a Canadian crossing the Atlantic to row against a man of Hawdon's proven skill. They backed their man heavily, not knowing that Hanlan's syndicate had matched him against Hawdon as a mere test, preparing for a more significant encounter with William Elliott, then the champion of England. When Hanlan began training on the Tyne, every effort was made to conceal his style from the bookies; but it was no use — by race time the odds were on Hanlan, two to one.

Here, for the first time, Hanlan indulged in some of the horseplay and gamesmanship that was to infuriate his English and Australian opponents. Hawdon started off at a vigorous thirty-eight to forty-two strokes a minute. Hanlan, with his longer and easier sweep, pulled at a little over thirty and took the lead. Soon he was three lengths ahead of Hawdon and the odds on the Canadian — for those who still wished to bet — rose to one hundred to one. As they passed the meadows, packed with spectators, Hanlan actually stopped to bail out his boat, nodding and laughing to the people who were running along the bank. "Poor Hawdon," wrote a reporter, "was painfully struggling along but in a piteous plight, thoroughly exhausted." As the crowd shouted and laughed, Hanlan allowed himself to fall back until he was only a couple of lengths ahead of his frustrated rival. Again he spurted forward, bowing and smiling to the cheering crowd. He finished four lengths in the lead, but had he wished he could have humiliated Hawdon by half a mile.

The match race with Elliott, the English champion, was set for June 16 on the same course. Scores of Canadians from Toronto, Montreal, Windsor and Belleville were on hand to cheer their man. The river was so black with boats that navigation was almost impossible. Hanlan appeared just before noon and took off his cap as the crowd cheered; he was wearing the familiar dark blue singlet and shorts, which had earned him the nickname of the Boy in Blue. Elliott was stripped to the waist. In the accounts of Hanlan's major races his opponents are always described as perspiring freely; but the Boy in Blue never doffed his singlet.

Hanlan was an easy favourite with the gamblers and quickly proved it. At first it seemed to Elliott's backers that the race would be tight; later they realized that the Canadian wasn't really trying. Elliott had not mastered the long slide and the swivelled rowlocks; his oars dug too deeply into the water, splashing and ploughing away in contrast to Hanlan's perfect style. "The style in which Hanlan moves his oars . . . must attract notice," one sportswriter noted. "The broad blades skim so close to the surface of the water that they are scarcely seen. . . . On the water Hanlan and his boat are as much in harmony as an animate and inanimate object can be. His sliding is as methodical and regular and as free from apparent effort as the motion of the driving shaft of a locomotive engine when running at a regular rate of speed." Hanlan beat the English champion by ten lengths and broke the course record by fifty-five seconds. To the sporting press of England he was "the most speedy and finished oarsman that was ever seen on the Thames or Tyne."

The new champion of England returned to a tumultuous welcome. He sailed to New York, took a train to Niagara and boarded the lake steamer *Chicora*. Ten miles out of Toronto, every conceivable craft that could be mustered was waiting to greet him: five large sidewheelers loaded to the gunwales with cheering people, all the yachts of the Royal Canadian Yacht Club and a scattering of small craft. As the *Chicora* steamed by, the entire flotilla lined up behind her, the whistles shrieking, the crowd yelling and the bands playing "Hail the Conquering Hero." Hanlan, standing on the roof of the pilot house, waved to the throngs cramming the Yonge Street wharf. That evening he appeared before an enormous gathering at the Horticultural Gardens to receive an address of welcome from the mayor.

All contemporary accounts describe Hanlan as a modest and totally moral man. An acquaintance recalled that, in all the years he knew him, he never heard him utter a vulgar word, nor had he been "party to a suggestive story. . . . Morally he was the cleanest man I had ever known." In 1933, a biographer wrote that "of all men, he combined the most likeable qualities. Unreserved, gracious, kindly, clean, humorous, honest and sporting, are just a few of the virtues attributed to the world's new demi-god. He is accredited with those two sterling qualities, friendliness and cleanliness of mind." Yet Hanlan's good name was certainly besmirched, if only temporarily, during the second of his notorious races with Charles Courtney.

The match was set for October 16, 1879, in the little upstate New York town of Mayville on Lake Chautauqua, which had given its name to the famous literary and scientific tent circuit. The promoter was A. T. Soule, of Rochester, the proprietor of a stomach tonic known as Hop Bitters and the owner of the Hop Bitters Baseball Team. Soule's plan was to bring Courtney and Hanlan to Mayville for a purse of six thousand dollars, if the businessmen of the town would pay him five per cent of the take they received from the tens of thousands who would surely arrive to watch the match. The locals needed no prompting. They built a grandstand two thousand feet long with seats for fifty thousand. A railroad, which built a special spur line, brought in an observation train half a mile long from which spectators could watch the race in comfort. Steamboats began to sell tickets and even old barges were patched up and made ready for the event at five dollars a seat.

On the eve of the race the little town of one thousand found itself swamped. Hotels raised their prices from a dollar a day to twelve dollars. It was said that five thousand people were forced to sleep on chairs, tables and floors. Others rented piano crates, bales of hay, corners of barns as sleeping accommodation.

The town sizzled with rumours. Courtney was said to have developed a new and secret method of training. Hanlan, it was whispered, had concealed a bellows in his shell for extra propulsion. The odds on both men shifted hourly. The referee, William Blaikie, complained that he had heard persistent rumours of a fix. He tried to close down the betting pools but pressure from the railway and from Soule, who was getting five per cent of everything, including the gamblers' take, forestalled him.

Courtney started as the favourite, but when the contestants' form was observed during the final day of training, the odds dropped to even money: both men seemed to be in the peak of condition. After that the betting went crazy. The odds swung back to Courtney in the teeth of new rumours: one hundred to ninety, one hundred to seventy-five, even one hundred to fifty. It was said that the Canadians, possessed of information that their man would throw the race, were desperately trying to hedge their bets. At one point odds could be obtained on Courtney at one betting box, on Hanlan at another. Finally, the sheriff agreed to close the boxes; when they were allowed to reopen, two hours later, some gamblers refused all further bets because they had no idea what odds to offer. The New York *Sportsman* reported that "the fancy could not find out who had fixed whom to do what."

Few were able to sleep during the stifling night that followed. The following morning, at nine, a stunning piece of news shook the community. Down Main Street on a velocipede came a tinhorn gambler crying: "Boys, it's all off! Charley Courtney's boat's been sawed."

A terrifying scene followed as hundreds of furious men choked Main Street for three blocks attempting to find out what had happened. They soon learned that the news was correct: both Courtney's skiff, *Hop Bitters,* and his practice shell, had been sawn in half at a time when the two watchmen, entrusted with guarding the boathouse, had unaccountably left their post and gone to the village to "play a little casino."

The rage of the crowd was understandable. Courtney was cornered and interrogated. He denied all knowledge of the incident. His trainer had discovered the damage the previous evening but said he hadn't wished to disturb Courtney's night's rest. Nor had he informed the press or anybody else of the disaster. Attempts were made to force Courtney to race in a borrowed shell. He bluntly refused. Blaikie, the referee, his face white with anger, announced that the match would be held anyway.

And so Hanlan sculled the five-mile course alone — and magnificently. He finished in 33 minutes, 56¼ seconds, breaking the record by 1 minute, 14¼ seconds. He was formally declared the winner, but his victory was Pyrrhic; Soule departed, after withdrawing all his money from the local bank, leaving Hanlan with a rubber cheque for six thousand dollars. The gambling pools also declared all bets off and returned the bettors' wagers, minus a one per cent handling charge. Nobody involved with the race, with the exception of Blaikie, emerged untainted.

Who had sawn Courtney's boat, and why? There is little doubt that the contest was fixed from the start. In order to get Courtney to race at all, Hanlan's backers had had to promise that he would win the second of the three matches. As David Ward, of the Hanlan Club, said, "How else would we have got Courtney to the scratch? A log chain wouldn't have dragged him there unless he knew he could win." The stumbling block was Hanlan himself, who had not been told of the arrangement. The Boy in Blue had no intention of throwing the race; one rumour said that he had already turned down a gambler's fifty thousand dollar bribe to lose. Undoubtedly the Toronto contingent knew this, because one of Ward's friends tried to place a quiet bet on Hanlan the day before the contest. But the secret leaked out. The Courtney camp discovered the double cross and told Courtney that the Canadians were welshing on their promises to ensure his win. The boats were undoubtedly sawn with Courtney's knowledge, and perhaps at his instigation, to prevent his further humiliation and, more important, to save all the money that had been staked on the outcome.

One thing is certain: Courtney was never a match for Hanlan. In spite of their discomfiting experience with Courtney and Soule, Hanlan's backers signed him up for a third race set for May 19, 1880, again under the sponsorship of the Hop Bitters salesman. This time, however, they had another oarsman on hand, just in case Courtney backed out. Sure enough, a few hours before the contest, Courtney developed a "blinding headache." His backers forced him into the contest and he actually started off in the lead. He wavered swiftly, stopped to bathe his brow in the water, fell back, and after two miles, quit altogether as the crowd howled in derision. That was the end of Courtney as a single-scull racer.

That November, Hanlan rowed the race of his career in England against the self-styled champion of the world, Edward A. Trickett, of Sydney, Australia. William Harding, the *Police Gazette's* sporting reporter, wrote that "perhaps in the history of boating there never was so much excitement over a race, or such a vast amount of money wagered."

Trickett was a six-foot, four-inch giant — jumpy, anxious and sullen. Hanlan was fifty pounds lighter and five years younger. Trickett, having defeated the English champion, Joseph Sadler, was claiming to be the world's greatest oarsman, even though he had never raced a North American sculler. He knew Hanlan was the man to beat, had even had a shell built and rigged like Hanlan's and had tried, not very successfully, to emulate the Hanlan style. His backers, the Thompson brothers, well-known Melbourne bookmakers, believed their man could beat any sculler in the world. Even after watching Hanlan's impressive training sprints on the Thames, they did not change their minds. "It is almost incomprehensible," Harding wrote, "that so many intelligent men could have been so strangely wrong."

The race was to be held over the famous Oxford and Cambridge boat race course from Putney to Mortlake on the Thames. Every bridge, on that unpromising November morning, was crowded from first light with spectators, peering through the fog and drizzle. Thousands more blackened the riverbanks for the entire four and a quarter miles of the course. Half a million dollars had been wagered on the outcome, with the English joining the Australians in backing Trickett. In Canada, the wise money was on Hanlan. Two days before the race the queue of people buying bank drafts for that purpose ran two blocks down Yonge Street from the Bank of Montreal in Toronto. In that city alone, forty-two thousand dollars was wagered on the Boy in Blue, enough to cause a last-minute shift in the odds.

But in truth, what had been billed as the Race of the Century turned out to be a farce, enlivened only by Hanlan's showmanship. The two men set off at 12:14 p.m. From the start Trickett appeared tense and anxious; clearly he was overtrained. Hanlan, by contrast, gambolled to the stake boat, apparently unconcerned about the outcome. At the moment he got underway he appeared to be criticizing his opponent; it was not until well after the starting signal that he turned his attention to the stern of his skiff and began to devote his energies to the race.

At the end of the first mile Hanlan was two lengths ahead of his rival. Trickett, labouring heavily, was observably outclassed. At Biffen's boathouse, Hanlan began to clown. He stopped rowing for a moment, leaned back in his boat, indulged in a leisurely survey of the scenery, and then took up the oars in a half-hearted way, "as though he would prefer to linger did not circumstances compel his progressing." He moved thirty yards, stopped again, moved on again, stopped again and thus continued by fits and starts down the course.

Trickett's face was pale, his expression wild. Hanlan, four lengths in the lead, now indulged in "a piece of harlequinade, the like of which has never before been witnessed in a race." He dropped his sculls clumsily into the water, fell forward onto his face and lay there for a moment or so — long enough to elicit groans from the spectators, who thought he had suffered some sort of seizure. Suddenly he sprang upright, resumed his oars and went back to work, laughing. There was an answering roar of relieved laughter from the crowd.

During this display, Hanlan's straining rival had almost overtaken him. Again Hanlan skimmed merrily away. Now he began to row with alternate oars, stopping repeatedly, looking cheerfully about, dawdling and clowning. He spotted his old rival, Elliott, in a boat beside the course, rowed over to him and chatted as they moved along side by side.

The Bull's Head Inn, Hanlan's headquarters, hove into view. His backers cheered. Hanlan produced a white handkerchief and waved cheerfully. As one of them later remarked: "I fully expected him to stand up in his boat and dance the Highland Fling." He won the race by seven seconds; he could probably have won it by a mile. In this contest, which saw more money wagered than had ever been bet on a sculling race, Trickett never had the ghost of a chance. There were some that day who seriously suggested that Hanlan's skiff was propelled by some kind of hidden machine. Nonetheless the audience was satisfied. "Hanlan's sculling was worth travelling a hundred miles to see," declared a writer for the London publication *Sporting Life*.

Hanlan now carried the official title of Champion Oarsman of the World. He was probably the first bona fide world's champion of anything. Except for boating there were as yet no international sports contests. The modern Olympic Games, which would introduce the idea of world championships, were still sixteen years in the future. But Hanlan was an international figure, handsome, clean-cut, still boyish but, with his fashionable new soupstrainer mustache, mature enough to be mobbed by women. His picture and his name were reproduced on Hanlan scarves, Hanlan shirts, Hanlan belts, Hanlan ties and, of course, Hanlan snuff boxes. It was said, truly, that no other Canadian was so well known in the English-speaking world. In Australia, a town was named Toronto to honour Hanlan's prowess.

Hanlan successfully defended his world title six times. Elias Laycock of Sydney, Australia, who had won the International Thames Regatta, was the first of the challengers. The race took place on May 22, 1881, on the Nepean river at Pendrith, Australia. En route, the champion staged profitable exhibitions: at Honolulu, for instance, hundreds of curious natives swam around his boat to watch him as he rowed. But Australia was an anticlimax. The odds on Hanlan were four to one; few would risk a wager. The promoters had invested heavily on the course, fencing in a space along each bank of the river with corrugated iron and erecting a big grandstand near the winning post. But the crowd was not as big as expected; Hanlan was too good. In the race that followed, his sweating opponent removed his jersey halfway down the course, but Hanlan stayed cool. A hundred yards from the winning post he allowed Laycock to catch up. When the two men were level he shot ahead with three or four powerful strokes and, amidst great excitement, won by a bare length. He had now won the Aquatic Championship Challenge Cup three times — from Elliott, from Trickett and from Laycock. Under the conditions of this race it was his forever. It can be seen today in Toronto's Marine Museum.

He raced Trickett again on the Thames on May 1, 1882. In Toronto, the *Globe's* headline told the story:

THE INEVITABLE PROCESSION OF TWO RE-PEATED/VERY LITTLE BETTING AND LESS EXCITEMENT. Hanlan was a five to one favourite; Trickett again seemed anxious and nervous. In the race that followed, the Canadian played his usual cat and mouse game, rowing all the way to the finish line and then turning back to his rival, rowing even with him and spurting ahead to beat him by a length. "Never was there a victory so thorough and complete," the *Globe* reported. Trickett never appeared again in a major race.

Hanlan kept his title for four years, and then the inevitable decline began. If it is true that great champions experience ecstasies of triumph not given to the common herd, it is equally true that they must face a concomitant bitterness of defeat. Each loss becomes a little death, and as age advances, the losses can only accelerate. Hanlan was finally beaten at twenty-nine by an Australian ferryman named William Beach. His backers were astonished and chagrined. Hanlan blamed the climate and the treacherous and unfamiliar Paramatta River. Others blamed the round of banquets and receptions that had preceded the match. But the real culprit was time. Hanlan tried twice more to beat Beach; twice more he lost. Smaller races, more frequent defeats followed. Crowds still turned out to watch his demonstration of trick sculling. But the adulation slowly died. As late as 1897, Hanlan, who never admitted or believed he could be beaten, was still issuing challenges. By then there were no takers.

Yet he never lost his popularity. The citizens of Toronto presented him with a twenty thousand dollar house and a piece of freehold property on Toronto Island where he built a hotel. It is still known as Hanlan's Point. They hung a gigantic portrait of him ten feet high and six feet wide, in their city hall. In 1898, when he finally rested his oars, they elected him alderman for Ward Four. When he died on January 4, 1908, at the comparatively young age of fifty-two, ten thousand people filed past his bier. Almost two decades later, Hanlan was still remembered. In 1926, Toronto financed, at a cost of seventeen thousand dollars, a twenty-foot statue to him on the grounds of the Canadian National Exhibition — the only statue in the world ever erected to a sculler. On it is engraved this tribute: "Edward Hanlan, the most renowned oarsman of any age whose victorious career has no parallel in the annals of sport." It has been said of Canadian heroes that they are rarely honoured in their own country. Happily, that was never the fate of the Boy in Blue.

12

The First Commando Raid

The story of Pierre, Chevelier de Troyes and his successful guerrilla attack on three English forts on James Bay has all the qualities of a bad movie — one of those gaudy, swashbuckling adventures that Hollywood churned out in the forties. In the saga of de Troyes, the good guys (the noble, daring French) always win; the bad guys (the dumb, incompetent English) always lose. One longs for some setback: a blunder, possibly, by a flawed lieutenant, which almost loses the day; an act of treachery by a turncoat in the French camp; the tragic death, perhaps, of one of de Troyes' trusted comrades. But there is none of this. De Troyes' saga is just too pat; it could only happen in the movies.

Still, it *did* happen. In 1686 the governor of New France sent this consummate soldier and a hundred men on a twelve-week canoe trip into totally unknown country with the task of capturing three supposedly impregnable forts, bristling with cannon. No riskier or more reckless venture can be imagined. A few dozen men — half-starved, living on weeds part of the time, armed only with muskets, swords and pikes — outmanoeuvred their foes, subdued all three strongholds, and captured an armed naval vessel without losing a single man in battle.

We have no idea what de Troyes looked like. His incandescent appearance on the Canadian scene was too brief for any painter to capture his likeness. But we know what he *ought* to have looked like: a lithe, tough soldier with the eyes of a rogue, flashing teeth and a mustache turned into a smile to match the *mouche* on his lower lip — Errol Flynn, in short, got up as d'Artagnan. A good deal of de Troyes' heroics are pure Dumas, and there are, of course, the three dauntless Le Moyne brothers by his side to sustain the comparison. The rest is pure de Mille. The story can almost be told in press agent superlatives: *See the mighty Canadian forest in flames! See the incredible dash through the foaming rapids! See the battering ram attack on the fort, the capture of the armed ship, the molten lead raining down on Fort Albany! See the flashing swordplay as determined men redden the soil of the Northwoods in a savage battle to wrest control of the fur country for New France!* A box office smasheroo.

It is necessary to get the history out of the way before beginning the adventure. In the latter half of the seventeenth century, the fur trade had become the single most important factor in the Canadian economy. The English, with their prior claims to Hudson Bay, controlled it. The French, through the newly formed Compagnie du Nord, were struggling to expand but could not get a foothold in the north. At this point the ragged figure of Pierre Radisson enters the story. As every schoolchild knows, it was Radisson and his brother-in-law, the Sieur des Groseilliers, whose explorations led to the founding of the Hudson's Bay Company. It is doubtful, however, if a more untrustworthy *coureur de bois* ever existed. Having set himself up as a kind of marketing consultant for a gigantic English enterprise, Radisson switched sides, gained a pardon from the French king, Louis XIV, and helped establish a rival firm in French Canada. He and Groseilliers went on to build a fort deep in Hudson's Bay territory (Fort Bourbon they called it) at the mouth of the Bourbon (or Nelson) River. Skirmishes followed with the rival Hudson's Bay post just four miles away — skirmishes which Radisson won. Now perfidy was piled upon perfidy. Taxed out of his profits, Radisson again turned his coat. He rejoined the Hudson's Bay Company, attacked Fort Bourbon and, in 1684, captured it from his own nephew. He renamed it Fort Nelson and successfully barred his former compatriots from trading on Hudson Bay.

It was Radisson's treachery that gave the incoming governor of New France, Jacques de Brisay, Marquis de Denonville, an excuse to mount an attack that he hoped would drive the English out of James Bay. It is a principle of guerrilla warfare that unorthodox methods are often successful, that deception is the best weapon and surprise essential for victory. It was these commando tactics that were first used on the North American continent by the man charged with harassing the English: Pierre, Chevalier de Troyes.

Denonville was circumspect in the orders he issued de Troyes. The expedition was to "occupy posts on the shores of the bay of the North" and to bring back Radisson and his adherents to face charges of desertion and treason.

The governor was careful not to order the capture of any English or to name specifically any posts except Fort Bourbon-Nelson which had, of course, originally been French. Thus his official orders could not be construed as a declaration of war against the English. What de Troyes did was de Troyes' affair. Like many politicians before and since, Denonville did not want to know the sordid details. De Troyes did not have to be told, at least in writing, what was expected of him. He had no intention of going after Fort Bourbon: it was far away on the west shore of Hudson Bay, unreachable by land. His objectives from the outset were the three Hudson's Bay forts on the southern shores of James Bay: Albany, Moose and Rupert.

Denonville's machinations were Machiavellian, to say the least. England and France were not at war. There was a live-and-let-live understanding between the two nations over their respective trading zones. The Hudson's Bay forts were manned not by soldiers but by traders and clerks recruited in London. Denonville, pretending to get a trading foothold in the north, was sending an armed expedition to do the job. It was scarcely sporting; but then, there is very little that is sporting in the long, and often grisly, history of fur trade rivalry in Canada.

The Chevalier was newly arrived from France, the son of a Paris attorney, and a former captain in the French regulars: tough, competent, totally professional. He had no experience at all in the Canadian wilderness, and knew none of the men who would go with him on the adventure. But he knew how to lead, how to organize, how to delegate. The governor gave him thirty marines; the rest of the force consisted of seventy Canadian canoemen with Canadian officers. The total cost was underwritten by the Compagnie du Nord, one of whose founders had been Charles Le Moyne, the Montreal merchant who sired the most famous family in French Canada. Three of Le Moyne's remarkable sons took part in the expedition. Jacques, Sieur de Ste. Hélène, aged twenty-seven, was de Troyes' second-in-command. Pierre, Sieur d'Iberville, was his second lieutenant. This would be his first encounter with the English, but by no means his last — he would wage sea war against them from Newfoundland to the Gulf of Mexico; at the moment, however, he was glad to leave Montreal to evade a paternity suit brought against him

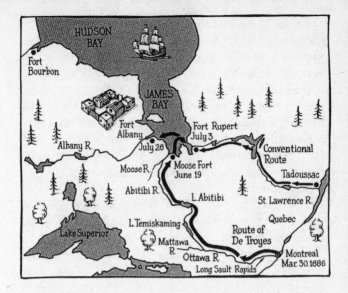

by the father of a teenage girl he had seduced. A third Le Moyne brother, Paul, Sieur de Maricourt, was de Troyes' adjutant. In addition, de Troyes took along an experienced navigator, Pierre Allemand, to command the English ships he hoped to capture; a scout, St. Germain, who knew the route; and a Jesuit chaplain, Father Antoine Silvy, whose years as a missionary among the Indians made him invaluable.

There were two routes to James Bay: the obvious one, taken by earlier expeditions, from Tadoussac through northern Quebec to Rupert House, and a less obvious one much farther to the west leading up the Ottawa River. De Troyes chose the Ottawa route, first because the English would not expect an attack from the west, and secondly, because the waters to the west, unlike the others, were navigable in mid-April. He wanted to reach James Bay just at spring breakup, weeks before ships from England could arrive from the north.

Although he intended to attack forts protected by cannon, de Troyes carried no weapons heavier than muskets: cannon could not be loaded into canoes. He was gambling that he could capture one fort by surprise and use its own cannon and ships to attack the others. His canoeists, all seasoned voyageurs, included tradesmen who would be useful after the capture: a carpenter, a blacksmith and a gunner, for example. By the time they reached their objective, they were burned so deeply by the sun that the local Indians thought they were Iroquois.

The expedition set off on March 30, 1686. The ice was so soft that two oxen pulling a sledload of baggage broke through and had to be hauled out. The following day they broke through again; de Troyes, in exasperation, sent the oxen back to Montreal. But his men were also breaking through the ice. On the second day they moved scarcely more than two miles because they spent most of the time rescuing one another.

But they struggled on, lining and poling their canoes up the famous Long Sault rapids, where Adam Dollard and his sixteen companions had been besieged and killed by Iroquois in 1660. After several days of travail, they next faced a series of impassable ice jams, with crevasses so wide that they were forced to build bridges to get their canoes and supplies across.

De Troyes, meanwhile, was hammering his undisciplined Canadians into an unaccustomed but necessary military organization, working out a marching order of three brigades with three squads each, appointing Canadian non-commissioned officers, and working out a regimented camp routine. "Thus," he wrote, "I subjected the men little by little to the discipline which military life demands, and which alone is lacking from the natural merit of the Canadians."

The trip was rough, even for experienced voyageurs. A shifting montage of incidents and images illuminates de Troyes' journal: the men, waist deep in the freezing waters, and sometimes neck deep, hauling on their loaded canoes like pack beasts; three nearly drowned when one craft strikes a rock in midstream and breaks up; de Troyes struggling along the shore through a braided tangle of fallen timber, thick brush and gigantic boulders, "frightening in its loneliness." A series of personal close-ups punctuates the montage: a man burns his hand in a fire, another cuts off his finger with a hatchet, several others sicken and come close to death from exposure.

In such conditions, discipline was all-important. When one Canadian made an insulting remark, de Troyes forestalled the incipient mutiny by tying him to a tree; in the regular army he would have been flogged, but the commander was too wise for that. "The character of Canadians," he wrote, ironically, "hardly accords with submission. . . ."

Two hundred and fifty miles out of Montreal the expedition reached the Mattawa and paddled and portaged its way up the right branch, sometimes smashing their canoes in the vicious rapids. On reaching Lake Temiskaming, they encountered, on an island, one of the Compagnie's trading posts. De Troyes left four of his men behind to augment its numbers and continued on north.

Forest fire! It is late in the afternoon of May 30; the weary expedition has covered twelve miles and made eight portages since morning. But somebody has left the breakfast fire burning. Racing round the lakeshore on a strong wind, it catches up with the rearguard just as it reaches the last portage, a fifteen-hundred-foot strip of land between two lakes. The men at the rear fling their

289

gunpowder and themselves into canoes to escape the flames; but the lake is so narrow that they are still in danger of being roasted. They cover themselves with soaking blankets and are saved.

The fire races on across the portage, pursuing more fleeing men. De Troyes and Father Silvy are caught three-quarters of the way across, running with all their strength, the flames pressing so closely that the sleeves of the commander's shirt are singed. At the lake ahead, the advance party is already hurling supplies and equipment into canoes, but de Troyes isn't safe yet. The clearing is only twenty feet wide and so soggy that he and his companions sink to their knees in the mud. They clamber, dishevelled, into the canoes and paddle desperately to the centre of the lake. Here the water is only thirty feet wide and the flames sweep like a torrent over their heads, igniting the bush on the opposite side. The canoes, made of birchbark and cedar strips, seem ready to burst into flames. There is only one way out — to flee back the way they have come, into the scorched and blackened forest through which the fire has already passed. This action probably saves their lives.

After the fire, the way led upward toward the height of land that divides the James Bay watershed from that of the St. Lawrence. Here the rapids and waterfalls climb the Precambrian shield like steps, acting as natural locks. On May 31, de Troyes stood on the divide and looked down on the rocky, beautiful countryside stretching off to the north, mantled in its spring mist of larch green and speckled by a thousand little lakes, glistening in the sunlight between the sombre ridges of gneiss and granite: English territory, all of it — enemy territory.

De Troyes' orders were to build a new trading post for the Compagnie du Nord on the English side of the divide. The site he chose, on Lake Abitibi, was so suitable that the post has been maintained ever since, first by the French, then by the North West Company and, since 1821, by the Hudson's Bay Company.

While his men were constructing the fort — the task took three days — their commander busied himself by laying out, with stakes and string, models of the English forts he intended to attack. One marvels at his sense of organization and even more at his conceit: he had to make do with models, he wrote blandly, "because I had not been able to find a suitable open clearing for building full-size replicas"! Now, he was able to show his officers exactly what part each man would play in the coming battle. "Subsequent events," he commented dryly, "showed me that this exercise was far from useless."

De Troyes left four more men in charge of the new post and paddled north on Lake Abitibi and down the Abitibi River into the Moose River. On June 10, one of his voyageurs, Noel Leblanc, an expert canoeist, was lost trying to shoot a series of rapids with Iberville. Like most of his comrades, Leblanc couldn't swim. Iberville was saved but lost most of his provisions, as well as his guns and clothes. Since it was standard on such expeditions for each man to carry his own rations, de Troyes shared his own with his second officer.

The way grew wearier. The men, slogging across gullies cluttered with falling timber, began to drop from exhaustion. De Troyes' two Indian guides deserted. Hardened though they were to forest travel, some of the voyageurs could not negotiate the final portage at day's end.

On June 19, they reached the junction of the Abitibi and the Moose rivers. Where, exactly, was Moose Fort? De Troyes questioned local Indians and sent Iberville and St. Germain to reconnoitre ahead. The following night, Iberville was able to lead the party to an island a little more than a mile from the Hudson's Bay post at the mouth of the Moose.

At daybreak, St. Germain rejoined the party. Going without food for twenty-four hours, he had found out how the fort was constructed and what the English were up to. He reported that the English had a ship, the *Craven,* anchored about four miles below the fort. De Troyes sent a detachment to guard the canoes, set up another as a rearguard and began, methodically, to plan the coming attack.

Moose Fort, a log castle standing on an island at the river's mouth, seemed impregnable. The thick palisades were eighteen feet high. The walls, each one hundred and thirty feet long, were guarded at the four corners by bastions, strongly constructed of earth, stakes and planks. Each bastion was armed with three seven-pound cannon that fired through slits which could be closed by sliding panels. Inside the walls was a three-storey redoubt (a strongpoint armed with three two-pounder cannon and one eight-pounder) towering above the walls of the fort so that its cannon could fire into the country beyond from all sides. The main door of the fort faced the river; it was six inches thick, reinforced by nails, strap hinges and iron bars. There was a similar door in the rear wall. Such was the stronghold that de Troyes intended to subdue with a force of about seventy men armed only with muskets and swords.

But de Troyes knew exactly what he was doing. First he sent for two canoes, one of which he loaded with picks, shovels, spades, ladders and planks. On the other he placed a newly constructed battering ram. The canoes were to follow de Troyes and his men who would march along the foreshore of the fortress island to their objective.

Ste. Hélène and Iberville, with eighteen men, were ordered to attack the two bastions that protected the rear wall, while the Sieur de la Liberté with six men was to make a diversionary attack on the bastions protecting the right wall. De Troyes' orders to La Liberté were explicit: three men were to attack each bastion, two of them firing continuously at the slits to neutralize the cannon, while the third hacked away at the palisade. The remainder of the party was grouped in three detachments for the major assault. Two of these detachments were ordered to keep up the hottest possible fire on the forward walls and bastions in order to interfere with the accuracy of the cannon, while the third would smash down the main gate with the battering ram.

Ste. Hélène immediately asked permission to leap over the palisade at the rear. De Troyes replied that when one gave orders to capture a fortress it did not matter how one entered it. Ste. Hélène took him literally and when the attack came, he and his two brothers and half a dozen others, swords in hand, climbed the palisade, seized several cannon and opened the rear door.

Meanwhile, de Troyes' orders were being carried out to the letter. The fire was so brutal, the fighting so confused that some of the attackers mistook Ste. Hélène's men on the inside for defending Englishmen and actually shot one in the loins. Shortly after, the battering ram smashed the main gate and de Troyes entered the fort at the head of his men, ordering them to keep up a withering fire on the gun ports, windows and other openings in the redoubt. While this was going on, de Troyes managed to turn one of the cannon against the interior stronghold, only to find that it was empty, with no balls available.

It did not matter. The others had smashed in the door of the redoubt and the English within were already asking for quarter. De Troyes had some difficulty dampening down his Canadian voyageurs who were whooping like Indians and wielding knives. Finally, he managed to have his interpreter call out that if the enemy surrendered they would be given quarter. One Englishman shouted that he wished to fight, but in doing so revealed his position; Ste. Hélène shot him dead.

With that the attack resumed. Again the English asked for quarter. The battering ram at that moment smashed in the door of the redoubt and Iberville was through in an instant, a sword in one hand, a musket in the other. The door was still on its hinges, however, and the English managed to slam it shut again. Iberville found himself alone with the enemy who swarmed over him. He fought back, wounding several in the face with his sword, until the battering ram completed its work and his comrades poured through the ruined door, ending the battle. De Troyes had taken the fortress with its seventeen defenders in exactly half an hour.

The English, still in their nightshirts, had been totally unprepared for any attack. The governor, John Bridgar, and all his officers had gone to Fort Rupert, leaving Moose virtually unguarded. Even sentinels had not been considered necessary. Now with his prisoners safely locked away in the hold of an abandoned ship and the fort guarded by his own men, de Troyes could turn his attention to the capture of the other two Hudson's Bay posts on southern James Bay: Forts Albany and Rupert.

The prisoners told him there was no watch or guard on Rupert, but it was a hundred miles to the east over a bad route and almost empty of supplies. Albany, on the other hand, seventy-five miles to the west, was well guarded and supplied, fortified with twenty-five cannon and manned by thirty men. Clearly de Troyes could not capture it without artillery. However, he could not convey cannon in his canoes, and so made his decision to attack Rupert first. He had learned that the *Craven,* which St. Germain had earlier observed a few miles away, had sailed for Rupert. De Troyes' plan was to seize the ship before it proceeded on to its next stop at Albany. Then he could use it to carry the cannon.

He took sixty men with him, leaving the others at Moose Fort under St. Germain. Ste. Hélène and Iberville commanded an advance party, taking along an Indian guide, some food, tools and two small cannon removed from their carriages. A passing canoe party of Indians confirmed that the *Craven* was anchored offshore from Rupert.

De Troyes knew that he must move in stealth. He and the main party crept towards the fort in darkness, concealing their canoes in a small bay. Ste. Hélène returned to report that their objective was a copy of the fortress at Moose. No cannon were visible in the bastions and no sentinels. The ship was moored where the Indians had spotted it — directly in front of the fort.

De Troyes again laid out his plan. Iberville was given thirteen men and ordered to capture the ship. Another detachment, under a sergeant, would provide covering fire from the shore. Ste. Hélène would attack the main gate with the battering ram. Once the door was down, de Troyes would lead the main force into the compound.

Slipping silently along the shoreline in their canoes in the early light of July 3, the men moved into the attack. The battering ram did its work. De Troyes led his followers into the courtyard, the men firing steadily at all the slits and openings in the redoubt. Ste. Hélène, the best shot in the party, put a ball between the eyes of one of the gunners as he tried to load a cannon with glass shards.

As the musket fire grew hotter, the English within could be heard crying out for quarter. De Troyes accepted their surrender, whereupon the commander, Hugh Verner, "approached me in fear and trembling, clutching me by the arm as though he would be safe in my presence." (Again, a cheap adventure film comes to mind; even the ship, be it noted, was called the *Craven*.) "In this posture," wrote de Troyes, "I dragged him to the gate of the fort, where I asked him everything that I needed to know." Verner warned him against musket fire from the ship and was astonished to find that the *Craven* was already in French hands.

Iberville had boarded the vessel from a canoe on the starboard side while the crew and one sentry were snoring peacefully on the deck. The French stamped their feet to wake them up, then shot the sentry. A man charged out of the cabin; Iberville slashed him across the head with a sabre. The Englishman plunged on; Iberville gave him a second cut across the body. Meanwhile his followers had chopped holes in the cabin with their axes and were pouring musket balls through the opening. This brought a speedy surrender. Iberville locked his prisoners in the hold. De Troyes' captives, who included the newly appointed governor of James Bay, John Bridgar, were locked away in the hold of another abandoned ship, aground near the fort.

The men loaded five iron cannon and a good deal of loot from the fort aboard the captured ship. De Troyes then ordered one of his captives, a shipwrecked captain named Outlaw, to sail the prize back to Moose, while he and some of his men returned by canoe. It was a hellish journey. The fog was so thick that the canoes lost contact with each other. De Troyes, caught in "an abyss of waves," had no idea where he was. Reaching an unknown shore, exhausted and half-starved, the company lived on weeds to keep alive. One man, sent off to hunt for game, was never seen again. Finally, much weakened, the party reached Moose Fort.

There de Troyes turned his attention to his third objective, Fort Albany, which lay in the opposite direction from Fort Rupert. The journey by canoe along the shoreline was complicated by the fact that no one knew exactly where the fort was. Fortunately, the English had the habit of firing off their cannon at sundown and these muffled reports, carried over the waters, told de Troyes when he was nearing the mouth of the Albany River. He brought his canoes into shore and sent Ste. Hélène with twenty men to reconnoitre. Shortly after this, the captured ship, loaded with cannon, arrived with Iberville in command.

The next day, following Ste. Hélène's directions, the party moved up to a position not far from Fort Albany, which lay beyond the woods across the marshy river. De Troyes and ten men crept closer until they were a musket-shot away. Here the commander found a spot where he could set up his cannon. By this time his men were worn out and famished. Worse, the fort was aware of his presence and had fired off a warning shot; de Troyes would no longer enjoy the advantage of surprise.

He sent an interpreter to treat with the enemy. The French demanded the release of three prisoners captured the previous year (they had long since been freed) and the surrender of the fort. The governor equivocated. De Troyes called for the cannon to be unloaded, but unfortunately the sea was too rough to make that possible. There was some sporadic shooting: musket fire came from de Troyes' guerrillas concealed in the bush; in reply cannon balls from the fort whistled harmlessly over their heads. Stalemate.

At this point, de Troyes and his men were running out of food. Every hour now was precious. Fortunately the wind died down and he managed at last to unload eight cannon. On July 25, he fired his first volley at the governor's house, which had been identified for him by his English captives. It was the dinner hour, and the governor was at table with his wife and a clergyman. The governor's lady was reaching for a glass of wine when two cannon balls whizzed past her face. She fainted dead away. A servant leaned forward to pour more wine; a third cannonball passed just under his arm. He dropped his pitcher in terror. The man of the cloth dropped his glass. The entire dinner company hastily left the room.

The following day de Troyes, now in a desperate situation himself, turned all his light cannons on the fort. In less than an hour he had fired more than one hundred and forty cannon balls "which roasted the place on all sides." He was running short of ammunition. To keep up their sagging spirits, his men began to shout "Vive le Roi!" The English shouted the same phrase back, indicating that they no longer had the stomach to fight. However, none was prepared to brave the cannon long enough to climb out of the redoubt and strike the flag. One who attempted the feat was forced to dart back quickly.

De Troyes was out of food. To keep alive, his exhausted followers were gathering and eating Macedonian parsley, a weed resembling Queen Anne's Lace. It was their only food. At the same time de Troyes was attempting to make more cannon balls from a wooden mould. The fort, he knew, must be taken quickly if it was to be taken at all; and it must be taken by bluff rather than force of arms.

One of his scouts returned to report that a party with a white flag was setting out from the opposite shore. De Troyes hastily lined up sixty armed men on the shoreline to greet them. The others were ordered to bustle around the camp in the rear, making noises as of a large force.

He and Father Silvy went out to meet the English party. At its head was the Reverend John French, the first clergyman sent to James Bay by the Hudson's Bay Company. French informed de Troyes that the governor wished to speak to him. With magnificent aplomb, de Troyes replied that the governor could come to his camp in perfect safety — something he secretly hoped to avoid, as "I was scarcely anxious to receive him there for fear he would discover our sorry state." As expected, French suggested a compromise: why not meet halfway in boats in the centre of the river? De Troyes pretended to consider the matter, shrugged and, at length, agreed. The clergyman bowed deeply and replied that the governor would be ready in an hour. De Troyes retorted that he had better be ready in half an hour, or his men would root him out. The shaken envoy replied that the governor would come at once.

De Troyes left a few men to guard the base camp and marched the remainder to the battery of cannon he had assembled on the shoreline. He marshalled his men under arms in full view of the fort, with two cannon loaded and aimed directly at the redoubt and the rest ready with short matches lit to fire. Then, observing the articles of war to the letter, he picked the same number of men as were embarking from the far shore and set out to parley with the enemy.

The two boats met in mid-stream and cast anchors. Governor John Sergeant came aboard the French craft and, with great ceremony, opened a bottle of Spanish wine to toast the health of the kings of France and England. De Troyes and Iberville responded. The governor, who had brought several more bottles with him, wished to continue the ceremony, but de Troyes told him bluntly that he had not come to carouse, that he

299

was not short of refreshments and that if the governor so wished he might come to the French camp where he would be offered much better wine! In truth, all de Troyes had was a half-litre of brandy, saved for an emergency.

The parley immediately got down to business. The governor agreed to surrender the fort "under suitable articles of capitulation," meaning that the prisoners would be well-treated. The capture was effected with much pomp and ceremony and beating of drums. De Troyes immediately razed all four of the fort's bastions, rendering it militarily ineffective. He and his men were now in charge of the three English strongholds in the area and James Bay, for the moment at least, was a French lake.

Various arrangements, not all of them satisfactory or even humane, were made for the prisoners. (The wretched governor, Sergeant, was eventually charged with cowardice in London and dismissed from the service of the Company.) Iberville and Ste. Hélène were left to hold the Bay with forty men. De Troyes and the others returned to Montreal almost immediately and arrived without incident.

The commander's victory had been total and it was due largely to his own brilliance and organizational ability. New to the country, unfamiliar with the terrain, knowing nothing of the perils and limitations of canoe travel, he had picked good men, and organized them into a strongly disciplined force. Thus did the Chevalier de Troyes set the pattern of warfare in Canada for the next half century, until the Seven Years' War brought European generals and troops and more formal methods of conflict to the New World. Until the mid-1750s, both the French and the English were to use de Troyes' guerrilla tactics of "le petite guerre," in which lightly equipped troops moved through the wilderness, using surprise and ambush as their basic strategy — an Indian pattern that later helped give the North West Company an advantage over its rival in the struggle for the fur trade.

The forts on James Bay continued to change hands by treaty and cannon fire in the years that followed. De Troyes had no part in this long wrangle between England and France. Sent to command the garrison at Fort Niagara, he was doomed by the problem that had almost ruined him at James Bay — a lack of provisions. It is possible that he never understood the stringency of a Canadian winter. Whatever the reason, his garrison was isolated during the 1687-88 season without fresh vegetables. All but a handful of men perished from scurvy or starvation. De Troyes himself died on May 8, 1688, not much more than two years after he had set off into the north to humble the English.

Some of his comrades in arms fared better, notably Pierre Le Moyne d'Iberville, the most famous son of New France, the man who established the first French colony in Louisiana, who founded the modern city of Mobile, Alabama, and captured the island of Guadaloupe from the English. Part colonizer, part explorer, part pirate, part smuggler — seducer, entrepreneur, naval genius, adventurer — Iberville was the quintessential swashbuckler and his story is one of the gaudiest in all Canadian history.

But that, of course, is a different movie.

13

The Mysterious Safari of Charles Bedaux

It is not possible to contemplate the long list of luxuries that Charles Bedaux insisted on taking into the bush of British Columbia in the summer of 1934 without a small tingle of admiration. There was folly in it, of course; idiocy might be a better word. But the sheer *panache* of it! Here was a man reputedly setting out to explore country that was only partially mapped — country so rugged that it had defeated the Klondike stampeders with their iron rations of bacon and beans: country that had driven a party of Mounted Police to despair and exhaustion when they tried to hack a trail through it: a land of tangled forests, raging cataracts, gloomy swamps and chill mountain peaks. Yet Charles Bedaux had no more intention of roughing it than an Indian rajah setting out on a tiger hunt. The famous Nile picnic that the Duke of Sutherland once gave for the future Edward VII springs to mind: the provisions on that occasion included three thousand bottles of champagne, four thousand bottles of wine and liquors and twenty thousand bottles of soda water. The Nile is not the Rocky Mountain Trench, but Bedaux's own list of life's necessities, which he proposed to take into the Peace River and across the top of British Columbia to tidewater on the Alaska Panhandle, comes close to rivalling the Edwardian shopping list.

There was champagne, of course, cases of it; and French wines, both red and white, of good vintages. And case after case of those particular comestibles without which life would be scarcely bearable: pâté de foie gras and caviar, truffles and chicken livers, Devonshire cream and candied fruits. And the equipment! Fireproof tents woven from asbestos fibre; folding tables of aluminum; chairs, beds, bathtubs and patented washbowls; bush toilets of the latest design; nests of French cooking pots; rugs and cushions, tropical suits, cashmere sweaters, fur parkas and quilted pants, all of which Bedaux felt that he and his companions would require while roughing it in the bush. Twenty tons of gear and provisions! Entire armies have travelled on less. The Bedaux army consisted of forty-three persons, including a Spanish maid. The equipment was loaded into five Citroën half-tracks, and later, when these failed, onto no fewer than one hundred and thirty pack-horses. One horse carried nothing but ladies' shoes. Another was loaded down with a small library of French novels. If nothing else, Bedaux had style.

That, alas, is the only commendable thing about him. Had Bedaux been an engaging eccentric one might warm to him. Unfortunately he was a hateful man, apparently without humour, a martinet and a fascist, with all the bad qualities of a self-made millionaire and few of the good.

He was a creature of his period, a genuine Mystery Man of International Intrigue, the kind of shadowy figure that kept popping up in the novels of E. Phillips Oppenheim. When he died, by his own hand, the *New York Times* remarked that "there was an element of fantasy about his involved existence, a maze of loose ends, as there was about the lives of Sir Basil Zaharoff, Ivar Krueger, Serge Stavisky and Alfred Loewenstein." The *Times* went on to point out that Bedaux was the fourth of that group to meet with an unnatural end. Only the enigmatic Sir Basil died in bed of natural causes.

Bedaux moved in the same circles as these fallen titans — a world of international finance and government, of kingmakers and kingbreakers, of backstage manipulations and political wheeler-dealing, both democratic and totalitarian. His highly placed cronies included Herr von Ribbentrop, the Duke of Windsor and Pierre Laval. As John A. Macdonald once said of the Canadian steamship king, Hugh Allan, his only politics was money. In the end that would be Bedaux's undoing.

But when he arrived in Canada in 1934, few people knew much about Charles Eugene Bedaux, and what they were told, thanks to his own carefully orchestrated publicity, was all flattering. His lunatic escapade into the forests and muskegs of British Columbia was hailed by the Canadian Geographical Journal as "a scientific expedition made possible through [Bedaux's] . . . enlightened generosity."

Exactly who was this enlightened citizen? Where had he sprung from? How had he amassed a fortune so grand that he could afford a Fifth Avenue apartment in New York, sprayed daily with quarts of lilac water, an entire grouse moor in Scotland and a castle in France staffed by thirty liveried servants?

He was the son of an impoverished French railroad worker. At sixteen, he had emigrated to New York, with only a few dollars in his pocket. That year, 1906, he kept himself alive scrubbing bottles and glasses in a waterfront saloon. He moved up to a nine-dollar-a-week waiter; later he worked as a sandhog on the East River tunnel. He saved his money, became an American citizen, and focused what was obviously a first-class brain onto a peculiarly American problem: how to get people to work more efficiently.

Shortly before the Great War, Bedaux set himself up in Cleveland as a business efficiency expert and there he started to spread the gospel of what he called the B-Unit — a means of relating time to movement in factory operations. The B-Unit has been described as an efficiency squeeze system designed to exact the last ounce of sweat from the workingman; it was to make the name of Bedaux a stench in the nostrils of organized labour. It was also to make Charles Bedaux fabulously wealthy.

By 1920, the emperor of efficiency had moved his headquarters to New York, where he presently installed himself on the fifty-third floor of the Chrysler Building in an oak-panelled office got up as a medieval monastery. This was the centre of an international spider's web which soon reached into eighteen countries, where Bedaux's time-study experts offered advice and counsel to wealthy industrialists. Soon Bedaux acquired the additional adornment of a socially impeccable spouse in the person of Fern Lombard, the daughter of a Michigan tycoon. A lean and lanky woman, with a darkly handsome face, she towered over her chunky, bullet-headed husband. Bedaux was only five foot six inches tall, but he was determined to be a big man in other ways. His expensively tailored figure became a familiar sight on Bond Street, Park Avenue and the Rue de Rivoli. In his several homes on both sides of the Atlantic he entertained the moneyed elite. But these minor indulgences were not enough. Bedaux wanted to show the world he could do things that no one else could.

He had made two earlier expeditions through British Columbia in 1926 and 1932. In 1930 he drove ten thousand miles across North Africa from Mombasa on the Indian Ocean through the Sudan, Egypt, Libya, Algeria and Morocco to Casablanca on the Atlantic.

But these forays went generally unnoticed. Bedaux determined that the next one would make headlines and to that end hired a New York public relations man, Austin Carson, to build up press interest.

Why did he do it? Bedaux's most plausible explanation was that "I am just a nut who likes to do things first." A decade later, when his wartime connections with the Axis powers were revealed, some were to suggest, in hindsight, a more sinister motive. But Bedaux always insisted that his only interest was to challenge the impossible.

"It's fun to do things others call impossible," he said, at one of his press conferences. "Everyone says that to take a fleet of automobiles through the unmapped Rockies where there are no roads can't be done. I say it can. If I succeed, it will open up a vast region which has never been explored. The government hasn't much faith in me but I have done the impossible before."

Bedaux also talked of finding a northern outlet to the Pacific; about the possibility of prospecting for gold; about mounting big game heads for a Paris museum; and about testing tractors for Citroën, as he had done in Africa. Much of this was pure fantasy. There is no evidence that he did any prospecting or big game hunting. As for the Citroëns, he was soon to discover that northern British Columbia is not the Libyan desert. It was as if Rommel had attempted to fight a tank battle in the Alps.

Bedaux's route would lead from Edmonton to Fort St. John in the Peace River country of British Columbia, then northwest by way of the Prophet and the Muskwa rivers to the summit of the Rockies and thence on to Telegraph Creek and the Pacific. A good deal of this country was still a blank space on the map.

In February, Bedaux sailed to Paris to order the five tracked vehicles, especially built by the Citroën company for the venture. He had already engaged as his second-in-command an Edmonton geologist named John Bocock, who got clearance for the expedition from the British Columbia Department of Lands. The department also donated the services of two geographers, Ernest Lamarque and Frank Swannell, together with the princely sum of six hundred dollars. Since Bedaux was spending a quarter of a million on the expedition, this was hardly enough to pay for the chewing gum and cigarettes which Madame Bedaux handed out daily to the wranglers. For the hard-pressed department, it was a bargain — a heaven-sent opportunity to map some seventy miles of uncharted country lying between the Muskwa River and Dease Lake, mainly at Bedaux's expense.

In Vancouver, Bocock hired a surveyor, A. H. Phipps, and a radio operator, Bruce McCallum. In April, Lamarque took an advance party out of Fort St. John to mark the route, using small French tricolor flags as guideposts. Lamarque's party was followed by a second group of six men and fifty-six horses whose task was to hack a roadway of sorts for the tractors through the densely packed trees, brush and deadfalls. This party was led by a hefty Englishman, one Reginald Geake, a mysterious figure who seemed impervious to the elements; even on the coldest days he insisted on wearing khaki shorts and going hatless, his only adornment being a silk handkerchief tied around his head. A former British naval commander, Geake had ostensibly retired to Pouce Coupé in British Columbia; but his neighbours were firmly convinced that he was a member of the British secret service. The suspicion, never proved, was eventually given credence when Geake was mysteriously murdered in Mexico. No reader of Oppenheim could fail to be intrigued by the seedy implausibility of his demise: he was reportedly searching for gold in the company of a blind man.

In Edmonton, the remainder of Bedaux's polygot entourage was assembling. This included his Scottish gamekeeper, Robert Chisholm; J. A. Weiss, a professional Alpine guide from Jasper; Floyd D. Crosby, a movie cameraman from New York and his assistant; Charles Balourdet, the Citroën company's top mechanic; an Italian-Swiss countess, Signora Bilonha Chiesa, described as a big game hunter; Bedaux's wife, Fern; and her Spanish maid, Josefina Daly.

In June, Bedaux announced that this cosmopolitan assemblage would move to Jasper Park for "training."

"I suppose it sounds funny training for such a journey, but there's nothing like being fit when tackling something hard. We'll go up there and climb mountains and chase mountain sheep for a few days and that'll take the fat off us."

Much of the fat that came off must certainly have gone back on in the series of champagne parties and banquets that followed. In Edmonton, that June, the citizens became used to the spectacle of the newly arrived tractors, with their gleaming white paint and their nickel-plated accessories, rumbling around town on practice spins.

Finally, on July 6, the Bedaux Sub-Arctic (Citroën) Expedition was ready to depart. First, however, there was the inevitable champagne breakfast for Edmonton's upper crust; then, a full-dress parade down Jasper Avenue; and, after that, a farewell speech by the Lieutenant-Governor. When these civilities drew to their graceful close, the expedition rumbled off on the first leg of its journey — a five hundred and fifty mile run over a muddy, unpaved road to Fort St. John.

The tractors, spewing mud and pulling loaded trailers, crawled along at an average speed of four miles an hour. At the French-Canadian settlements of St. Albert and Morinville over the grinding of the gears came the sound of cheers. "Vive Bedaux!" the local citizens cried, waving tricolor flags. At Grande Prairie, the populace thrust up a ceremonial arch beneath which the mayor delivered a welcoming speech. And why not? It was the worst year of the Depression but Bedaux was spending good money for lodgings in small hotels and private homes.

The going was not easy, for that summer was one of the wettest on record. The fruitful Peace River soil, which has produced a succession of international wheat-growing champions, had already turned to gumbo, slippery as ice, thicker than glue. Clogged by mud, feed pipes and transmissions, differentials and brakedrums refused to function. Under these circumstances Bedaux was no longer the charming bon vivant. There was a nasty little scene at Tupper Creek involving a young dental student named Bill Murray who had been hired at the last minute. Bedaux was underneath one of the stranded half-tracks, trying to scrape off some of the mud. Murray was talking to a group of local girls. When Bedaux emerged, mud-stained, one or two of the girls made the mistake of giggling. Bedaux fired Murray on the spot.

Frank Swannell, the B.C. government surveyor, soon discovered that Bedaux was not really serious about mapping unknown country. When one of the tractors bogged down in a mudhole, Bedaux threw out a hundred pounds of Swannell's equipment rather than dispense with any of his own luxuries. As if that was not enough, the leader appropriated Swannell's surveying assistant, Al Phipps, and turned him into a personal servant.

On July 17, the expedition lumbered into the farming village of Fort St. John. Bedaux pitched his asbestos fibre tents in a local baseball field and, in a gesture which was literally flamboyant, attempted to set them on fire to prove their resistance. The locals gasped appreciatively; the well-heeled stranger was bringing prosperity to a town sunk in the depths of depression despair. He was offering four dollars a day (twice the going rate) to anyone who knew how to handle a horse, and seventy-five dollars (three times the going rate) for the horses. He purchased seventy-five animals and took on a dozen wranglers to handle them. That was merely the beginning: he had fifty steel tanks especially made in which the horses would carry gasoline for the Citroëns. Then he masterminded a farewell scene by his cameraman, Floyd Crosby, who had worked with the famous documentary film-maker, Robert Flaherty. Every one of the several score of men, women and children taking part in the scene was presented with a ten-dollar bill. It was estimated that Bedaux left something on the order of forty-five thousand dollars in Fort St. John; no wonder the Board of Trade threw a banquet for him.

The expedition was held up repairing the Citroëns until July 22. The departure, however, was delayed until three that afternoon in order to accommodate both speech-making and movie-making. The entire company spent an hour and a half standing in the mud of the main street while the newly broken ponies bucked off packs, riders and gas tanks. Indians arrived and were included in Bedaux's filmed epic. Finally, the expedition lurched forward for eight miles and at 9:30 p.m. set up camp.

The following day there was an altercation over the Citroëns between Bedaux and the French mechanic, Balourdet. The expedition had come to a stop before a small creek. The bridge was washed out and Bedaux, over Balourdet's objections, insisted that the half-tracks ford the four-foot-deep stream. The first car tilted over at a forty-five-degree angle and stuck fast. An attempt was made to bring the second one across on a floating bridge; it, too, tilted and was almost washed away. Finally, the crew set to felling trees to rebuild the bridge, while the two marooned vehicles were winched out of the creek bed and hauled across by cable.

The following day all five vehicles floundered in three hundred yards of swamp and had to be dragged out by cable. It took four hours to move one quarter of a mile. The front wheels of one of the trailers, overloaded with fourteen hundred pounds of winch and cable, splayed apart at the top of a slope; a day later it was ditched. The tree-cutting party up ahead had failed to cut low enough so that the tractors were constantly jamming their axles against raw stumps. On July 25, each car had to have a separate road cut for it through a swamp near Cache Creek. The day's run was no more than two miles and the tractors were in such bad condition that the company was not able to move again until the end of the month. In all that time they had moved a mere fifty miles beyond Fort St. John.

Meanwhile, to everybody's bafflement, Bedaux fired Bruce McCallum, his radio operator, his explanation being that the radio didn't work well enough to justify its extra weight, not to mention the food that its operator was consuming. As a result, the expedition was now out of touch with civilization. Bedaux attempted to solve the problem by sending back couriers from time to time with dispatches which were telegraphed from Fort St. John to New York and Paris. Without the radio, of course, Swannell could no longer get a Greenwich time signal and had to depend on the stars to chart the expedition's course.

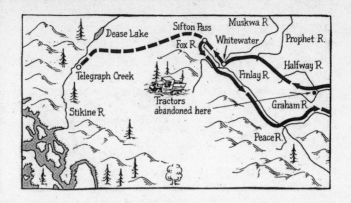

All this time Floyd Crosby was grinding away with his camera under Bedaux's direction. One would have thought that the problem rafting the Citroëns across the streams, hauling them out of muskegs, dragging them through the tangle of alder and willow, and winching them over precipices would have provided lively and dramatic fare. But the reality was not good enough for Bedaux. Over and over again he staged fictional scenes for the camera.

In camp, during that final week in July, for instance, one of the half-tracks was shown lumbering through the young poplars. Balourdet was at the controls while Swannell and Ev Withrow, the camera assistant, clung to the sidesteps, axes in hand, looks of grim determination on their faces. Al Phipps, Swannell's assistant, was then shown shouting a warning. As the half-track screeched to a stop, all the men leaped from it, dashed forward and began hacking a trail through the trees, watched by a band of baffled Indians.

The expedition struggled off again on July 31, leaving another ruined trailer in its wake. By this time the whole country was a quagmire. The rain never seemed to let up; in the first thirty-seven days, there were only

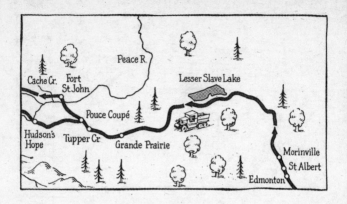

five which might be described as dry. On some days the tractors could not move more than a mile.

Clearly, this was not Citroën country and it was tacitly decided that the vehicles would have to be abandoned. Two men were sent forward on a two-hundred-mile dash to tell Geake and his men to stop hacking out a road for the tractors; a packtrail would be sufficient. Meanwhile Bedaux busied himself with more scenes for his movie, as Swannell's diary entry for August 4 reports:

"Afternoon spent by our chiefs in rifle practice. In the evening a movie by flares simulating a fire in camp. I dash across in frantic haste to save my tent — this is the cue for our buckaroo cowboys to drive the pack train in front of the camera. The others dash out of the tents with dunnage and Josefina finally emerges screaming. All went well except the pack horses stampeded and wouldn't face the flames."

Bedaux had conveniently glossed over the fireproof qualities of his asbestos tents.

On August 7, when the expedition reached the junction of the Graham and Halfway rivers, about ninety

314

miles from Fort St. John, it became clear that the tractors could go no further. The previous evening, Swannell had recorded "cooks quarrelling and everybody grumbling." But Bedaux intended to make the most of adversity. He spent the next four days making preparations for a spectacular movie sequence detailing the destruction of the tractors. He ordered that a rock bluff, rising a hundred and twenty feet above the Halfway River, be undermined. On August 11, two of the tractors were driven to the lip of the precipice and, as the cameras ground, the hill caved in and the cars made a spectacular plunge into the river as the drivers jumped free at the last moment and loads of empty boxes burst forth and spilled into the gorge below.

At four that same afternoon, Bedaux ordered his exhausted men to move the entire camp across the river. A frantic struggle followed to get the tents pitched before darkness fell. Everything had to be loaded aboard a raft and winched across by one of the tractors. It was 10:30 before the tents were raised but breakfast was scheduled for 6:45 the following morning because Bedaux was planning another movie sequence.

This time he set his men to work drilling dynamite holes in the cliffs above a series of rapids. Bedaux's idea was to place one of the tractors on the raft, slash the cable and then, as the raft smashed into the bank, detonate the dynamite which would cause the entire cliff to collapse, submerging the raft and tractor. The plan went awry: the cameras whirred away behind screens of brush but the raft missed the cliff, swung clear and charged down the river for some twenty miles before it came to ground on a sandbar. (Some months later the machine was salvaged by a local rancher.) The blasting was also a fizzle; in Swannell's words, "the drill holes merely erupting upward like squibs." For Floyd Crosby, however, it was a useful practice session; he

later went to Hollywood where he worked on everything from documentaries to horror pictures.

These minor setbacks did not appear to faze Bedaux.
If the tractor hadn't actually been swamped by a falling
cliff, it *ought* to have been. He reported all these spu-
rious incidents as genuine accidents. The drowning of a
packhorse became the drowning of a man. When one of
his wranglers, Jim Blackman, took a rest at a nearby
ranch, Bedaux, through his New York publicity agent,
blew it up into a tale of a cowboy gone missing in the
wilderness.

With the tractors gone, Bedaux bought thirty more
packhorses. He now insisted on military discipline.
Members of the expedition mounted their steeds at
Bedaux's cry of "Aux chevaux!" and dismounted on
his order, "Aux pieds!". The Prussian symmetry of
these spectacles was marred, however, by the refusal of
Madame Bedaux and Signora Chiesa to be hurried. The
ladies did not mingle with the common herd; the so-
called "big game hunter," in fact, vanished into her tent
as soon as it was pitched and there is no evidence that
she so much as shot a rabbit. The women's interminable toilets each morning, at the hands of Josefina the
maid, caused maddening delays. At first the horses
were saddled and ready at six, but when it was found
that they had to stand around loaded for hours, the start
time was advanced to ten. This did no good; the women
merely drew out their preparations and were rarely
ready to set off before noon. Bedaux made no attempt
to hurry them.

As the long train of packhorses struggled toward the
Rocky Mountains, the route grew rougher and mar-
shier. The animals began to suffer from hoof rot,
brought on by the constant immersion in mud; few days
went by without at least one being shot. When that
happened, some of the kit had to be abandoned, but

Bedaux refused to part with personal comforts. Several horses continued to stumble along loaded down with French wines, books and women's shoes. One afternoon, Bocock insisted that several hundred rounds of ammunition be discarded. Bedaux couldn't bear to leave it lying around in the wilderness; he had his cowboys fire it off into the air — "the craziest scene you ever saw," to quote Swannell.

On September 1, the party reached the Muskwa River and entered unmapped country. The mornings were chill and there were small flurries of snow. Bedaux decided that the time had come for his Swiss-born guide, Weiss, to make a quick reconnaissance on skis. Poor Weiss was forced to mount a horse every morning and ride in great discomfort with a pair of skis strapped to his back. The opportunity to use them never arose.

Balourdet, the elite Citroën mechanic, was now a man without a job. Bedaux put him in charge of the lanterns, a crushing blow to his dignity. The plight of the horses, scrabbling for meagre feed, worried him. Swannell recorded his concern, as the animals strayed farther and farther from camp in search of pasture: "Waire 'ee going, ze 'orses, for eating?" Sometimes it took four hours to round the horses up again in the chilly mornings.

The expedition had caught up with the trail-blazing party when it reached the Muskwa and now numbered forty-three men and women and about one hundred and thirty horses. The cowboys began secretly dumping whole cases of canned food, blankets, cook stoves and unused reels of movie film. On September 13, when Bedaux reached Whitewater (now Ware) at the junction of the Fox and Findlay rivers, he was clearly preparing himself for failure. Lamarque and an Indian guide had been sent ahead seeking a route through the mountains to the expedition's objective of Telegraph Creek. If they found one, they were to telegraph Victoria which would relay the message by a broadcast to Whitewater. But the deadline for the message passed without any word. Bedaux dispatched two of his men to rent some power boats and then led the party up the Fox River to Sifton Pass on his own, believing Lamarque to be lost.

The expedition reached the pass on September 19, trekked on through heavy snow to the Drift Pile River and stopped. Food supplies were low. Horses were being shot daily. Some of the men were reduced to ploughing along on foot because there weren't enough fit animals for everybody. Bedaux decided that all must turn back.

He did not, however, neglect his motion picture epic. Floyd Crosby and his helper continued to grind out scenes devised by their master. At the Fox Pass, the missing geographer, Lamarque, arrived back at camp to witness a mind-boggling spectacle: all of Bedaux's cowboys were crawling around the campsite on their stomachs as if in the final throes of fatigue. Lamarque was anxious to inform Bedaux that he could now lead the party to Telegraph Creek but Bedaux began shouting at him and his Indian guide: "Go back into the bush and come into the scene on your hands and knees." Lamarque stolidly refused to be part of the charade. As for Bedaux, he did not share Lamarque's enthusiasm for the rest of the trip. (The telegram had been sent to Whitewater but it had never arrived.) Six power boats were waiting on the Findlay to bear him swiftly homeward. It was a nine days' trek back through the snow and that was enough for him. On October 10, the entire entourage boarded the power boats at Whitewater and made the cold, dangerous journey down the Findlay and into the Peace River to Hudson's Hope (covering in thirteen days by water a journey that had taken fifty-nine by land). There the wranglers were paid off while

Bedaux and his guests left by truck for Pouce Coupé and the railhead.

Bedaux's retreat through the wilds of British Columbia had some resemblance to Napoleon's from Moscow. Dead horses, wrecked vehicles, tents, clothing, saddles, pack gear and cases of food littered the route. Some of the cowboys backtracked to salvage the more serviceable equipment. Bedaux himself, when paying them off, divided up the extra rifles, binoculars, stoves, saddles and cameras. Bert Bowes, the Fort St. John garage-owner, recovered four of the tractors. One served his garage as a wrecker until the early 1950s; another was employed all through World War Two as a tractor on a ranch. Parts from the others were used to reconstruct another which later found its way to a museum in Saskatoon.

Bedaux, however, still retained enough personal equipment to fill three trucks and two taxis. Bert Bowes' bill to move it all to the railroad station at Pouce Coupé came to two hundred dollars. Bedaux tipped him an extra fifty.

On October 22, at Pouce Coupé, the erstwhile explorer held a press conference in which he jauntily blamed the failure of his expedition on bad weather. He insisted that the original idea was sound, though he admitted that the Citroën half-tracks had not lived up to expectations. But some day, he prophesied, a highway would be built in the wake of the trail that he had blazed. In that he was partially correct; eight years later the Alaska Highway paralleled some of the same route taken by his expedition.

To Bedaux, this was a mere incident in a life crowded with adventure and intrigue. He followed up his British Columbia safari with later expeditions to India, Tibet and Persia. In 1937, he made headlines again when the Duke and Duchess of Windsor were married in his

château in the south of France. That same year he tried
to organize a tour of America for their highnesses; a
bitter outcry from organized labour, which attacked his
speed-up system and accused him of fascist sympa-
thies, caused his speedy withdrawal from the venture.
The charge of fascism was not hollow; later that year,
Bedaux rented a summer home near Hitler's eyrie in
Berchtesgaden and began to develop close associations
with several leading Nazis including von Ribbentrop,
the foreign minister, and Hjalmar Schacht, Hitler's
financial wizard. In the war that followed, Bedaux acted
as an intermediary between Pierre Laval's Vichy government and Berlin.

In 1941 he devised a plan for the German protection
of the Persian Gulf oil refineries from Allied bombing.
(The Germans had expected that Rommel's drive into
Egypt would be successful.) After the United States
entered the war, Bedaux gave the Germans valuable
information from the files of his international company
at Amsterdam. In the summer of 1943, he undertook,
on Laval's authority, to construct a pipeline across the
Sahara, which he had once explored in Citroën tractors.
Its purpose was to relieve the scarcity of edible oils in
the Reich. He had begun to assemble men and equipment for this task when the American army, in December 1943, overran the area and Bedaux was
captured.

He was arrested and flown back to the United States
just before Christmas, charged with trading with the
enemy. He was kept in a cell in the immigration bureau
where he regularly asked for sleeping pills to counteract
his chronic insomnia. On Valentine's Day, Charles E.
Bedaux was dead by his own hand, the victim of an
overdose of the hoarded barbiturates.

When the news reached Fort St. John, people shook
their heads sagely and declared that they had known all

along that Bedaux was engaged in espionage. "Looking back on it," said Bert Bowes, the garage-owner, "the man was obviously a spy." In hindsight the entire expedition took on a sinister aspect: the firing of the radio operator, the fake movie-making (no one ever saw the film), the strategic importance of the route itself, the presence of the mysterious Geake — all these bits and pieces of evidence were dredged up to bolster the view that Bedaux was in the pay of the Axis powers, trying to find out if Alaska could be defended successfully from the interior.

If true, the Bedaux expedition must have been the most expensive and cumbersome cover operation ever mounted and Bedaux himself must go down as one of the most inept spies in history. But the real explanation, surely, is simpler. Charles Bedaux, *circa* 1934, was exactly what he claimed to be: a rich nut who liked to do the impossible; a self-made success squandering his funds on a fantasy; a middle-aged man trying to capture a childhood he had never known, playing with grown-up toys like movie cameras and nickel-plated tractors; a five-foot-six egotist trying desperately, and not very effectively, to be noticed.

14

The Man Who Invented Dan McGrew

His log cabin stood directly across the dusty road from our own home in Dawson City. It was the town's chief tourist attraction. Each summer, when the visitors poured off the sternwheelers, they boarded a yellow bus, which drove them directly to the poet's shrine. We children lay hidden in the long grass, peering at the strangers who squeezed through the door. We did not think to enter the cabin ourselves; I was fifty years old and a tourist myself before I saw its interior. It was, after all, no different from thousands of similar cabins that were strewn over every hillside for fifty miles out of Dawson, empty monuments, all of them, to the days of the great stampede.

We knew all about Robert W. Service, of course. A special edition of *Songs of a Sourdough,* his first and most famous work, lay in the parlour, specially bound in fringed caribou hide with real gold nuggets pressed into the picture of a gold pan that was burned onto the cover. He had left Dawson forever almost twenty years before but there were scores who remembered him — the diffident young teller, weighing gold in the Bank of Commerce, the man on the bicycle peddling alone along the old Klondike road, the recluse, retired to his cabin, scribbling verses with a carpenter's pencil on rolls of wallpaper. He had escorted my mother to a dance in the days when she was a young kindergarten teacher; he had even read the newest of his ballads to her — the one about Blasphemous Bill. She had told him it was awfully reminiscent of the one about Dan McGrew. He had agreed; that, he said, was what the public wanted.

In school we recited Service's verses. They were as real to us as the grey river, rolling past the town on its long journey to the Bering Sea.

> The summer — no sweeter was ever;
> The sunshiny woods all athrill;
> The grayling aleap on the river,
> The bighorn asleep on the hill.

Tintern Abbey and Dover Beach were light years away, but every one of us had seen the grayling leaping in the cold Klondike waters and knew exactly what a bighorn sheep looked like.

> The winter! the brightness that blinds you,
> The white land locked tight as a drum,
> The cold fear that follows and finds you,
> The silence that bludgeons you dumb.

Which one of us had not stood, hip-deep in the crusted snows, high on those wooded hills beyond the town and *heard* the silence of winter? None of us had ever seen Wordsworth's host of waving daffodils (they wouldn't grow in the Yukon) but each of us had "gazed on naked grandeur when there's nothing else to gaze on." Service's verse grew out of an experience we all shared. I remember, for instance, reading the first lines of "The Telegraph Operator":

> I will not wash my face;
> I will not brush my hair,

I "pig" about the place —
There's nobody to care.
Nothing but rock and tree;
Nothing but wood and stone;
Oh, God, it's hell to be
Alone, alone, alone!

And I remember, at the age of six, drifting down the river with my family and encountering just such a man. I can see him now, wildly dishevelled, running down from his telegrapher's shack on the bank, pleading with us to stop, stay, have dinner, stay overnight, eat breakfast. Stay for days ... for weeks ... as long as we wanted. And when, after our brief meeting we had to move on, running along the bank, crying out: Don't go yet ... please ... You've only just come. Please, don't go!

Service, in his lifetime, wrote some two thousand poems. Four, at least, are imperishable — and that is not a bad record. These are "The Law of the Yukon," "The Spell of the Yukon," "The Cremation of Sam McGee" and "The Shooting of Dan McGrew." The titles are part of the language and the stanzas are shouted, declaimed, whispered, carolled, parodied and mumbled by men and women, drunk and sober, boys and girls, comedians and actors, from school stages, in church halls, around campfires, in front of microphones, at father and son banquets, stag parties, smokers, reunions, in moments of high carnival and nights of revel wherever the English language is spoken.

Of the four, "The Shooting of Dan McGrew," is the most familiar. It has twice been made into a motion picture, was the subject of the first original Canadian ballet, was parodied by everybody from Bobby Clarke, the Broadway comic, to Guy Lombardo, has been recorded close to a dozen times and lives on in several obscene versions.

Tens of thousands of people are convinced that the story is true and these have included a suspicious number of Klondikers. In February 1934, the Canadian Press interviewed, in Regina, one Philip Gershel, aged seventy-one, who claimed he was the Ragtime Kid of the ballad. "I knew Dan McGrew and all the others," Gershel declared and went on to describe the Lady That's Known as Lou as a big blonde, "tough but big-hearted — a grand lady." Gershel said that the incident had taken place in the Monte Carlo Saloon in Dawson City and that Lou was married and living in Sioux Falls, North Dakota. Two years later, Mike Mahoney, whose story was to be chronicled in a bestseller, *Klondike Mike*, announced that he, too, had been an eyewitness to the fatal shooting. "I was right there when it happened in the Dominion Saloon," said Mahoney, who claimed that Lou was still alive in Dawson City. In 1940, the *Toronto Star* published what it claimed was an authentic account of the shooting which, it said, took place in Dawson in 1897. In 1942, in a motion picture version of *The Spoilers,* Rex Beach's famous novel about Nome, Alaska, the poet is shown sitting in a smoke-filled saloon, actually writing about Dan McGrew. The version was given added credence by the fact that Service played the role himself.

The facts are somewhat different. There was no Malemute Saloon in Dawson, no lady called Lou, no Dan McGrew and no shoot-outs. Service made up the story before he actually saw the Klondike. Of all his verses it is the least characteristic of the Canadian north. It is pure romance, based on Service's boyhood reading about the American Wild West and his own experiences in the camps of the coastal United States. It irked Service that of all the poems he published, it was this first one that made his name. He himself had long since tried to forget it. "I loathe it," he said. "I was sick of it the moment I finished writing it." Yet wherever he went and was known, he was asked to recite it.

A good many people, including several Klondike historians, find it difficult to believe that Service wasn't within five thousand miles of Dawson City during the gold rush era. When the news of the great strike reached the outside world in July of 1897, he was a hobo in California. While others rushed north, Service headed for Mexico. For the next decade he was a drifter. In his remarkably vague memoirs (there is scarcely a single date) he tells us that he was variously a gardener in a rural bordello, a miner, a sandhog, a fruit picker, and a bum, eating food picked from gutters or begged at back doors or handed out at gospel saloons. Much of this must be taken with a shaker of salt. Service also suggested in his memoirs that he was raised in poverty in Scotland in a flat infested with rats, mice and cockroaches. This account so antagonized his several brothers and sisters that some of them were estranged from him. Service was not raised in anything approaching luxury, but the Glasgow district in which he was brought up was no slum. His grandfather was a postmaster, his father a bank teller. His mother inherited a small legacy and Service himself was weaned on the classics of English literature. After a spell as a bank clerk, he emigrated to North America hoping to be a cowboy in Canada, practising, over and over again, the quick draw from the hip with an air pistol. Instead, he found himself digging potatoes on Vancouver Island for fifteen dollars a month.

After the turn of the century, Service drifted back from the South to Canada. In 1903, he walked into the Vancouver branch of the Canadian Bank of Commerce, hauled out a dog-eared testimonial from his former bank manager in Glasgow, and was given a job. He worked successively in Vancouver, Victoria and Kamloops and then, in the fall of 1904, was sent to the bank's branch in Whitehorse, then a tiny village at the head of navigation on the Yukon River, some four hundred miles, as the salmon swims, from Dawson City.

For a man who was to become famous for his rough-and-tumble verse, Service presented a remarkably mild face to the world. In the hard-drinking Yukon, he remained a teetotaller, saving his pennies in the hopes of becoming financially independent. A lifelong agnostic, he agreed to act as a deacon in the church. A shy loner, he preferred solitary walks among the birches and aspens that fringed Miles Canyon, to the lively parties that whiled away the long winter. After his ballads were published Service had to face the astonishment of strangers who could not match his unassuming personality with the virility of his writing. ("His face is mild to the point of disbelief," one Canadian reporter wrote. And in Hollywood, the casting department at Universal balked at the idea of him playing himself; they said he wasn't the Robert Service type.)

At the church concerts in Whitehorse, the young bank clerk played the banjo, took part in amateur theatricals, produced a play and recited "Casey at the Bat" and "Gunga Din." Since childhood he had been attracted by the stage and all his life he revelled in role playing. When he first arrived in Canada he immediately donned a Buffalo Bill costume his father had bought for him. On a brief stint as a lumberman "I wore the rough overalls of the toiler, the denim shirt and heavy boots, but was prouder of them than I would have been of a suit from Savile Row." Each job, to Service, was a drama; and he tended to take jobs that allowed him time to dream. "The world has been a stage for me," he wrote, "and I have played the parts my imagination conceived. Rarely have I confronted reality. . . ."

In Whitehorse, with another church concert coming up, E.J. "Stroller" White, the colourful editor of the *Whitehorse Star*, suggested that, instead of reciting Kipling, Service might like to do something of his own. The idea appealed to Service; after all, in his younger days, he had written scores of poems, many of which had been published in Scotland; and in California, sitting around the hobo fires, he had sung many of his own songs. It was years since he had tried his hand at verse but he needed no prompting. Walking past the saloons on a Saturday evening and hearing the sounds of revelry a line popped into his head: "A bunch of the boys were whooping it up . . ."

The rest came easily. When he reached the bank (the clerks lived in rooms on the second floor) Service decided to seek the quiet of the teller's cage to finish his ballad. There, he tells us, a bank guard, believing him to be an intruder, fired a shot from his pistol, which happily missed. "With the sensation of a bullet whizzing past my head, and a detonation ringing in my ears, the ballad was achieved."

Service, who never let the truth get in the way of a good story, admitted in the last year of his life that this particular incident was pure hokum. What followed, however, was as dramatic as fiction.

Service was told that "The Shooting of Dan McGrew" was too raw to recite in church and so, believing it worthless, he stuffed it away in a bottom drawer under some shirts. He continued, however, to write verse for his own amusement. A month later he met a mining man from Dawson who, removing a stogie from his face, suddenly turned to him and said: "I'll tell you a story Jack London never got," and thereupon spun a yarn about a prospector who had cremated his partner. Everybody laughed except Service who saw it as the core of a new ballad. In a six-hour walk in the moonlight he composed "The Cremation of Sam McGee," borrowing the name of the hero from the bank's ledger of customers. For the rest of his life, until he died in 1940 in Beiseker, Alberta, scarcely a day passed without the wretched McGee encountering somebody who asked: "Is it warm enough for you?" As a result of the poem, McGee's obituary made the *New York Times* and his cabin, like Service's, became a shrine in Whitehorse.

Service tucked the new ballad away in the same drawer, then went on to write more poems until the inspiration ceased. Some months later he showed his work to the bank manager's wife; she suggested he might make up a little souvenir booklet of some of his poems for friends at Christmas. Service decided to squander his hundred-dollar Yuletide bonus on the venture and suggested to a Scottish friend that he take a half interest. With a single crude phrase, the canny acquaintance did himself out of a fortune: "Ye can jist stick yer poetry up yer bonny wee behind," said he.

Service sent his cheque and his poems to his father, who had emigrated to Toronto. The elder Service took the manuscript to the unlikeliest of all publishing houses, William Briggs, a firm that specialized exclusively in Methodist hymnbooks but which also did job printing on the side. There, an astonishing thing happened: the firm's own employees went crazy over Service's poems. The composing room foreman noticed it first: he had never seen type set so fast; the printers were actually reciting the verses at their machines. One of the travellers grabbed the first proofs and he, too, began to recite out loud. The Briggs firm scarcely knew what hit them; they received seventeen hundred orders for the book from the galleys alone. On the train west, in January 1907, their traveller, R. B. Bond, let his meal grow cold as he read the proofs, while passengers crowded around to hear him declaim. Briggs hurriedly sent Service's cheque back. The poet was chagrined. Shortly after, however, he received an offer of a ten per cent royalty. When the book actually reached Whitehorse, however, he was embarrassed; his own minister reproached him for writing about bad women. Only when the summer came and the tourists started to demand his autograph did Service and the town begin to comprehend his celebrity.

The book, published in Canada as *Songs of a Sourdough* and in New York by Barse and Hopkins as *The Spell of the Yukon,* ran into seven editions before publication day and twenty-four by 1912. Since that time it has sold close to two million copies. It helped make Service not just the wealthiest poet ever to come out of Canada but also the wealthiest writer of any kind. Within a decade he was hailed by the *New York Times* as one of the two best-known living poets in the English language, the other being Edgar Guest.

The publication of his first book rocked the literary world. Aesthetes such as T. P. O'Connor, the Irish poet, praised it. Shackleton the explorer took it with him to the Antarctic. Others attacked the author as a mere versifier, a writer of doggerel, a poor man's Kipling, pandering to popular taste. Service did not disagree, then or later. "Rhyming has my ruin been," he was to write, "with less deftness I might have produced real poetry." More than thirty years after *Songs of a Sourdough* was published, the author wandered into a lecture room to hear himself reviled in the course of a talk on contemporary poetry. When the lecturer had finished, Service rose from the back and said that he knew the poet in question and that he would be the first to "disclaim the imputation that he was a writer of poetry." Service never used the word poet to describe himself; he was, he said, a rhymer.

In the spring of 1908, to Service's delight, the bank posted him to Dawson. He arrived with the mail, which contained a royalty cheque for one thousand dollars; the resultant welcome by his fellow bank clerks was appropriately Rabelaisian. Dawson, once a city of thirty thousand, had declined to four thousand. Service walked the wooden sidewalks, trying to "summon up the ghosts of the argonauts," and listened endlessly to the yarns of men who had climbed the Chilkoot and prospected on Last Chance. In four months, working from midnight until three in the morning, he finished his second book, *Ballads of a Cheechako*. By the rules of literary success, this obvious sequel should have been a flop; it turned out to be another bestseller. First, however, Service became involved in a wrangle with his publishers, who didn't want to distribute the book at all because they thought the material too raw. He compromised and removed one objectionable poem in return for an additional five per cent royalty.

Ballads, which contains such classics as "The Man from Eldorado" and "Clancy of the Mounted," confirmed Service as a superb story-teller in verse. They have everything; the surprise ending, the humorous twist, the raw adventure, and, more than once, a whiff of the supernatural. Some of his openings are marvellously gripping:

> There was Claw-fingered Kitty and Windy
>   Ike living the life of shame
> When unto them in the Long, Long Night
>   came the man-who-had-no-name
> Bearing his prize of the black fox pelt, out of
>   the Wild he came.

Others, in a single line, caught the essence of the insanity that gripped North America when a ship arrived out of the Arctic with a ton of Klondike gold aboard:

> Gold! We leapt from our benches. Gold! We
> sprang from our stools
> Gold! We wheeled in the furrow, fired by the
> faith of fools.

Service was just far enough removed from the manic days of the stampede to stand back and see the romance, the tragedy, the adventure and the folly. His verses sprang out of incidents that were common occurrences in the Dawson of that time: Clancy, the policeman, mushing into the north to bring back a crazed prospector; the Man from Eldorado hitting town, flinging his money away and ending up in the gutter; Hard Luck Henry, who gets a love message in an egg, and tracks down the sender only to find that she has been married for months because Dawson-bound eggs are ripe with age.

This was not fiction, as "Dan McGrew" was. As a boy in Dawson I watched Sergeant Cronkhite of the Mounted Police, his parka sugared with frost, mush into town with a crazy man in a straight jacket lashed to his sled. As a teenager, working on the gold creeks, I saw a prospector on a binge light his cigar with a ten-dollar bill, fling all his loose change in the gutter and lose his year's take in a blackjack game. The eggs we ate, like Hard Luck Henry's, came in over the ice, packed in waterglass, strong as cheese, orange as the setting sun.

After *Ballads*, Service decided to write a novel based on the great stampede. Before he could begin he learned to his horror that the bank was about to promote him to manager of its Whitehorse branch. He did not want the responsibility and he did not want to leave Dawson.

After some soul-searching he quit. He rented a hillside log cabin (never realizing that half a century later, the Canadian government would restore it in painstaking detail and at enormous expense) and then began to walk the hills, soaking up atmosphere for the book.

He had no idea of the plot when he began to write. He lifted the name of the heroine, Berna, from the label of a can of condensed milk. He scrawled his story on anything that came to hand — copy books, typing paper, building paper, wrapping paper, wallpaper. After five months he had completed *The Trail of '98*, which immediately became a raging bestseller and was later a blockbuster of a motion picture, employing as many as fifteen thousand extras in a single scene. No one reads the novel today: it is a mawkish and saccharine piece of work. It is hard to believe that Service's New York publishers, Dodd, Mead, thought it too bawdy (a seduction scene had to be cut out) and that it was actually banned in Boston.

Service took the manuscript personally to New York, leaving it twice on park benches where, happily for him, if not for posterity, it was twice retrieved. His publishers were astonished to find their Yukon author looking so tame. "Why didn't you arrive in mukluks and a parka, driving a dog team down Fifth Avenue?" he was asked. "It would have made a great ad."

He did not return to the Yukon for a year. Instead he walked all the way from New York to New Orleans and then took a boat to Cuba, where he lived in luxury and boredom. It is typical of Service that, on reading a magazine article about motherhood one day, he recalled that his own mother, whom he had not seen in thirteen years, was now on the same side of the Atlantic, living on a farm near Edmonton. Back he went to Canada and jingled up to the farmhouse in a hired sleigh. One of his sisters answered the door. Service introduced himself to her as an encyclopaedia sales-man. His mother was not deceived: "Why," said she, "if it isn't our Willie!"

That spring he decided to return to the Yukon. Characteristically he took the most difficult but also the most romantically adventurous route — the "all-Canadian route" of the Edmonton Trail of '98. He travelled by stage coach to Athabasca Landing, by canoe to Fort McMurray, by Hudson's Bay barge to Fort Smith, by birchbark canoe to Great Slave Lake and then proceeded on down the Mackenzie by steamer. He crossed the Mackenzie divide by canoe and portage, slipped down the Porcupine to Fort Yukon on the steamer *Tanana* and reached Dawson on August 11, "with a face ambushed in an ebony thicket of three weeks' growth, nose broiled to lobster red, hands a Mongolian shade, trousers shredded," to quote the *Dawson News*.

The durability of Service's work was never better illustrated than by his composition, during this long trek, of a song entitled "When the Iceworms Nest Again." This is, perhaps, the best-known folk song in all the north. It has been quoted in various versions in several anthologies. For years there was speculation about its origin. In 1934, the *Northwest Miner* put it into print and credited it to Anon. In 1938, the Yellowknife *Prospector* published it and attributed it to a riverboat crew in 1919. I heard it sung in Yukon mining camps in the late 1930s, but nobody then knew where it had come from. The song was actually composed by Service and sung to the crew of the *Tanana* in that summer of 1911. In 1939 he published it in a book of songs called *Bathtub Ballads* his original version differing considerably from the one handed down orally over three decades.

Back in Dawson, Service settled down once again in the same log cabin, nestling under the hill on Eighth Avenue. Here he began to compose the verse for his third collection, *Rhymes of a Rolling Stone.* Another extraordinary bestseller, it was his Yukon swan song. In *The Spell of the Yukon* he had written: "There's a land — oh, it beckons and beckons. And I want to go back — and I will." But in the autumn of 1912, when the buckbrush on the hilltops had changed to purple, Robert Service took the last steamboat out of Dawson never to return. In the forty-six years that followed he never gave the slightest indication that he ever wanted to see the Yukon again.

By his own account, he continued to lead an adventure-packed life. The *Toronto Star* sent him to cover the Balkan war, where he also served in the Turkish Red Cross. He moved on to Paris, costumed himself in a broad-brimmed hat, a butterfly tie and a velveteen jacket and mingled with artists, models and writers of the order of Gelett Burgess and Jeffery Farnol. Of those days, he was to write: "Like an actor, I was never happy

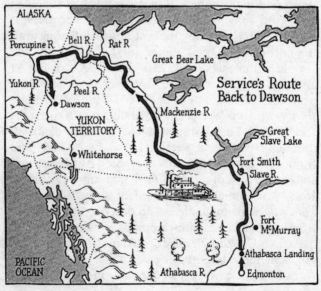

unless I was playing a part. Most people play one character in their lives; I have enacted a dozen and always with my whole heart."

In Paris, Service fitted easily into the role of an impoverished poet. One day in 1913, he rescued a young Frenchwoman from a mob after a streetcar accident. She married him without having the slightest idea who he was, shared his garret on the Boulevard Montparnasse and scrimped for groceries while he wrote his second novel, an autobiographical work aptly named *The Pretender.* She had no idea that her husband was a wealthy man until he took her on a bicycle trip through Brittany, knocked boldly on the door of a luxurious mansion, was welcomed by the concierge who had dinner prepared, and then revealed to her that he had bought the house with the proceeds of his verse.

In the Great War that followed, Service worked as a Red Cross man for the Americans and then as an intelligence officer in the Canadian army. During an illness, he produced another book of verse, *Rhymes of a Red Cross Man,* the most popular collection of war poems to be published in North America. In 1917 and again in 1918, it headed the non-fiction bestseller lists. It also received adulatory reviews from some unexpected sources. Several literary magazines hailed Service as the new Kipling. In *The Dial,* the poet Witter Bynner wrote: "We have been inquiring for the poetry of war. In my judgement, here it is." Service was rapidly attaining a respectability that he had never sought. The Norwegian journalist, Carl J. Hainbro, later president of the League of Nations, translated his verse into his native tongue and castigated his countrymen for ignoring the Yukon bard. Louis Untermeyer praised Service in *The Bookman.* "Like Burns," he wrote, "he took the curse off effeminacy in poetry."

By this time, even pale copies of Service's verse was bringing his imitators a modicum of fame. In 1921, *Vanity Fair* published "The Ballad of Yukon Jake, The Hermit of Shark Tooth Shoal." This parody of Service's style by a young Yale graduate was so successful that the magazine republished it in 1926 and again in 1934 and filled requests for thousands of photostatted copies. Eventually the parody appeared in book form and earned its author, Edward E. Paramore, Jr., an invitation to join the Adventurer's Club of Los Angeles, whose board apparently assumed that he was a seasoned Yukon explorer.

When Untermeyer published his *Collected Parodies* in 1926 several of Service's fans complained that he was making sport of a man who couldn't defend himself. By this time it was widely believed that Service was dead. Shortly after the war, *The Times* of London had published an article about writers and artists who had been lost in trenches. The Bard of the Yukon was included. Service did nothing to contradict the assumption; on the contrary, he was amused and a little relieved by it; there was less mail to answer. His French neighbours in Brittany and later in Monte Carlo had no idea who he was and he didn't bother to tell them. Meanwhile, he occupied himself by churning out more novels and books of verse — nine of them between 1920 and 1940, including a curious work on physical fitness — and by travelling the world from Tahiti to the Soviet Union. When he returned to North America in 1940, after fleeing France a few steps ahead of the invading Germans, Service began to encounter people who thought they were seeing a ghost. These included some of his own brothers and sisters. He had, by this time, forgotten how many of them there were (or so he says in his autobiography) and often failed to recognize them when they came up to shake his hand. Two of them, whom he met in hotel lobbies in Canada, opened with the identical salutation: "My God, Bob, I thought you were dead."

Even his two volumes of autobiography, *Ploughman of the Moon,* published in 1945, and *Harper of Heaven,* in 1948, did not entirely dispel the myth of his passing. In the postwar years, Service produced eight more books of verse to an ever-diminishing audience, but his original Yukon poems, anthologized and re-anthologized by his publishers under a variety of titles, continued to enjoy a healthy sale. He spent his winters in Monte Carlo and his summers in the same house in Brittany which he had bought years before for his bride. Money had ceased to have any meaning for him; early in the game, the one-time bank teller had sunk all his royalties into annuities. He had no idea what he was worth and he didn't care; his whole idea was to live as long as possible to beat the insurance tables. The health and physical fitness book *Why Not Grow Young,* which he wrote in the 1920s, long before its time, was republished in the 1950s. Among other things, it urged the consumption of vast quantities of potatoes; Service himself claimed to eat twenty-two thousand a year, a statement that even the most devoted follower must have found hard to swallow. None the less, he was a living advertisement for his own theories, a chipper octogenarian, still working daily at his typewriter turning out verse after verse.

I met him, at last, in the spring of 1958, when he had reached the age of eighty-four. The Canadian Broadcasting Corporation asked me to visit him in Monte Carlo and prepare a half-hour filmed interview for television. There was some difficulty in clearing the assignment since several members of the upper echelon were convinced that Service had died years before. A letter from the corpse, however, made it clear that he welcomed the proposal:

For me this will be probably a unique television show as I am now crowding eighty-five, and the ancient carcass will soon cease to function. For that reason I hope you will bring it off successfully. My home here makes a nice setting for an interview which if well planned could be quite attractive.

Patrick Watson and I arrived with a television crew in May. The poet met us at the door of his Villa Aurore, overlooking the warm Mediterranean. He was casually dressed in a sleeveless sweater and slacks, a small, birdlike man with brightly veined cheeks, a sharp nose and a mild, Scottish accent. We started to discuss the interview, but Service held up his hand.

"It's all arranged," he said. "I've spent the week writing it up. Here's your script — I'm afraid you've got the smaller part because, you see, this is *my* show!"

He handed me two sheafs of paper, stapled and folded. "It's in two parts," he said. "We can do the first part after lunch. Now you boys go back to your hotel and *you* (to me) learn your lines. I already know mine, letter perfect. Come back this afternoon and we'll do it."

I looked at Watson. This is not the way spontaneous television interviews are conducted. He gave a kind of helpless shrug and we left.

"What do we do now?" I asked.

"I guess we'd better read what he's written," said Watson.

What Service had written, it turned out, was pretty good — lively, witty, self-effacing, romantic:

I'm crowding eighty-five now (he had written) *and I guess this will be my last show on the screen. Oh, I'm*

340

feeling fine though I'm a bit of a cardiac. In middle age I strained my heart trying to walk on my hands. After sixty a man shouldn't try to be an athlete. Only yesterday I was talking politics to a chap in the street. I'm Right and he was Left so we got to shouting, when suddenly I felt the old ticker conk on me, and I had to go home in a taxi, chewing white pills. Say, wouldn't it be a sensation if I croaked in the middle of this interview?

When we returned Service was easily persuaded to submit to a less formal interview. But whenever one of my questions coincided with one in his script he gave me a letter-perfect answer — even to the line about croaking on television. Service, the actor, managed to make even that sound spontaneous.

We spent three days with Robert Service, his wife and his daughter, filming, in his own words, his own version of his long, checkered life, including, of course, the familiar story of how he wrote "The Shooting of Dan McGrew." In between camera set-ups, Service and I talked together about the Yukon. He remembered my mother very well and talked about Lousetown, the tenderloin district across the Klondike River. "We used to go down the line every Saturday night," he said, a little wistfully. I asked him why he had never returned to the Yukon. His wife and daughter had made a pilgrimage to the famous cabin during the war years when Service was in Hollywood but the poet himself had stubbornly refused to go. "It would be too sad for me," he said. "I wanted to remember it as it was." My own feeling is that Service just couldn't be bothered. The past did not intrigue him; he lived for the present. He never looked back, never reread any of his work, could not remember any of it. He did not even bother to read the galleys of his books; he paid somebody else to do that because he found them monumentally boring.

Only one thing concerned him and that was the work at hand; his greatest poem, to him, was always the one which he was in the act of composing. The Yukon, which had given him fame and of which he had written with so much love and passion, belonged to another era, it seemed, to another man; its spell did not grip Service. "Oh, it's too cold," he told me. "I'm a sun lover."

When the filming was completed, Service, with great ceremony, opened a bottle of champagne which he had been saving for the occasion. All during the filming he had been an enthusiastic interview subject, lively, loquacious, ebullient. "It's made me young again," he said at one point. "I'm just loving it."

Now, as we toasted him, he seemed cast down.

"Is it really over?" he said. "Haven't you got any more questions? I could go on, you know."

But the crew was already packing up the equipment.

"Oh, I do wish we could go on," said Service. "I wish it didn't have to end."

He stood in his dressing gown in the doorway of his villa and the wind, catching the silver of his hair and blowing it over his face, gave him an oddly dishevelled look.

"I wish it could go on forever," said Robert Service, and I caught, briefly, the image of the telegraph operator, running along the riverbank, pleading with us to stay just a little longer.

The interview was shown on the CBC television program *Close-up* in June and was a great success. Almost everybody commented on Service's spontaneous remark about croaking on television. Imagine him saying that! What a character!

It was, indeed, his last performance. That September, in Brittany, Robert Service's heart gave out and he was buried under the sun he loved so well and far, far from those cold snows, which he disliked so heartily, even though they made his fortune.

15

The Search for Gun-an-noot

There are no sad songs for Gun-an-noot, the invisible
Indian. No banjos or electric guitars twang out the tale
of his long exile in the mountains of British Columbia.
Ira Hayes had his Johnny Cash but Gun-an-noot, who
vanished for thirteen years, eluding all efforts to capture
him, has yet to find his balladeer. Perhaps it is as well;
he was a man of dignity and his saga would only be
cheapened by the simplicities of the country and western circuit.

Yet this is the stuff from which folk songs are fashioned: the story of a man who shadowed his own pursuers, who regularly managed to visit his wife and family, who sired five children when he was on the run from
the police. No one ever captured Gun-an-noot; when
the time came he gave himself up, voluntarily.

The song of Gun-an-noot would have to be in a
minor key. Beat the drum slowly for the Indian who
wanted to live like a white man but was forced to revert
to the ways of his forbears. Play the pipes lowly for
Simon Gun-an-noot, who triumphed over his pursuers,
but whose life, in its fullest flower, was wasted. Thirteen
years is a long time to spend in caverns and in canyons,
hiding out in the freezing cold of winter and the blast
furnace of summer. Gun-an-noot might have become
the most prosperous Indian in all British Columbia —
rancher, merchant, solid citizen. Instead, his life was

wrenched into a different channel. He was never to be the most prosperous; he certainly became the most famous. But for Gun-an-noot that kind of fame was ashes in the mouth.

He was a Kispiox of the Carrier Nation (so called because their widows carried the cremated ashes of their husbands' bones in a small pouch over their loins for two or three years after the death). His name, originally Zhumpmin-hoot, heavily Anglicized to make it pronounceable, meant "the little bear that climbs trees." He was born in 1874 in the village of Kispiox not far from the junction of the Skeena and the Kispiox rivers — totem pole country, some five hundred miles north of Vancouver.

For centuries his people had followed the customs of the Carrier Nation, a culture preserved as if in amber until the white presence began seeping through the forests, like ink on blotting paper. Now the loggers were coming in to hack away at the great cedars. White farmers were blasting out the stumps and churning up the soil. Roman Catholic missionaries arrived to give children Christian names — like Simon Peter. The members of the tribe began to wear the suits and sweaters of the white man, to abandon the old communal lodges in favour of single family shacks, to renounce the deliciously pagan ceremony of the potlatch. Simon Peter Gun-an-noot always wore his church medallion; more significantly, he began to believe that the best course for an Indian was to live as a white man.

In his childhood he had hunted and trapped on his family's traditional preserve, a hundred miles to the east at Bear Lake. But as he grew older he ranged farther afield until he came to know a vast area, ten thousand square miles in size, as well as most men know their own neighbourhoods. At twenty-one, he was a re-markable human specimen: six feet tall in his moc-casins, two hundred pounds, light as a cougar on his feet and just as swift. With his Winchester .30-.30 he was a dead shot. It was said that he had once killed a bear with a knife and that he could straighten out a horseshoe with his bare hands. Gun-an-noot, growing a mustache like a white man, inspired that kind of tale.

But there was more to Gun-an-noot. Unlike so many of his fellow Indians he was an astute businessman. When he brought his pelts into the Hudson's Bay store, he did not accept the first offer. He bargained for cash and if the price wasn't right, he went elsewhere; some-times he went as far as Vancouver.

He saved his money. In 1901, when he had enough to marry he took his bride, Sarah, and their first baby to Vancouver to buy supplies. Gun-an-noot had decided to embark on a venture that, for an Indian, was unheard of. He planned to open a store in his village.

He prospered. In the winter, the family closed the store and went trapping together. In the spring, they sold their pelts, bought more stock, increased their cash reserves. Gun-an-noot kept building up his equity; he bought a part interest in a sawmill, started a ranch on the Skeena, raised horses and cattle — a pillar of the community, until the world fell in on him.

In the winter of 1905, Sarah, newly delivered of her second child, elected to run the store while Gun-an-noot and his brother-in-law, Peter Hi-ma-dan, went trapping for the winter. They returned the following June, loaded with pelts, sold them for cash, and stopped for a brief celebration at the Two Mile House, halfway between the Indian village and Hazelton.

The community was then on the very edge of a boom. Real estate fever was sweeping the west, sparked by the construction of two new transcontinental railways. The

Grand Trunk Pacific was due to pass directly through Hazelton on the way to its western terminus of Prince Rupert. The little village of two hundred souls was swelling and changing under the impact of the newcomers, one of whom, Jim "The Geezer" Cameron, had founded the Two Mile House to cater to the hard-drinking trappers, hunters, guides and Indians. It did not matter to Cameron that the law forbade him to serve natives. He had two charges pending against him already for that offence and another for operating an illegal gambling house. He felt no compunction about serving Simon Gun-an-noot and Peter Hi-ma-dan.

The incident that touched off the saga of Simon Gun-an-noot occurred that night and it involved Alex McIntosh, a member of the Charleston and Barrett mule train, camped nearby at Two Mile Creek. McIntosh was a pugnacious miner and half-breed, known for his willingness to brawl. Late that evening he got into a fierce struggle with Gun-an-noot and Hi-ma-dan over some remarks he made about Simon's wife. Gun-an-noot mangled McIntosh's finger but took a bad beating in return. He left the tavern vowing to "fix" McIntosh.

Years later, an Indian boy, Peter Barney, was to testify under oath that he had seen the unarmed Gun-an-noot ride off north toward Kispiox village. Later, he watched McIntosh ride off in a different direction — west — toward the hospital at Hazelton to have his finger dressed.

McIntosh reached the hospital, had his injuries attended to and headed back toward the pack train camp. He never reached it. Next morning his body was found on the trail, some distance west of Two Mile House. He had been shot in the back, apparently from an ambush. A short time later another body was found on the opposite side of Two Mile House, about a mile and a half to the north on another road leading out of

Hazelton toward Kisgegas. It, too, was face up and it, too, had a bullet in the back. The corpse was later identified as that of a Frenchman, Max LeClair, one-time seaman, now a rancher and guide, who had only recently moved to Hazelton and was not well known in the area. A postmortem revealed that both men had been shot between six and seven in the morning and that the shots, to the lower spine, were almost identical.

Constable James Kirby of the B.C. Provincial Police immediately jumped to the conclusion that Gun-an-noot was the murderer. He did not bother to search for cartridges of bullets or possible tracks left by the killer or killers. He arranged for an immediate inquest and some twenty men with hangovers turned up that morning, their recollection of the previous night's events understandably confused. Gun-an-noot and his brother-in-law did not appear. This together with Gun-an-noot's threat caused the jury to name him as McIntosh's murderer. The jury believed that the two men were also probably responsible for the murder of Max LeClair.

Gun-an-noot, apparently, was convinced that he would not get a fair trial from an all-white jury in Hazelton. Yet it is doubtful that either Indian could have been convicted on the evidence, which was both circumstantial and flimsy. Certainly, both men had a motive for killing McIntosh. But McIntosh, who had a criminal record and was a known molester of Indian women, had many other enemies. Moreover, Gun-an-noot had been seen riding in a different direction, unarmed, from his supposed enemy. Even more baffling was the murder of LeClair, a mild-mannered man whom the two Indians scarcely knew and who was almost a stranger in Hazelton. LeClair had not even been present at the tavern brawl the previous evening. Equally confusing was the position of the two bodies.

McIntosh's corpse had been found west of the tavern on the Bulkley River road out of Hazelton. LeClair's had been discovered a mile and a half to the north on a different road. How was is possible for the same murderer to dash from one spot to the other and set up an ambush without being seen? Yet the nature of the bullet wounds suggested that both men had been felled by the same killer — an experienced and deadly marksman.

There was another curious occurrence which in retrospect seemed odd, though nobody thought to investigate it at the time. Jim the Geezer, summonsed once again for selling liquor to the Indians, vanished from town, never to return.

When Kirby and his deputies rushed to Gun-an-noot's store to arrest him they found that he and Peter Hi-ma-dan had fled. Unaccountably, Gun-an-noot had killed four of his horses. Why? Was it, as some believed, to prevent his pursuers from using them? But they had horses of their own.

On the way back to town Kirby encountered Nah-gun, the wanted man's father. Kirby clapped him into jail, hoping perhaps that this would draw the fugitive back into town. Then he set off on a two-week search, riding at the head of a posse in true frontier style, while a scene of pure farce was enacted back at the stockade. Kirby had deputized one Jake Ashman, a one-time coal miner from Nanaimo, to guard Nah-gun. The Indian sized up his prison and discovered that the outer wall of the latrine extended beyond the stockade. He told Ashman that he needed to use the outdoor facility. Ashman accompanied him. Nah-gun handed the guard his coat and vest, stepped inside the outhouse, closed the door, pried off two loose boards and slipped away into the mountains, leaving Ashman still holding the clothes and wondering what was taking Nah-gun so long.

With a fellow constable at his side, and six deputies close behind, Kirby was riding in hot pursuit of Gun-an-noot. Crossing the Kispiox River the posse was greeted by a chorus of howls; there, tied to trees, were Gun-an-noot's fourteen pack dogs. Kirby shot them all on the spot.

Constable Kirby mounted a series of searches in the summer and fall of 1906. All proved fruitless. The Indian Agency organized another party. It returned to Hazelton exhausted. For the next thirteen years, in spite of valiant attempts by much better men to smoke him out, Gun-an-noot remained at large, an invisible Indian, creating a growing legend. His hiding place was a vast rectangle, ten thousand miles square, a jungle of mountains and muskegs, lakes and trenches, rivers and canyons, plateaus and forests, stretching from the Nass River in the west to the Omineca Mountains in the east, from the Stikine in the north to the Nechako in the south. Gun-an-noot knew it as well as a taxi driver knows his own city.

The two Indians lived off the land, snared rabbits, shot grouse, deer and moose, angled for fish. Those who hunted them were not as mobile. The police carried their food in boxes; in wintertime when they could not use horses, they were forced to pack all their equipment on their backs.

Gun-an-noot did not lack for friends. In all those thirteen years no man, white or Indian, sought to claim the reward for his capture, even though it was raised from five hundred to twenty-three hundred dollars. The police, from time to time, tried bribery to discover the fugitives' whereabouts; the tribesmen remained totally loyal. One hundred skilled trappers roamed the Upper Skeena country; almost any one of them could

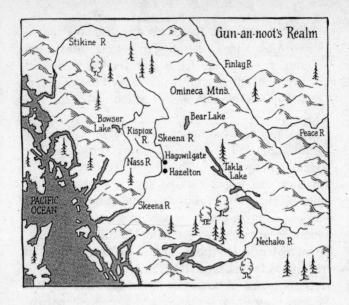

easily have brought Gun-an-noot in. Instead, their grapevine worked for him, warning him when his pursuers were getting too close.

On many occasions Gun-an-noot was able to slip back to his home to visit his family. They in turn spent more and more time with him in the bush as the years went by. Unlike most men on the run he was able from the beginning to continue to support his wife and children. He trapped furs and sold them through intermediaries, who passed the money on to Sarah. Gun-an-noot was even able to afford a tutor for his offspring.

Intensive efforts were made to bring Gun-an-noot to justice by a government that feared his example would have a two-pronged effect, first on other Indians who might be inspired by it, and secondly on prospective settlers who might be frightened off by the thought of a dangerous fugitive at large in the wilderness.

The most experienced woodsman in the service of the B.C. police, Otway Wilkie, was selected to bring back the wanted men. Wilkie, who had a reputation for successfully tracking outlaws, launched his first expedition in the winter of 1906-7. Although he plunged deep into the heart of Gun-an-noot country, as far as Bear Lake, and although he came upon several of Gun-an-noot's caches and talked to men who claimed to have seen the two men, he emerged from the bush convinced that further searching was fruitless.

However he tried again the following winter, mounting a double-barrelled attack with two posses, one of which moved south from the Upper Skeena country and the other pushing northeast again to Bear Lake, the traditional trapping grounds of the Gun-an-noot family. His men combed the shoreline by raft and found nothing. Wilkie, with three others, then headed down the Bear and Stuart rivers and, although he did not learn about it for another dozen years, almost captured his quarry.

The two fugitives were setting rabbit snares in a box canyon near the headwaters of the Skeena. Just as they turned to leave, they saw Wilkie and another man approaching the canyon's mouth. A few more steps and their pursuers would see their snowshoe tracks, leading into the defile. Hi-ma-dan sighted Wilkie in his rifle and cocked the hammer. On an impulse, Gun-an-noot stuck his thumb under the hammer to prevent his partner from shooting. It was a fortunate move. At that instant Wilkie stopped, spoke a few words to his comrade and then, unaccountably, turned away and vanished into the twilight.

Gun-an-noot had learned his lesson. Never again would he be caught unaware. He could not afford to have men stalking him. From that point on, he determined that *he* would be the stalker. As Wilkie and his partner struggled back through the blizzard to Bear Lake, two shadows followed silently in their path.

The winter that followed was ghastly. Game was scarce, the cold almost unbearable. Many times the two fugitives were tempted to surrender themselves to the warmer, better-fed searchers in the valley below. But the hunters were often in as bad straits as the hunted. "Constable Jack Graham returned to us . . . exhausted and half-frozen," Wilkie wrote in his journal two days before Christmas. "His snowshoes had gone to pieces, his feet are in bad condition, and it took him twelve days to make the return trip from the fourth cabin of the Telegraph Line."

By January, Wilkie and his men were almost out of food. Two prospectors gave them frozen goat meat. They searched Kitkeah Pass, the Kettle and Otseka rivers and returned again to Bear Lake, empty-handed. Frostbite was taking its toll. On January 31, Wilkie was forced to call off the search, which he called the most difficult he had undertaken in thirty years of police work.

The searches continued; but no one came forward to betray Simon Gun-an-noot. His friends knew where he was and could always find him. One of these was George Beirnes, a Hazelton rancher who packed supplies on the old telegraph trail. When Gun-an-noot learned that the agent who was selling his furs was not passing on a price increase, he persuaded Beirnes to act for him. He left his pelts in a cache along the trail and his friend picked them up at regular intervals.

The Great War came and the search for Gun-an-noot was temporarily suspended. When the Grand Trunk Pacific was completed through Hazelton to the coast the boom died. The British Columbia Provincial Police moved their headquarters out of the Hazelton district to Smithers. Kirby had long gone. A new and different kind of policeman, Sergeant Sperry "Dutch" Cline, was in sole charge of the Hazelton post.

Cline had lived in Hazelton for years before joining the police in 1914. One of his first moves was to take down the faded *WANTED* poster that had hung in the office for so long. He was trying to change the official attitude to make it easier for Gun-an-noot to come in. He stopped the badgering of Gun-an-noot's fellow tribesmen and he began to let slip a few complimentary remarks about the fugitive.

George Beirnes was also working on Gun-an-noot. In 1917, with the Indian's permission, he began to explore the possibilities of a surrender, taking Cline into his confidence. Cline gave him some advice: tell Gun-an-noot to get a good lawyer.

An ingenious plan now began to take shape with Cline, Beirnes and Stuart Henderson of Victoria as co-conspirators. Henderson was the leading criminal lawyer in the province, the son of a Scottish stonecutter, who specialized in defending Indians. With Gun-an-noot's permission, Cline and Beirnes had approached him to conduct the Indian's defence, when and if he should decide to surrender. Their idea, brilliant in its simplicity, was that Beirnes would "capture" Gun-an-noot, claim the twenty-three hundred dollar reward and turn it over to Henderson for his legal fees.

But Gun-an-noot refused to go through the charade of a faked capture. If he came in, he said, it would be of his own free will. That meant that he would have to trap for furs to pay for his own defence.

Two more years passed before Gun-an-noot was prepared to give in. Finally, on June 24, 1919, Beirnes and Henderson rode out to an abandoned cabin at Poison Mountain where Gun-an-noot was waiting. When the party reached Hazelton, Gun-an-noot insisted on riding alone to the police post. Cline that week had been called to a trial at Prince Rupert, and Constable John Kelly was sent from Smithers to replace him. The constable could not resist a nervous glance at the gun rack. Gun-an-noot reassured him: "You have nothing to fear," he said. "If I wanted to kill you, I could have shot you many times on the trail."

He was lodged in the Hazelton jail. Cline returned from Prince Rupert to find that his prisoner, after thirteen years in the open wilds, was suffering from claustrophobia. When Kelly put him into the cell he had broken out in a cold sweat, soaking himself so thoroughly that he needed a change of clothing. In return for Gun-an-noot's word of honour not to attempt an escape Cline stopped locking the jail. One night he discovered that it had been locked by accident. He rushed through the building, unbolted the door as quietly as possible and then walked into the cell where Gun-an-noot was sitting. Cline always remembered the spectacle that confronted him.

"He was crouched like a caged beast ready to spring, eyes aflame, every muscle tensed. I realized that I had to do something and do it quickly. So I turned my back to him and said, 'We're keeping the back door open, now. Come, I'll show you the way out . . . I guess Mr. Kelly forgot to tell you.' " Gun-an-noot followed him out into the yard and Cline left him there to relax.

Henderson had the trial moved to Vancouver, away from the passions that the murders had inspired in Hazelton. The charge was the murder of McIntosh, but the verdict was a foregone conclusion. Out of the past came a host of witnesses. Peter Barney helped to bury the case when he testified that the accused and his alleged victim had ridden off in opposite directions after leaving Two Mile House. Henderson did not put Gun-an-noot on the stand.

In his summation to the jury, Henderson said: "The prisoner has already been punished for a crime he did not commit by thirteen years of exile in a harsh northern wilderness. Throughout that time he has provided for his family. He endured an exile because he was afraid he would not receive justice in a white man's courtroom. It remains for you, the jury, to prove to him his fears were groundless."

The jury took fifteen minutes to acquit. Peter Hi-madan, who surrendered a few months later, was freed following a preliminary hearing in Hazelton.

That is the gist of the story that I told in the original edition of *My Country*. But in a sense the story was unsatisfactory because several questions nagged. Who really killed the two men? Was there one murderer or two? What, if any, was the connection between McIntosh and LeClair? And if no connection, how was it that both were murdered in identical fashion within an hour? And why did Gun-an-noot kill all his horses?

Then, in the spring of 1977, I learned that Gun-an-noot's son David felt the time had come to tell the real story. But what *was* the real story? To find out I had to travel to the little mining town of Stewart, which nestles below the mountains at the head of the long Pacific fiord known as the Portland Canal. And there in the King Edward Hotel I found myself sitting on the edge of my chair listening to the eloquence of David Gun-an-noot who is also, by virtue of his mother's lineage, Chief Legap of the Gitksan band of the Carrier Nation.

I found him to be a remarkable man — a man who had never had a single day of schooling because he was brought up in the wilderness. "My teacher," he told me "was an old gramophone." He learned English by playing old records over and over again and he taught himself to read by buying the appropriate sheet music and fitting the syllables of the lyrics to the recorded sounds. All his active life was spent out of doors. Until his mid-sixties he trapped and hunted for a living. Less than a decade before he had been alert enough and bold enough to accomplish the almost impossible feat of stopping an attacking grizzly bear while armed only with a .22 rifle.

At 71, he was suffering from heart trouble and was partially deaf and half blind. But when he told his story he did it without faltering and with none of those rambling excursions from the narrative that so often characterize the reminiscences of the aged. The oral tradition is engrained in his people. His voice, which tended to waver in ordinary conversation, grew stronger as he talked so that the tale, complete with dialogue, emerged with force and drama.

In the winter of his life, David Gun-an-noot wanted to tell at last the account his mother gave to him more than half a century ago, when she swore him to secrecy.

And what is the secret? The secret is that his father did it — did it and was proud of it; killed both McIntosh and LeClair and got away with it; changed the mode of his life only in degree: walked boldly down the streets of Hazelton and of Kispiox, the Indian village; shopped for rum at the Hudson's Bay post; lived on his ranch at Kisgegas; fathered a clutch of children, only one of whom (contrary to legend) failed to survive in the wild; trapped, hunted, and sold his furs to buyers who knew exactly who the vendor was.

David Gun-an-noot's account begins on that May night, seventy-one years ago, with his father walking into the Two Mile House hoping to buy some spring salmon. The place is crowded. Gun-an-noot does not really want a drink, but his pockets are full of money from the sale of his winter's catch and the women are imploring him to stand round after round of drinks.

The evening grows boisterous. McIntosh, the packer, begins to pick on Peter Hi-ma-dan, who has preceded his brother-in-law to the tavern. There is a struggle. Peter is knocked to the ground. Gun-an-noot intercedes, whereupon McIntosh pulls a knife and taunts him.

"I can sleep with your wife any time," David Gun-an-noot quotes him as saying, and the words hiss from his lips as he recreates the incident. "You'll never do anything about it. You'll never scratch my skin!"

A struggle follows; McIntosh goes down, but not before his knife has bloodied the Indian's face. More taunts by McIntosh about Sarah Gun-an-noot follow. Hi-ma-dan tries to break up the fight but by now his brother-in-law is in a fury.

"Before the light comes you'll be frozen blood!" he shouts at McIntosh.

"Run!" says Hi-ma-dan to the packer. "You better run! Hide! When he makes a promise you can bet he's going to keep it. He don't miss his promise!"

"Fuck him!" says McIntosh. "Fuck him! You'll never see an Indian scratch a white man's skin."

"He'll scratch your skin alright," Hi-ma-dan warns as he and Gun-an-noot leave the tavern. "You better go."

But McIntosh stays while Gun-an-noot rides to Kispiox village a couple of miles to the north.

Simon Gun-an-noot is in a black rage. He enters his house, seizes a rifle and mounts his favourite horse, Frank. There is no doubt that he wants to have it out with McIntosh. His sister-in-law Christine, Peter Hi-ma-dan's wife, fears the worst. She has managed to twist and loosen the cinch on Frank's saddle so that when Simon mounts the saddle turns turtle and he tumbles to the ground. This only increases his fury. The horses, startled, scatter. Simon seizes his rifle and shoots four of them. He mounts the fifth and dashes off toward Two Mile House.

Now, David explains, the tavern lies on the arm of a dog leg in the road between Hazelton and Kispiox. But a trail through the bush, wide enough for a single rider, acts as a short cut. Gun-an-noot takes the short cut and emerges on the main road west of Two Mile House.

Fate now takes a hand. If Alex McIntosh had not come riding past at that exact moment on his way back from the hospital, if he had stopped to argue when Gun-an-noot shouted at him, he might have lived, or so David Gun-an-noot believes. But when Gun-an-noot cries: "Alex! Stop! Remember what I told you!" McIntosh spurs his horse and the Indian, his fury increasing, drops him with a single shot.

Gun-an-noot turns back along the short cut, emerging again on the Kisgegas Road well to the north of Two Mile House. Again chance decides the course of events. At that exact moment Max LeClair comes driving past on a buckboard. He sees the blood from MacIntosh's knife drying on Gun-an-noot's cheeks and, without thinking, taunts him: "Hey, you Indian! Fighting again, eh? Look at the blood on your face."

It is too much. Gun-an-noot raises his rifle and shoots LeClair dead. Thus begins the long exile of Simon Gun-an-noot and his family.

Yet, in David Gun-an-noot's telling, it is not quite the ordeal that most writers, including this one, have described. One must tread warily here. For his first thirteen years David knew no other kind of life. He did not know his father was a fugitive. For a long time he thought everybody in the world lived in tents warmed by B.C. heaters. The family thought nothing of moving a hundred miles in a single day, sometimes directly across mountain ranges. What would be a harrowing ordeal for a city-bred boy was, for him, a normal existence.

After the murder, they lost no time in leaving the Hazelton area, fleeing to the ranch at Kisgegas, more than fifty miles to the north. More than once Gun-an-noot doubled back on the trail to smoke out pursuers.

"What are you going to do — shoot them?" Sarah asked.

"Only if they put a gun on me," he told her. His son remembers that he always carried a 9 mm. pistol stuffed into his belt.

Gun-an-noot's father, Nah-Gun, so David Gun-an-noot believed, had been purposely allowed to escape in the hope that he would lead the police to the wanted men. But Nah-Gun, realizing he was being followed, hid in a hollow cottonwood log, evaded his pursuers and made his way to the ranch at Kisgegas. Here Gun-an-noot built a raft, took his entire family across the swollen Skeena, hacked a trail through the mountains and vanished.

The remarkable thing, in David Gun-an-noot's telling of the tale, is not so much that this tight group of men, women and children survived for thirteen years in the wilderness; it is that they spent so much of their time in civilization. David remembers wondering why his father always cast a careful eye about him when emerging from the woods onto a river bank; but he also remembers the later years when the entire family moved freely about in Kispiox and Hazelton.

Once, walking down the main street of Hazelton, Gun-an-noot almost ran into two of the Pinkerton detectives hired to flush him out of hiding. They did not recognize him but the Indian, taking no chances, vaulted a fence and vanished.

In Kispiox, David remembers, his father actually held an auction in order to get the best prices for his furs. The Hudson's Bay Company sent two buyers who bid against an independent. The Bay won. And Gun-an-noot also bought rum by the keg from the Hudson's Bay store, slipping in by the back door after dark. Meanwhile members of his family became familiar figures in Hazelton and Kispiox picking up groceries and other supplies.

Nobody ever turned them in. Early in the chase, two of Kirby's Indian deputies actually caught up with the fugitives. David's grandmother's remark at the time was told with great relish in later years to the younger children.

"Better pack your blankets and go home," she warned the two. "Or your shit will be cold by morning." They took her advice.

Gun-an-noot's most brazen public appearance took place when the first silent movie came to Hazelton in the days before the Great War. Everybody was talking about the new device that flashed moving pictures onto a white screen. Gun-an-noot could not contain his curiosity. He had his hair cut and his mustache trimmed. Then he bought himself a new suit, a good white shirt and a smart tie. Thus attired, he marched boldly into the movie house and saw the picture. All around him people were asking in whispers who the distinguished-looking stranger might be.

The family's headquarters was the ranch at Kisgegas on the Skeena. But their life was nomadic. They moved to Bowser Lake in the west, to Bear Lake in the east, crossing torrents, canyons, swamps and mountain peaks in the way city people cross roadways. When babies were born in the wilderness, Sarah slung them in a blanket and the family moved on.

David has never forgotten the day his father gave himself up. Though there had been negotiations with George Beirnes and the lawyer, Stuart Henderson,

David Gun-an-noot believes that his father's ultimate decision to surrender was again triggered by pride, as the murders were. He had been, so David remembers, taunted by a fellow Indian, Moses Slamgeest. By 1919 his legend had assumed superhuman proportions and it may well be that the tale of the phantom Indian was used to frighten small children. At any rate, Moses was heard to sneer at Gun-an-noot, behind his back, in Kispiox.

"What's the use of him running around scaring people?" he asked. When those words came back to Gun-an-noot, the fugitive picked up a gun, rode into the village and confronted Moses, who promptly shut up. But the taunt rankled and one day Simon told his family: "I'm going to give myself up. I'm tired of people making up stories behind my back. If they're going to hang me, well, let them hang me. I've got to die some time."

David Gun-an-noot, aged 13, clung to his father.

"No, no" he cried. "I'm not going to let these white men hang you up."

"You're too young to understand," his father replied. "Look how many years it's been. You'll never fit into my tracks. You'll never be like that."

"For all my life," David Gun-an-noot told me, "I have remembered those words."

Most of the rest of the story is on the record. David remembers his mother telling him: "You're not going to live in this tent no more. You're going to sleep in a house and you're not going to use that candle no more. You're going to use a lamp on the wall."

In David Gun-an-noot's account the years that followed differed only in degree from the earlier ones. His father trapped at Bear Lake, and the family spent much of their time at Kisgegas. Gun-an-noot died in 1933, not of tuberculosis, as some have said, but of pneumonia, caught on the winter trail after his dogs broke away to chase a bear, leaving him alone without blankets or matches.

"I don't want to be buried in a town," said Simon Gun-an-noot. Appropriately, they were his last words. At his own request his tribesmen carried his body to the lake and laid it to rest beside that of his father, Nah-gun. Even then, Gun-an-noot's domain remained isolated from the world; it took four months for the news of his death to percolate out to civilization.

It remains wild, untravelled country to this day, far off the beaten tourist pathways, unmarred by asphalt, unscarred by campfires. Here the invisible Indian's name lives on in Mount Gun-an-noot and in Lake Gun-an-noot and in the legends of the Kispiox, who do not need a pinpoint on a map to honour his memory. It probably would not matter to Gun-an-noot that a mountain and a lake were chosen to mark his passage, though it might have amused him; during his lifetime all of the lakes and the mountains were his. Still, one can be certain that he would have preferred these natural monuments to the ephemeral accolade of a folk song in the Top Fifty.

16

Blondin Walks Niagara's Gorge

It is a commonplace to remark that Niagara Falls attracts daredevils the way raw meat attracts bluebottles. From Sam Patch in 1829 through Red Hill and his notorious barrel in 1910, to the final, tragic tomfoolery of Red's son in his impossibly pneumatic vessel in 1951, the Falls and its gorge have been a magnet for assorted stunt artists, daredevils, mercenary acrobats and plain nuts. Men and women have minced across the chasm on tightropes, plunged over the cataract in barrels, shot the rapids and the whirlpool in all manner of queer craft, and even tried to swim the foaming torrent. Some have lived, some have perished; but only one man can be said to have reaped the expected harvest of fame and fortune. He was born Jean François Gravelet, but all the world knew him as Blondin.

In the summers of 1859 and 1860, the Prince of Manila, as he was then called, made his way across the boiling chasm on fifteen hundred feet of taut rope cable — not just walking gingerly, but in every possible fashion, skipping, dancing, somersaulting, pretending to slip, hobbled, chained, swathed in sacking, wearing buckets for boots, even carrying a terrified man on his back while, far below, tens of thousands of upturned faces gawped and gasped, Victorian ladies fainted gracefully away, gamblers placed fivers on the certainty of horrible death, and everybody who was anybody from ex-president Millard Fillmore to the Prince of Wales sobbed in terror, sighed in relief and cheered in unison, as the Monarch of the Cable, clad in pink tights, mastered Niagara's gorge.

It was Niagara that made Blondin. Ever after, when he toured the world in a huge roofless tent, rendering heathens and Christians alike sick at the stomach with his feats, it was the memory of the Falls that drew the crowd. In the great central transept of London's Crystal Palace immediately following his Canadian triumph he performed on a rope stretched high above the cascading fountains to simulate the spectacle at the gorge. He was the Hero of Niagara on the billboards and he caused such a furore that one woman tried to commit suicide because her husband would not take her to see Blondin joust with death. For that was the secret of his act: had he stretched his rope a few feet above the ground, or draped a net beneath him, few would have cared. What the crowd wanted was blood, or at least the possibility of blood — the vision of a mangled body hurled from on high. Blondin gave them their money's worth. There were few performances in which he did not seem to totter from his perch.

"Horror!" wrote a journalist with the uncommon by-line of Albany Fonblanque, Jun., after viewing Blondin's imitation of Niagara at the Crystal Palace in 1861. "We have seen enough (we are not ashamed to own it) to set our pulses thumping painfully, to send a cold, sickening terror crawling along our veins, to make us very glad to look anywhere but at that figure on the rope. . . ." As the writer turned from the nerve-wracking spectacle, ladies fainted dead away, while "several others had their faces in their hands, and many a strong man averted his gaze from sight."

The man who inspired all this exquisite terror — the "dilated eyes, quivering lips, clenched hands, loudly beating hearts" — had been an acrobat since the age of five when, inspired by a circus stunt, he tied a rope to the backs of two chairs and tried to walk on it. The little boy, born in 1824 at St. Omer of an acrobat father, promptly tumbled off. But he persevered; a gatepost, a stouter cord, a fishing pole for balance were all called upon until eventually he succeeded, showing such natural talent that his parents were pleased to enroll him in the Ecole de Gymnaste at Lyons. There, after only a few months' instruction, he made his first public appearance as "The Little Wonder."

Within a few years the boy had become a distinguished member of various European acrobatic troops, known under his stage name of Blondin, having inherited both the sobriquet and the flaxen hair from his father. He was an accomplished somersaulter and jumper, able to leap with ease over a double rank of soldiers. That, by itself, did not titillate the audience; it was the rifles with fixed bayonets, which seemed almost to scrape his buttocks, that caused the gasps of appreciation.

In Paris in 1851, when Blondin was twenty-seven, the celebrated gymnast, Gabriel Ravel, offered to take him to America. Blondin signed a two-year contract, which was later extended to eight years. En route to America a storm sprang up and a young nobleman was swept overboard; Blondin leaped into the waves and saved his life. It was a propitious beginning.

It is said that Blondin invented the tightrope. Until he came along acrobats wobbled precariously on a swaying slack wire. By the time he had his first view of the Falls, in 1858, he was an accomplished master of the new medium. His troupe had been appearing in Buffalo, and Blondin visited Niagara with Ravel on his

Sunday off. Standing on the dizzy edge of the gorge and looking down into the maelstrom, he turned to his colleague and remarked: "What a splendid place to bridge a tightrope."

At first Ravel thought he was joking. It took him some time to realize that Blondin, who was now casting his eyes about seeking a likely anchoring spot for the rope, was in deadly earnest. Ravel had horrible visions of his premier attraction disappearing into the mists of the canyon. There were heated words: *Idiot! Fou! Dément! Dérangé!* Blondin pretended to drop the idea. He knew that his contract was up the following year and was prepared to bide his time. But as soon as the trumpets sounded the finish of his last performance he headed straight for Niagara.

First, he had to find a suitable site for his exhibition. After considerable reconnaissance he decided to string his rope from a plot on the American side known as White's Pleasure Ground over to the Clifton House on the Canadian side. There were diplomatic difficulties caused by the British consul, who insisted on getting permission from the Foreign Office before Blondin was allowed to kill himself. The Foreign Office, however, remained silent and the Englishman yielded; he would pretend, officially, that nothing was going on — a miraculous act of blindness considering the furore that was about to take place.

Blondin's financial problems also threatened to frustrate the venture. The rope alone would cost thirteen hundred dollars and no common acrobat had that kind of money. Nor would any sane man advance money to an obvious lunatic. But a fellow lunatic was finally uncovered in a certain Mr. Hamblin, who not only put up the cash but also, in a moment of undisguised philanthropy, urged Blondin not to jeopardize his life on his, Hamblin's, account: if the acrobat had any qualms, he was to abandon the crossing. Blondin had no qualms at all.

He did face a considerable engineering problem. The rope was to be stretched in an area between the Falls and the Niagara rapids, at a spot where the gorge is fairly narrow. But how to get it across? A dozen years before, a little boat, romantically called *The Maid of the Mist* had been put into service to give its oil-skinned passengers a whiff of Niagara's spray. This craft was now engaged to drag a cable, five-eighths of an inch thick, across the river. To this rope was attached a second cable, two inches thick, and when that was dragged through the water, a third rope was hauled over. This last was to be the narrow bridge on which Blondin would cross the gorge. It came in two sections, each one thousand feet long, united by a single splice — manila hemp wound around a steel core, three inches in thickness: about the size of a man's wrist.

To fasten the cable, Blondin's crew drilled holes into the solid rock of the cliffs on the Canadian side. Three axletrees were placed in these holes, one behind the other, and around them the rope was tied. Eleven hundred feet distant, on the American side, horses heaved and strained as a windlass pulled the rope taut.

The long process of stringing the tightrope was watched with high excitement by press and public. On June 25, 1859, with the large rope within two hundred feet of the Canadian side, the *Buffalo Express* reported doubts as to whether the smaller line was strong enough to pull the larger, heavier one up the sloping one hundred and seventy feet to the clifftop. Blondin personally manoeuvred himself out onto the smaller line, attached a second drawing rope to the manila cable and then descended on a slack rope to the water's edge. The *Express* was all applause: "Those who saw it now give up and do not doubt his ability to walk across."

Once the rope was stretched across the gorge, the watchers below realized that Blondin could not make a level crossing: even though it had been pulled as taut as possible, the rope's own weight caused it to sag fifty feet at midpoint. Blondin would have to descend to the centre and then climb up again to the far side.

At this juncture, the acrobat faced a second engineering problem. To prevent it from swaying back and forth for hundreds of feet in the wind, the cable would have to be anchored by guy ropes — some forty thousand feet of them. These guys were spaced at intervals of twenty feet along the main cable and made taut by being fastened to the banks below. In addition, each guy would be weighted by a heavy bag of salt or sand to prevent the winds that roared through the gorge from blowing it upwards to strike the performer's balancing pole. To attach each guy to the main tightrope a little car was rigged to run under the cable. But Blondin, who oversaw everything personally, walked out on the cable himself to check each fastening, watched by hundreds of spectators. Said he: "When one's life depends on the security of the rope, it is better to put up that rope oneself, is it not?"

With the guy ropes in place, the river was spanned by a gigantic spider's web, which vibrated and swayed as much as fifty feet when the wind blew down the river. Blondin announced that he would cross on this tenuous, swinging bridge on June 30. Thousands were already pouring into town to watch him plummet to his death.

Then, as now, the Falls was the greatest natural wonder in all of North America, a hypnotic attraction for holiday-makers, gamblers, pickpockets, confidence men, entrepreneurs, salesmen, souvenir hunters, conventioners, lodge brothers, adulterers, fatcats and rubbernecks of every description. Honeymooners were beginning to discover Niagara, magnetized by the fury of the cataract and the cunning of the local boosters. Somebody conceived the bright idea of dubbing the small Luna Falls, between Goat and Luna islands, "the Bridal Veil." Another sharpie invented the legend of an Indian princess, shoved under the tumbling water as the Bride of God: he sold medallions to commemorate the pseudo-event. White stones found at the base of the Falls were peddled as "congealed mist" and when every stone had been looted from the gorge, boatloads more were imported from Derbyshire. On the Canadian side, the famous "Front," that incredible mile-long hodge-podge of bath houses, hotels, souvenir stands, taverns, museums, curio shops and pagodas was taking shape downriver from Table Rock. In Old Pol Davis's notorious Table Rock House, a combination souvenir shop and hostelry, the gullible, drawn by the cry that "everything inside is free," were forced to purchase worthless knicknacks under the threat of a physical beating.

Ballyhoo had its birth at the Falls: anything and everything was done to attract attention. In 1827, an entire ship, the *Michigan,* was sent plunging over the cataract with three bears, two foxes, a dog, a cat, a raccoon, four geese and a buffalo aboard. The bears climbed the mast and escaped: the other creatures plunged to their doom before the admiring throngs. Shortly after that date Sam Patch, of Rochester, a man who made pin money jumping off bridges, announced he would leap off a hundred-foot ladder into the river below the Falls. Thousands turned out to see Patch kill himself. Groans went up when it was announced that Patch had broken his leg and couldn't appear. It was too late to leave, and so everybody stayed overnight, guzzling beer, living high in the hotels, while the cabbies took kickbacks to steer their fares into the curio shops. The following day, Patch, his leg miraculously healed, made his jump and unaccountably lived; the suckers realized they had been doubly hoaxed.

This was the atmosphere in which Charles Blondin proposed to thrill the thrill-seekers. His feat that year would start the Falls on what some called its Golden Age. Every kind of daredevil act would follow Blondin's. None would achieve lasting fame. There is, after all, no substitute for being first.

Into the Falls poured the railway specials and the excursion steamers, crammed with the morbid, all scrambling for a view. They crawled onto the housetops, squeezed out of windows, jammed themselves onto the *Maid of the Mist*, packed all the bridges and squatted on the scaffolding especially erected for the day — twenty-five thousand souls in all. The betting was frenzied. Would Blondin make it or would he tumble dizzily to his death? The sums being wagered were large enough to make sabotage profitable. Blondin checked his ropes, personally re-testing every knot.

June 30, 1859. The sun flashes dizzily on the cascading water, causing rainbows to glow out of the mist. The vast audience on both sides of the gorge waits, scarcely breathing, for the moment. The hero of the day does not disappoint. He appears at the American end of the rope, a slight, agile, thirty-four-year-old, just five feet five inches tall, one hundred and forty pounds, blond and bewhiskered. Every eye is on him as he makes his preparations. The crowd is silent. Crinolines rustle. Hats come off, as if in prayer. Blondin tests the guys and a low murmur rises from the spectators. Now he is ready. Now he picks up his balancing pole, twenty-seven feet long,

*American ash, balanced to the nearest gram by small
lead weights. Now he steps out briskly onto the cable.*

*With disarming casualness he strolls down to the
midpoint. There he sits down, calmly surveying the
crowd. He rises, advances a few feet, stops again, lies
down on his back, the pole horizontally across his chest.
The crowd gulps, swallows, holds its breath. Suddenly
the small figure on the rope turns a back somersault and
lands upright on his feet. A long gasp from twenty-five
thousand throats. But he has already walked swiftly
upward to the landing stage on the Canadian side. The
band begins to play La Marseillaise but it cannot be
heard. The roar of the crowd even drowns out the sound
of the Falls.*

The time would come when this feat by Blondin
would seem commonplace in the light of later excursions on the rope. The acrobat was all showman; he
knew the value of building his act, performing the easi-
est feats first, the more difficult ones later, though it is
probable that no feat performed at Niagara was ever
difficult in Blondin's eyes.

He waited for twenty minutes, building expectancy;
the crowd waited with him. Now he reappeared. This
time he was carrying a camera and a tripod. Two hundred feet out on the tightrope, he lashed his balance pole
to the cable, unstrapped the camera and took a picture
of the crowd. Then he shouldered the cumbersome
device (cameras were only twenty years old), unlashed
the pole and returned to Canada.

Blondin was no Sam Patch. He intended to give his
audience good value. Out he set for a third time, carrying a heavy chair. One-third of the way across the rope,
he put the chair down, sat on it, crossed his legs and,
with a look of magnificent unconcern, gazed calmly
about him. Moving towards the American shore, he

repeated the feat with a variation: this time he *stood* on the chair. Now the women below began to have fainting spells; but by the time the smelling salts were produced, the acrobat had stepped, calm and smiling, onto the American shore. The entire performance had lasted one hour. "His name," announced the *Niagara Falls Gazette*, "stands at the head of the most wonderful gymnasts of the age."

Blondin had only begun to entertain. He crossed the gorge on three more occasions that summer — on July 4, July 14 and August 4 — before attempting his greatest feat. Each time out the stunts grew more daring: he blindfolded himself with a heavy sack of blankets; he bicycled across; he pushed a wheelbarrow; he stood on his head; one night he crossed after dark in the glare of locomotive headlights. There seemed to be no further surprises, but Blondin had one more rope trick left. He meant to carry a man on his back across the gorge.

An imitator, one Delave, threatened to forestall him. He proposed to stretch a rope across the Genesee Falls at Rochester and carry a man over with him on his shoulders. Being first is what counts: Blondin immediately offered a reward to anyone who would volunteer to ride on his back across Niagara.

Volunteers stepped forward at once, took one look at the surging waters below, swallowed, stepped back, remembered previous appointments. Blondin was not surprised; he had already had his eyes focused on one of his own kind, a one-time whaler from Chicago named Harry Colcord. Colcord, who was Blondin's manager, had already ridden on the acrobat's back on lesser ropes and in smaller theatres, but never across a pit as gaping as this one.

How did Blondin talk Colcord into such madness? The question was on many lips. In an interview he gave three years before his death, Blondin revealed his secret. Colcord, he insisted, knew from the beginning that he would not fall off his back, because the acrobat had conducted an impressive experiment. He stood on a pole resting on two supports and challenged Colcord to dislodge him. Colcord pushed, shoved, prodded, sweated; Blondin could not be budged. It was a reassuring gesture, but there would be moments when Colcord, clinging to those slippery, silk-clad shoulders, one hundred and seventy feet above the maelstrom, would not be so certain of his master's iron control.

The public was sceptical from the first. Captain John Travis, a famous pistol shot who had performed with Blondin, wrote to the acrobat to make sure the attempt would be made; Blondin assured him that it would, even offering to carry Travis across. The sharpshooter demurred. He had a different sort of diversion planned, which he suggested to Blondin; the acrobat readily agreed to take part in the scheme.

Those gamblers who had lost heavily over Blondin's insistence on staying alive were cheered. It was difficult enough for a man to struggle along on level ground lugging his own weight. But up an incline of swaying rope? Impossible! Blondin weighed one hundred and forty pounds; Colcord, one hundred and thirty-five. To that must be added the additional weight — forty pounds — of the balancing rod. And then there was the chance that Colcord, an amateur, would lose his balance. The odds against Blondin were formidable. Greenbacks began to change hands.

All the world, it seemed, was jammed into the twin cities clustered around the Falls. Entire organizations made field trips to Niagara — the Bethel Sunday school of Buffalo, for instance, and the volunteer firemen of Toronto, red-shirted, marching in a parade. Indians came in feathers, Southern gentlemen in lace cuffs, midwesterners in clawhammer coats and stovepipe hats. Excursion trains chuffed in from upstate New York; nine cars from Buffalo, ten from Lewiston, twenty from Rochester. A Great Western locomotive pulling thirty-five cars choked with humanity from various Upper Canadian centres arrived. The crack steamer *Arrow* debouched twelve hundred passengers downriver, went back for twelve hundred more. Carriages by the hundreds blocked the streets; omnibuses, horse-drawn, forced their ungainly way through the press of people. The crowd swelled by the hour. How many were there? The newspapers estimated three hundred thousand, but one must remember that reporters tend to build up a story by inflating the estimates. Still, it is safe to say that never before and never again has such a human mass thronged to the gorge of Niagara.

The swindlers were out in force. Three-card monte men slipped among the gullible. Strangers cajoled other strangers to trust their fortunes to the turn of a card at faro bank. Ladies found their portmanteaus snatched. Thimblerig operators and pickpockets slid through the thousands who picnicked on the grass, reducing it to straw. At makeshift booths, wide-boys served fake lemonade at a quarter a glass — a rate that boosted the price of tartaric acid to four hundred dollars a pound. There were long lunch queues for all except the very rich, who glided around the dance floors in the posh hotels. It was a merry, merry time. Some of the Toronto firemen got into an argument with a drunk and pushed him into the river where he drowned. It failed to dampen the holiday mood.

The stagings could not hold the crowd which spilled over once again onto the limbs of trees and the sills of windows, onto verandahs, porches and eaves and the crumbling shores of the gorge itself.

Suddenly all eyes swivelled to the spot on the American side where a small, neat figure in pink tights and rough-dressed buckskin moccasins could be seen stepping out onto the rope. Blondin tantalized the crowd with an anthology of acrobatic legerdemain: head stands, somersaults, a trip across without a balancing pole, another trip across suspended from below, like an ape, hand over hand. These were mere warm-up stunts.

But when next he appeared, after a fifteen-minute rest on the Canadian side, the crowd's buzz was silenced. Hooks could be seen hanging from various parts of his costume. This was to be the main event. Harry Colcord, in formal dress, appeared beside him and, ignoring the hooks, leapt nimbly on his back. The time had come.

In spite of what Blondin had told him, Colcord suspected that the acrobat was not quite as confident of success as he appeared, partly because of the additional weight, but also because he could not control a human error on Colcord's part.

"Harry," he had told him, "be sure and let yourself rest like a dead weight on my back. If I should sway or stumble, on no account attempt to balance yourself." Colcord listened carefully; his life, after all, was at stake.

As they started off, he looked down and felt a little shiver. The sharp tops of pine trees bristled far below, between cliff and river; they seemed more terrifying than the water itself. Blondin was moving with maddening slowness, step by careful step down the long incline of the rope; to Colcord, nothing had ever seemed so dreadfully slow.

Worse was to come. Blondin required periodic rests to gather his strength. Colcord later described what this entailed: "Just think of the situation — getting down off a man's back, feeling with your foot for a taut, vibrating rope, then standing on the same, while it is swung to and fro, some hundreds of feet in the air, and holding on to a man in front of you, clad in slippery tights, when the least false move or loss of presence of mind can plunge you both into eternity, and then climbing again on his back — and this has to be repeated seven times!"

Below, Colcord could see the seething current; it produced an odd optical effect, as if he, Blondin, the rope and guys, were all moving at express train speed upriver, but making little progress to the far bank. To him, the roar of the waters below "rose like the united voices of a thousand demons."

The two men approached the centre of the humming rope. Danger lurked, because for a space of forty feet there were no guy lines. Blondin had manoeuvred ten feet into this no-man's land when he suddenly tottered, swayed and made a furious effort to walk straight, working his pole as if it were a pair of wings. Colcord later claimed that Blondin had lost his balance; one suspects, knowing the acrobat's ability at both balance and showmanship, that he was totally in control, simply giving the crowd the extra thrill he always provided. Colcord, remembering his instructions, hung from his shoulders like a dead man.

Apparently unable to regain his balance, Blondin ran along the rope, the momentum keeping him upright, the pole thrashing madly up and down, until he reached the nearest guy line on the American side, thirty feet away. He stepped on the line to steady himself. A huge gasp escaped from the open mouths below: the line snapped and the main rope, tugged by the corresponding guy on the opposite side, was jerked sideways. Blondin recovered himself, gained enough equilibrium to continue his run to the next brace of guys, twenty feet distant, and halted.

"Get off, quick," Colcord remembered his saying.

"He was like a marble statue; every muscle was tense and rigid; large beads of perspiration trickled from him. It was then that I admired his wonderful grit and coolness. Neither by voice or sign did he manifest his knowledge of the fact that a dastardly attempt had just been made to kill us, probably by some unscrupulous and murderous gambler or gamblers who had adopted this method of trying to save their miserable stakes."

So Colcord told his Boswell, Mr. Justice Jervis Blume. He did not explain, however, how any gambler could have crept all the way out to the middle of that swaying rope to tamper with lines that Blondin himself checked regularly. In his later years, Blondin made it clear that he never felt, personally, any danger at all. An aged lady once asked him how he performed his wonderful feats: what exercise, what diet? Blondin replied that he ate and drank as he pleased, smoked cigars; and took no exercise of any kind. "Madame," said he, "the fact is that when I am on the rope, my safety depends on my keeping my balance. So I keep it." To a London journalist he explained: "There is only one danger, and that is with respect to the safe adjustment of the rope, and to that I always give my minutest attention."

An incident occurred during this exhibition that sheds further light on the so-called sabotage of the rope. Blondin was carrying a top hat to provide an extra diversion; at one of the stops at the guy ropes he held it aloft. Waiting below, on the *Maid of the Mist,* was his fellow showman, John Travis, the marksman. Travis aimed his pistol at the hat and fired. He missed. He fired again; a second miss. A third shot rang out and Blondin waved the hat to signal a hit as the crowd applauded. Few questioned the logic of the hat trick; but certainly no pistol of that time could have fired a bullet at that angle and hit anything at that distance. The hat had been pierced long before Blondin set out. A souvenir hunter paid fifty dollars for it. That, as they say, is show business; and so, one must conclude, was the affair of the broken guy.

Colcord climbed once more upon his master's back and the two men began to toil up the long incline toward the American shore. Show business or not, it was hard work. Ahead of him Colcord was confronted with "a great sea of staring faces, fixed and intense with interest, alarm, fear. Some people shaded their eyes, as if dreading to see us fall; some held their arms extended as if to grasp us and keep us from falling; some excited men had tears streaming down their cheeks."

Colcord, at the last moment, realized that there was real danger from an unexpected source. The people, excited to a frenzy, were quite capable of rushing towards the two men and crowding them right over the bank. Even Blondin was nonplussed.

"What shall I do?" he asked.

"Make a rush and drive right through them," said Colcord.

The advice was good. The two men cleared the crowd. And then the world went mad.

Blondin's future was assured. He and Colcord were overnight heroes. Someone began composing a Blondin March. Niagara Falls struck a gold medal for him. New York City presented him with an inscribed, gold-headed cane. Indians from a nearby reservation insisted on spangling his costume with beadwork. Onlookers collected forty thousand dollars on the spot for the two men. People paid in gold coins for Colcord's autograph.

Now the acrobatic parade was on. Rope-walkers popped up, it seemed, at almost every canyon. To Niagara the following year came a formidable rival, the flamboyant Signor Farini, who strung a second rope some distance below Blondin's. The two men matched each other, feat for feat. Farini stood on his head; Blondin did back flips. Farini crossed over in a sack; Blondin walked his rope in chains. Farini lowered a wash-bucket from his rope, drew water from the gorge, and laundered a lady's handkerchief. Blondin cooked a meal on a Lilliputian stove and lowered it to a passenger on the *Maid of the Mist*. On August 29, 1860, Farini duplicated Blondin's feat by carrying a man on his back across the gorge. Alas for him, it only matters if you're first. Who now has heard of Farini?

It was Blondin that the future Edward VII wished to see perform. The young prince, not yet run to fat, arrived with much pomp on September 8. This time Blondin's rope was stretched below the suspension bridge, two hundred and thirty feet above the Whirlpool Rapids.

The Prince sat in a rustic lodge, his heavy-lidded eyes glued to a pair of field glasses. The acrobat was brought before him and introduced. "For Heaven's sake," said the Prince, in his guttural accent, "don't do anything extraordinary because I am here." Blondin immediately offered the extraordinary: he would take the Prince across on his back. Thanks, but no thanks, said His Royal Highness — or something to that effect.

Again Colcord was tabbed for the ride, his third. At the last resting place there was some sort of flurry. Colcord couldn't seem to get back onto Blondin's shoulders. The rope oscillated; the two showmen appeared to quarrel. *Get up immediately,* Blondin is said to have told his man, *or I'll leave you here on the rope!* Colcord remounted quickly. It was his last ride. Shortly after that he and Blondin parted forever.

The acrobat was not quite finished. He donned three-foot stilts and lumbered across the rope one more time. His Royal Highness seemed to be more exhausted than the performer. "Thank God it's all over," he was heard to mutter as the exhibition ended.

For Blondin, the triumphs never ended. The Crystal Palace beckoned and after that, the world. With his profits he bought himself an English country home, named it Niagara House, of course, and performed for the rest of his life. He was still bringing hearts into mouths when he gave his final performance in Belfast at the age of seventy-two. On February 22, 1897, a few days before his seventy-third birthday, he died.

Harry Colcord also lived to be seventy-two. He quit show business and became a landscape painter in Chicago. It was a quiet profession. His nights, however, were not always quiet. For the rest of his life, Harry Colcord was troubled by nightmares, always the same, always terrifying. He would start up in the dark, sweating profusely, reliving once again those heart-stopping moments when he stood on a thin strand of manila, stretched tight as a violin string, over the dark chasm of Niagara.

17

The Overlanders

The days of the great gold rushes are long gone. One cannot embark on a stampede in a twin-engine Otter or a helicopter. The gold country has been mapped and settled, the free colours are all panned away. There are no mysterious Eldorados left to lure romantics across a wild terrain, no dizzy Chilkoots to test the mettle of the tyro pioneer. Like so many other communicable diseases, gold fever has been wiped out; there is nowhere for the virus to breed.

But there was a time when the slightest whisper of a strike produced in otherwise sensible people a kind of insanity which, in a curious way, was also a kind of high courage. Men and women would dare anything for gold; or at least that was the excuse. Perhaps the real lure was simply the age-old desire for adventure beyond the horizon. No matter how far off the bonanza might be (and it was always desperately far), no matter how weary the route to reach it (and it was always hideously weary), the hordes pushed off, convincing themselves that the wealth of the ages lay just over the next hill. Gold fever produced a kind of mass blindness; its victims were ready to swallow the most preposterous absurdities on pure faith. Like supplicants at a camp meeting, or marks at a carnival, they *wanted* to believe.

Consider, for instance, this advertisement, published in English newspapers in the spring of 1862 at the height of the Cariboo gold rush:

The British Columbia Overland Transit Company will punctually dispatch . . . at 12 noon from Glasgow — in the first class and powerful screw steamship *United Kingdom*, 1,200 tons burden, 300 horsepower, James Clarke commander, a party of first and second class passengers for Quebec, Canada, and over the Grand Trunk Railway and continuous lines of railway to Chicago and St. Paul and via the Red River Settlements, in covered wagons, to British Columbia.

This is the speediest, safest and most economical route to the gold diggings. The land transit is through a lovely country unequalled for its beauty and salubrity of climate. More than half the distance from Quebec is by railway.

Through fares, £42 from England to British Columbia; saloon berths £5 extra.

Letters received from the agents in Canada announce that a first spring party of 52 in number have left for British Columbia by this route. About 1,000 carts annually travel along this line. There are numerous posts, missions and trading stations from the Red River Settlements along the Saskatchewan, now discovered to abound in vast gold deposits, to the Rocky Mountains. The route is constantly travelled with perfect safety. Full particulars can be had at the offices, 6 Cothall Court. . . .

The enterprise was a hoax. The company, which made one of the harshest of overland adventures seem like a pleasant Sunday outing (it claimed the journey would take only five weeks), welshed on almost all of its promises, as those who were caught up in the scheme discovered as soon as they reached Toronto. The climate might sometimes be salubrious, the scenery might indeed be unequalled; but when the rails ended men and women who had never saddled a horse found themselves on their own, facing a journey of more than four months across empty and often vicious terrain — a thousand miles of friendless prairie, and at the far end the implacable wall of the mountains. But such was the pull of gold that many of those who had fallen for the hoax refused to quit. As the *Globe* reported: "Though not pleased with the conduct of the company, the party now in Toronto are resolved to push on like brave men and we cannot help thinking they are in the right."

One of these Englishmen of whom we have record was a young nineteen-year-old biology student from Cornwall, named Eustace Pattison. His photograph in the Archives of British Columbia shows a Byronic youth, with a pageboy haircut, lidded eyes, sensitive nostrils and full lips. His pose is languorous and unselfconscious; he seems, indeed, to be day dreaming and perhaps he was. Contemporary accounts reinforce the impression left by the portrait: he was described by his friends as refined, shy and not very gregarious. What, then, impelled him to travel almost halfway round the globe in a mad rush for treasure? The gold? Or the romance?

Whatever the reason, young Pattison and his English companions became part of a larger group of Canadians travelling together for mutual protection and convenience who crossed Canada in the summer of 1862 and who are known to history as the Overlanders. Starting in mid-April, they travelled more than thirty-five hundred miles by rail, steamer, Red River cart, horseback, foot, canoe and raft to reach the gateway to the Cariboo goldfields in late September. The wonder is not that so many managed to reach their objective, but that only five perished in the attempt.

It is not possible to follow all of them as they rattle on greaseless axles through the waving buffalo grass. Nine separate parties were organized in the towns of Ontario and Quebec in the spring of '62 when news of the Cariboo strike trickled through to the east. These were joined, in St. Paul and Fort Garry, by other goldseekers, eager to reach British Columbia. Out of Fort Garry, the Overlanders coalesced into three main parties, one of which split in two at Tête Jaune Cache. Before that objective was reached some had defected and a natural leader had emerged, a teacher from Queenston, Ontario, named Thomas McMicking. His party's long odyssey is the best documented of all the Overlanders'; it is also the most eventful.

McMicking's portrait, taken when he was a student at Knox College, also survives in the archives but there is no languor in his pose. He sits bolt upright, gazing directly at the camera, a book on his knee, an academic gown over his shoulders. His Celtic features are marked by a strong jawline, a determined mouth and clear, unwavering eyes. The effect is one of serenity and confidence, twin qualities which were to make McMicking the undisputed leader and hero of the overland expedition. McMicking, who was thirty-three, was accompanied by his nineteen-year-old brother, Robert, who had been working for the Montreal Telegraph Company.

McMicking originally led the Queenston party of twenty-four men, a quasi-military group like all the others, with a tight set of rules and a five-dollar organization fee. Values change; five dollars in those days was for many more than a week's wages. The total per man cost of the 141-day journey across Canada, for McMicking's followers — including supplies and transportation — came to $97.65, all found.

All these men had a strong sense of community. In the 1860s, Canada was not a mobile nation. Men and women were born, schooled, married and buried in the same village; many never travelled more than a few miles from their birthplace. Friendships made as a child lasted for the rest of their lives. It is not surprising that the men from Acton, Huntington, Queenston and the other communities who started off together in April, shared the same rafts in the final dangerous dash down the Fraser and Thompson rivers in September. This kind of teamwork sets the story of the Overlanders apart from most other Canadian adventures, for this was probably the first community enterprise in which men worked in loose coalition, democratically organized for their own ends.

Steam travel, a century ago, was haphazard, uncomfortable and tedious. The McMicking party took more than a month to reach Fort Garry from St. Catharines in fits and starts, using a variety of railroads, steamboats and stagecoaches.

Consider, for instance, the trip to St. Paul, Minnesota. On April 23, at 11:40 a.m., the party left St. Catharines for Detroit by Great Western Railway. They arrived at 9:30 that evening and stayed overnight. On April 24, they boarded another railway, the Detroit and Milwaukee, and travelled 186 miles to Grand Haven on Lake Michigan. There they changed to a steamer, the *Detroit*, which took them 86 miles to Milwaukee, which they reached at two the following morning. At five that afternoon (April 27) they boarded the Milwaukee and LaCrosse Railway for a 201-mile journey to LaCrosse on the Mississippi River. They reached it at 10 p.m. on

April 28. Here, after another four-hour wait, they transferred to the steamer *Frank Steele* which took them, upriver to St. Paul.

St. Paul, then a town of ten thousand, was at the end of organized transport and also of civilization. Here, the various parties of Overlanders found their number swelled by eighteen young Englishmen, including Eustace Pattison, who had been lured by the B.C. Transit advertisements. There were something like two hundred people moving through St. Paul, heading for Fort Garry, and these all had to be transported, literally by stages, to Georgetown, the frontier village on the Red River, where a steamboat was being readied for them. Since the stagecoach could hold no more than ten at a time, the process went on for days.

In Georgetown there was another maddening wait. The steamboat, *International*, was not completed. Workmen hammered away on her superstructure, while the goldseekers, their numbers swelling daily, hunted, fished, and played ball. Finally, the sternwheeler was ready. There were so many passengers that scores had to sleep on the decks. The ship almost came to grief when, attempting to navigate a tight bend she crashed into the bank, smashed the pilot house and knocked off two funnels. But at last, on May 26, she reached Fort Garry. The McMicking party had been on the road for thirty-three days and the real journey had yet to begin.

Gold fever gripped Fort Garry. Residents and newcomers who had arrived by canoe or on foot clamoured to join one of the parties heading west. One of these was a German immigrant named Augustus Schubert. Schubert had left his native Dresden some years before, emigrated to the United States and married an Irish girl from County Down. Before coming north to Fort Garry, the two had run a beer hall in St. Paul. Now they had three children and Catherine Schubert was again pregnant. But her husband, wandering among the tents of the Overlanders at Long Lake, became obsessed with the idea of trekking to the goldfields. McMicking had no objection to taking him but balked when Mrs. Schubert appeared and insisted that she and the children share the perils of the journey with him. She must have been persuasive because McMicking waived his strict no-woman rule and agreed to take the entire family along. Had he known about Mrs. Schubert's condition he might not have been so accommodating. As it was he never had cause to regret his decision. As one of the members of his group was to write: "Her presence in the company helped to cultivate a kindly and more manly treatment of man to man." Equally important, perhaps, is the fact that the presence of a domestic group may easily have made the Overlanders' passage through Indian country easier; clearly, this was not a war party. The Schuberts packed their belongings in a covered spring democrat, drawn by an ox and a cow, and devised two basket cradles for the older children, Mary and Augustus, Jr. Mrs. Schubert rode horseback with a child in a cradle slung to each side of her saddle. The younger boy, Jimmie, aged three, was carried by his father.

By the time the Overlanders left Fort Garry, the nine groups from the various eastern Canadian communities had become three. McMicking's, with one hundred and thirty-eight men, plus Mrs. Schubert and her three children, was by far the largest. It also included Eustace Pattison, who had joined the Toronto group in St. Paul but switched to McMicking's party at Fort Garry.

A mass meeting, chaired by McMicking, hammered out an organization. Under the captain, there would be a committee of thirteen, each of these a leader of a subgroup. Schedules, starting times, hours and rate of travel, relations with the Indians and the arrangement of the wagon train were all laid down. On June 5, the party set off for Fort Edmonton, nine hundred miles to the west.

Like a great, jointed snake, the train of ninety-seven carts and one hundred and ten animals stretched for half a mile across the prairie, travelling for ten hours a day at a speed of two and a half miles an hour. At nights the carts were drawn up in a triangle, shafts out, animals tethered within the makeshift corral, guards posted. The Overlanders rose at 2:30 each morning, pushed off at three, halted at five for two hours to breakfast and feed the animals, halted again for a lunch break at eleven, and set out again from one until six in the evening. Sundays were sacrosanct, for these men took their religion seriously. On the Sabbath they halted, sang hymns, prayed aloud, listened to the scriptures and appointed one of their number to preach a sermon.

There wasn't a single bridge between the Red River and the Rockies — the Hudson's Bay Company had seen to that; the great fur enterprise did not want settlers moving into its territory and this was one method of

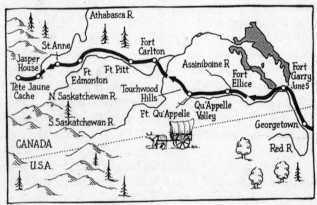

dissuading them. To cross the Assiniboine at Fort Ellice, McMicking's people borrowed a crude Hudson's Bay scow attached to a rawhide rope that stretched from bank to bank. It was only large enough to hold a single cart and ox. That meant more than a hundred crossings before the entire party was ferried over: it took six hours.

In the broad valley of the Qu'Appelle the rains had turned the long, steep slopes into greasy slides. Men and animals slipped, slid and were maimed. One unfortunate, W. W. Morrow of Montreal, was dragged downhill by his own ox; at the bottom a cartwheel ran over his head. A doctor patched the unconscious man together and he continued on with the party.

On June 18, the Overlanders awoke to find the prairie white with frost, the ice thick in the waterbuckets, and their guide gone: from this point on they would have to find their own way to Edmonton. But spirits remained high. The country was indeed lovely, and in the Touchwood Hills there were wild strawberries.

Then, on June 25, they left the shelter of the woods and burst out onto an immense and trackless plain. Few had thought to husband their fuel supply and not all had

brought nets to fight off the torture of the mosquitoes that swarmed over them. In spite of the rules, some groups began to scramble to reach the head of the wagon train: it was the last ones to cross a ford or a mudhole who had the most trouble. Some even abandoned their meals and rushed for the carts with cups of tea or pancakes still in their hands. Tempers began to fray; small, ignoble quarrels flared. Sunday could not come soon enough; the day of rest served a healing purpose. McMicking wrote that "the vigour with which our journey would be prosecuted, and the cordiality and good feeling that characterized our intercourse after our accustomed rest on the first day of the week, are sufficient evidence to us that the law of the Sabbath is of physical as well as moral obligation, and that its precepts cannot be violated with impunity."

McMicking never stooped to squabble. A man of principle, serious, a bit pedantic, he pressed forward, always reasonable, always forceful enough to command the majority of the expedition. He was, said one who knew him, "a true Christian gentleman, a genial companion, a ready writer and speaker, and withal a man of strong character."

On June 30, the party reached the South Saskatchewan River, three hundred yards wide. A single Hudson's Bay bateau was available to ferry all the carts, people and animals across. It lay on the far side of the river. A. C. Robertson, of Goderich, a jailkeeper's son, who was already emerging as one of McMicking's senior lieutenants, and who was the strongest swimmer of the party, swam the river and fetched the boat over with the help of one other man. It took ten hours to move the party across. Every beast had to be unharnessed, every cart unloaded, and the wheels pried off before it could be fitted onto the ferry. Back and forth the little boat laboured, carrying six carts at a time while the horses, oxen and cattle were forced to swim across. One man, Robert Kelso of Acton, almost drowned hazing laggard animals into the water. He was revived by artificial respiration, pummelled back to life, and the wagon train moved on.

At Fort Pitt, the Hudson's Bay factor warned McMicking of rough country, faint trails and unruly Indians ahead. A mass meeting tightened up the organization. McMicking was promoted to colonel; Robertson, the swimmer from Goderich, was named captain. The meeting decided that the party would split into four groups who would travel together in close order and that a guide would be hired to lead the way to Edmonton.

And then came the rain! It began in earnest a day out of Fort Pitt and did not let up for eleven days. No one who has not camped out night after night in an unending downpour can comprehend the misery this means: clothes soaked, tents saturated and leaking, blankets forever damp, provisions soggy, dry wood non-existent. On Saturday, July 12, the deluge grew so heavy that the party could not move. On Monday, it was forced to halt after two hours because the guide could not see the trail. Yet, in the midst of all this soggy discomfort, there was merriment. On July 16, after supper, in the centre of the corral, thirty-two Overlanders formed a musical society complete with vocalists, violinists, flautists and others. While the rain pelted down, the hastily organized orchestra and choir entertained the camp.

Now the rivers were transformed into torrents and even the smallest creeks were too dangerous to ford. Between July 18 and July 20, the party built eight bridges. The shortest was forty feet long; some exceeded one hundred feet. Once, when no trees were available, McMicking ordered the swollen creek filled with carts to form a passage.

July 19 was the worst day of all. Most of the party had been neck-deep in water and every one was soaked to the skin; every stitch of clothing, packed or worn, was dripping wet. In the tents the water was four inches deep. Men used wagon boards, piles of brush, buffalo robes — anything to raise themselves above the ooze. The following day was the Lord's but, for once, the Overlanders were forced to break their Sabbath rule. They threw a sixty-foot bridge across a roaring creek and fled to higher ground.

There was one further obstacle: a two-hundred-foot ravine with a foaming torrent at the bottom, its sides so steep that no man or animal could keep his feet while sliding downward. Trees had to be felled for a bridge, a trail opened up, and carts and cattle let down the flanks by ropes. On the far side, one of the men riding ahead spotted the palisades of Fort Edmonton in the distance and the party, revived by the spectacle, broke into cheers. Wrote McMicking:

"During the preceding eleven days our clothing had never been dry, we had just passed through what we considered a pretty tough time, and the toil-worn, jaded, forlorn and tattered appearance of the company was in striking and amusing contrast with our appearance a few months before; so marked, indeed, was the change that our most intimate friends at home would scarcely have recognized us. But our courage was still unbroken and, although we had been so much longer on the road than we anticipated, we had yet full confidence in our ability to reach the El Dorado of our hopes. . . ."

The inhabitants of Fort Edmonton, cut off from the world as if on another planet, greeted them eagerly for news. Here the Overlanders learned that the carts must be abandoned; the land rose steeply toward the mountains and only packhorses could make the journey. The prices of animals and saddles rose almost immediately on this intelligence, and some members of the group were forced to sell provisions to raise money. The Schuberts, for instance, sold their cow. But, like many others, they kept their ox as a pack animal; there weren't enough horses to go round.

Archibald Thompson from Queenston panned for gold in the river and claimed he'd found some colours; these were almost certainly mica. But a man named Timoleon Love, who said he was a seasoned prospector but who was, in actuality, a charlatan, insisted there were riches to be found on the eastern slopes of the Rockies. Twenty-five men peeled off from the main party to follow this will-o'-the-wisp; none found so much as a grain of gold.

For the remainder, the trail would lead through the Yellowhead Pass, the traditional fur traders' route to the interior of British Columbia. On July 29, the Overlanders broke camp and headed west in high spirits, refreshed at riding horseback, sure that they would reach the goldfields in a matter of weeks. Actually, the worst part of the journey lay before them.

They had one hundred and forty pack animals with them, but none knew how to adjust a saddle, balance a load or secure it with a diamond hitch. They learned these things on the trail. At St. Anne's they faced a river with all the timber on the opposite side. Four men caught two oxen, tied their clothes to the horns, drove them into the freezing waters, hung onto their tails, breasted the torrent and felled a gigantic poplar tree on which the others crossed. Here the unfortunate Morrow, still scarred by his earlier accident, was battered again: his steer bolted, he clung to its horns and was thrown to the ground, where the animal promptly stamped all over the face that had been bruised weeks before by a cartwheel. Morrow, however, was determined to get to the Cariboo. He recovered after eleven days at the St. Anne Mission and joined a second party of Overlanders following behind.

The trail grew worse. The forests were so dense that an advance party had to chop a passage through the coniferous jungle. Somebody had waited behind in Edmonton for the mail from Fort Garry. He rejoined the party on August 2, with a copy of the *Globe* of May 16. It was full of reports about the American Civil War. Great Britain had just recognized the Confederate states as belligerents. This was the last news the party had of the outside world until they reached the Cariboo.

In the chill mornings, the dew, freezing as it fell, hung from the leaves like icicles. One river was too deep to ford and too broad to bridge: everybody was forced to swim across. In the spruce swamps, the horses could only flounder until their packs were removed. The men themselves became beasts of burden, leaving behind them a trail of discarded tools. At the McLeod River two men, trying to ford on foot, were swept away and almost drowned, but saved at the last instant by their comrades.

Then, on August 13, the Overlanders got their first magic glimpse of the Rockies, one hundred miles ahead of them, the snowy peaks floating like clouds in the brilliant blue sky. They were enraptured; none had ever seen a mountain before. Five days later, camped in the foothills, McMicking could exclaim over "a view at once sublimely grand and overpowering."

The most dangerous section of trail lay dead ahead along the south side of the Athabasca River, up a high shoulder of Mount Miette, "with its cold and craggy cliffs, crowned with eternal snows." Near the top, the narrow defile led between a perpendicular wall of rock and a dizzy precipice. At fourteen hundred feet a pack-horse missed his footing and tumbled four hundred feet down the cliffside; he was hauled back up, miraculously unharmed. But later two more slid over the side and were lost.

The McMicking party was moving through history. Around them lay various crumbling monuments to the fur trade. From Mount Miette they could see the deserted Hudson's Bay post of Jasper House on the north side of the Athabasca. They passed it at midday and the next day happened upon the rotting logs that marked the site of Henry House, built in 1810. In one two-hour period that day, they crossed the raging torrent of the Miette River seven times. The following day, August 22, they passed over the continental divide and entered the crown colony of British Columbia.

They had expected to reach the Cariboo in two months from Fort Garry. Already they had spent three months on the trail and were only at the midpoint of the mountains. Their stock of food was perilously low; indeed, their pemmican had run out. Some parties slaughtered their oxen; the Schuberts killed one of their horses; others shot squirrels, a porcupine, and several small birds. On August 24, a Sunday, unable to find grazing land for the stock, they again broke the Sabbath stricture and travelled all day. With heavy irony, McMicking reported on their supper that night: "We dined this day upon a dish so delicate and rare that it might have tempted the palate of Epicurus himself; so nice, indeed, was it, that I have some little hesitation in naming it lest we might be censured for living too luxuriously by the way. It was a roasted skunk, which our guide prepared and served us in true Indian style."

Pastures became more difficult to find. The animals were beginning to fail. A few miles east of Tête Jaune Cache, a horse slipped into the Fraser and drowned, taking all his pack of cooking utensils with him. At this point the provisions were very low; many of the Overlanders had run out of flour and were subsisting on dried beef; Shuswap Indians appeared with fresh fish and serviceberries; the travellers were glad to trade ammunition, clothing — anything — for food.

The Cariboo beckoned; but where was the Cariboo? The Shuswaps had never heard of it. Most of the easterners had thought of a pass as an easy way through the mountains. Instead they were faced with a forested slope, flanked on both sides by huge precipices and torrential cataracts. It was all very beautiful in midsummer; windflowers, mountain roses, bluebells and cornflowers sparkled in the sunlight; the fragrance of grass and hemlocks rose sweetly to the nostrils. But there was danger ahead where the Fraser River lurked — that barbarous waterway whose discoverer had named it, for the best of reasons, the Bad River.

Ten days' travel down the Fraser, the Indians said, lay the trading post of Fort George. But the route was dangerous in the extreme, a nightmare of canyons and white water. The Indians shook their heads sadly at the idea of the Overlanders taking to the river. "Poor white men," they said. "No more see white men."

An alternative route lay directly to the south. Fourteen days' travel to the headwaters of the North Thompson would bring the travellers to the white man's pack road, a foot deep in snow. Was this the trail from Oregon to the Cariboo? The party was in a quandary. If they went south, they might be frozen in for the winter before they reached the goldfields. If they followed the Fraser in its great loop west, north and south again, they might all drown. After much palaver the party split in two. The larger group, under McMicking, would take a few cattle and challenge the Fraser in rafts and canoes. A smaller group, including the Schubert

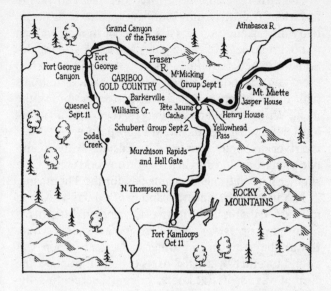

family (Mrs. Schubert was now heavy with child) would take most of the stock and head south for the Thompson.

These were different men from the eager, optimistic goldseekers who had set out so jauntily the previous May. Exhausted but hardened by travel, their faces gaunt, burned by sun and wind, their clothes in shreds, their food heavily rationed, they seemed to have lived a lifetime in a single summer. Look at them now as they prepared to face, without a tremor, a river that had for half a century daunted the most experienced explorers. The early fur traders had plunged down these hazardous rapids in canoes manned by seasoned Indian guides, but now a group of greenhorn easterners have arrived intent on running the rapids without any help in hollow cottonwood logs or on huge rafts with fences on the sides and cattle tethered to the decks.

The rafts they built were forty feet long and twenty feet wide. The men from Huntington, Ontario, fastened two rafts together — eighty-five feet of timber, enough to hold nine head of cattle plus passengers and freight. Some stitched buffalo hides together and stretched them over wooden frames. Many took live animals with them; others butchered their oxen and took the meat. With the Indians standing on the bank and uttering doleful warnings, the McMicking party set off down the river on September 1, led by Eustace Pattison and two men from Toronto in a big cottonwood canoe. The smaller party left the following day for the Thompson.

Thomas McMicking was captain of a thirty-two-man raft named for his home town of Queenston. Most of his fellow passengers were members of that original group. It was the same on the other rafts: each group was bound together by a sense of its own community. The current was a swift five knots, the course serpentine, the channel narrow, the weather cold and wet. The men cooked meals on the raft and sometimes ran at night. Each party chose its own camping time, so that the rafts kept passing and re-passing one another while the lighter canoes shot well ahead of the main body.

Eustace Pattison's canoe reached the rapids of the Grand Canyon of the Fraser a full two days ahead of the leading raft. It was obvious that the hollowed-out cottonwood log could not run the rapids, so the three men attached a lariat to its snout and tried to line it along the bank. The tow rope snapped and the canoe was swept away, carrying with it everything they owned. For two days Pattison and his two comrades lay out in the clothes they wore without food or bedding, exposed to rain and cold. The exposure began to tell on the nineteen-year-old. By the time the next craft arrived, forty-eight hours later, he was in a bad way.

Two canoes, lashed together, appeared in the white water, manned by Robertson, of Goderich, and two fellow townsmen. The snarling river seized their craft, ripped it apart and capsized both boats. Robertson, being the best swimmer, told the other two to hang onto one of the upturned canoes while he swam to shore to get help. Off he struggled only to be swept away into the icy waters, never to be seen again, a loss that shocked the party when the news was known. The canoe drifted onto a shoal in midstream. Shortly after that the big double Huntington raft appeared; these men had had the foresight to equip their craft with a canoe which they now used to pick up the stranded men. McMicking's raft, not far behind, picked up the ailing Pattison and his shivering companions.

When McMicking first approached the rapids at dawn on September 6 — the only warning was the terrible roaring of the waters breaking the morning stillness — he barely had time to get his raft ashore before being drawn into the maelstrom. The party pondered the situation, examining the shoreline for possible portages. But there was no way around: "We saw no alternative; we had either to run the rapids or starve where we were." Finally it was decided that ten men would remain on board the raft to handle the sweeps. The others would work their way along the shoreline, inching along narrow granite ledges, above the torrent, or taking hesitant advantage of the shaky footholds of treetrunks that the Indians had built where the cliffs fell sheer to the water's edge. The raft was untied and pushed out into the racing current. McMicking described the scene:

"Onward they sped like an arrow. They seemed to be rushing into the very jaws of death. Before them on the right rose a rocky reef against which the furious flood

401

was lashing itself into foam, threatening instant and unavoidable destruction and on the other side a seething and eddying whirlpool was ready to engulf in its greedy vortex any mortal who might venture within its reach. With fearful velocity they were hurried along directly towards the fatal rock. Their ruin seemed inevitable. It was a moment of painful suspense. Not a word was spoken except the necessary orders of the pilot, which were distinctly heard on shore above the din and tumult of the scene. Now was the critical moment. Everyone bent manfully to his oar. The raft shot closely past the rock, tearing away the stern rowlock, and glided safely into the eddy below. The agony was over. The gauntlet had been run and all survived. The issue of the ordeal was announced by an involuntary cheer from the brave hearts aboard the raft, which was heartily responded to by those on shore."

All the other rafts shot the rapids safely using similar techniques. Beyond the canyon, the river broadens and the current slows. To make up time, the McMicking raft floated all night, with only one man posted to watch. It was a terrible risk to take for, unknown to any, fifteen miles of continuous rapids lay ahead. Awakened hastily, the men struggled with the sweeps to keep a course through a channel studded with masses of rock. They did not succeed. The raft struck a rock and stuck fast. Three men immediately swam ashore with a line, secured it to a tree and managed to pull the raft free.

At 8:45 on the morning of September 8, the McMicking raft, having navigated the great curve of the Fraser, reached Fort George. Eustace Pattison was now seriously ill, apparently with diphtheria, his resistance badly weakened by exposure. That night he died, to be buried in a rough grave in a strange land, some six thousand miles from the home he had left, with such high hopes, the previous spring.

At the trading post McMicking was warned that the Fort George Canyon, fifteen miles downriver, was too dangerous to run. Emboldened by his earlier experience, he decided to chance it. All the rafts ran the rapids successfully, including the eighty-five-foot Huntington raft, which made the most difficult passage. A shelving of rock lay across the principal channel; the resulting cataract formed a whirlpool below. The big raft leaped over this fall and buried its nose in the waters below as the Indians, watching from the shoreline, threw up their arms and emitted a sad moan, believing all the white men to be drowned. Every man and animal on the raft was swimming but; having fastened themselves to the logs by ropes, retained their purchase as the raft, nosing out of the foaming water, raced down the remainder of the spillway like a toboggan on a slide.

There were more rapids and more adventures ahead, but all seemed tame compared with the ordeal of the Grand Canyon. Now the party began to get some hint that the goldfields were near: on the sandbars they came upon a party of curious pigtailed men in wide hats, mining with rockers. It was the first time that any of these easterners had set eyes on a Chinese.

The party reached Quesnel, the northern gateway to the gold country, on September 11. The remnants of the two other parties of Overlanders, who had left Fort Garry in May, followed some weeks behind along the same route. The last of the three parties lost two men in the Grand Canyon.

The thirty-two Overlanders and their hundred head of horses and cattle, who had separated from McMicking to head south for the North Thompson River, reached Fort Kamloops, far to the south, on October 11. All were in bad shape. One man had drowned and all their provisions and baggage had been lost in the nine-mile stretch of the Thompson known as the Murchison

Rapids. At the lower end of this cataract the banks narrow to enclose the river between two high, perpendicular rock walls, fifty feet apart. Through this crevice the river rushes at top speed and then makes a right-angle turn. It was here, at Hell Gate, that most of the rafts were smashed and lost.

This party, who trekked overland to Kamloops, was in pitiable shape, but its members were far more concerned for the Schubert family than for themselves. The Schuberts and several others had decided to continue on downriver by raft, Mrs. Schubert being so heavily pregnant that walking was a near impossibility. They had no food, and when they stopped at an Indian camp hoping for provisions, the Indians, who had never seen a white woman before, became hostile. One woman, seeing the cowhide rope to which the raft was tethered, accused Mrs. Schubert of trying to steal her cow, and tried to set the raft adrift.

The next Indian village was deserted. When the Schuberts went ashore they came upon a grisly spectacle; half-rotted corpses lay every which way, victims of the terrible smallpox epidemic of the previous year. Potatoes were ripening in the fields, unpicked, and for the next four days the Schuberts lived on nothing else. They reached Fort Kamloops, on the west side of the North Thompson, on October 13 — and not a moment too soon. Early the following morning, Catherine Schubert gave birth to the first white girl born in the interior of British Columbia. She named her Rose because, it was said, the family existed for several days on rose hips, an edible that Catherine remembered from her native Ireland. Thomas McMicking could not contain his admiration for her. He wrote that she "has accomplished a task to which few women are equal; and, with the additional care of three small children, which but few *men* would have the courage to undertake."

By mid-October, all of the goldseekers were within reach of the goldfields. Why, then, did they not rush to the Cariboo, eyes aflame, hearts beating wildly, to stake claims and work ground? For the irony is that only a tiny fraction of them bothered to seek the bonanza that, in the first instance, had taken them westward. The majority of the Queenston party took their rafts downstream to Fort Alexandria, where they went to work building the wagon road from Clinton to Soda Creek. Most of the others went immediately to Victoria and thence by boat to San Francisco and home.

Why? Part of it, no doubt, was disillusion brought on by the realization that, while they were struggling across the prairies and over the mountains, men much closer to the scene were staking the richest ground. Perhaps some of those who reached Quesnel on that triumphant day in September found their elation dampened by the spectacle of disenchanted men retreating on foot from the gold country, heading for the coast, dead broke. Only then did they understand that they had been hoaxed, not by fast-talking confidence men, but by their own false optimism.

That is not the whole story. Though some of the Overlanders left for the coast with a sour taste in their mouths, others clearly felt that they had triumphed in unexpected and more enduring ways. Perhaps, in their hearts, they had always known that the gold was a false lure, and that they had really travelled thirty-five hundred miles for reasons that had nothing to do with material gain. They had tested themselves and had not been found wanting. The long trek across the continent had brought out the very best in them. Others had passed that way before, and others would again, but these men were not explorers or fur traders; these were sedentary amateurs seeking adventure under the acceptable guise of business.

In the face of the discouraging reports leaking out of the Cariboo fields, the wonder is that some of them actually worked on the placer claims with varying degrees of success. It isn't surprising that one of these was Augustus Schubert, who stuck it out for eleven summers before rejoining his family in Lillooet, where his resourceful wife ran a hotel. Another who persevered was a veteran of the Huntington raft, James Wattie, who staked a claim on Williams Creek and got enough from it after two years of toil to open a woollen mill at Valleyfield, Quebec.

Dozens of others remained in British Columbia to ply their trades as blacksmiths, millwrights, contractors and storekeepers; some of these went on to become community leaders, aldermen and pillars of local society. Thomas McMicking became sheriff and county clerk in the city of New Westminster. There, in 1864, his wife and family joined him; and there, in 1868, ironic tragedy struck him down. The man who had survived the worst white water in all of British Columbia was drowned in a vain, noble attempt to rescue his little son from the same Fraser River which, just six years before, he himself had conquered.

Others of his party survived well into the twentieth century. His brother, Robert Burns McMicking, the young telegrapher, rose to become general manager of the B.C. Telephone Company; he died in 1915. Augustus Schubert survived until 1908 and his wife, a legend in her later years, lived on until 1918. All these people left their mark. Long after the colony had become a province and more than one railroad had reached the coast — when Fort George was a real estate man's paradise, the canyons of the Fraser had become tourist attractions and the goldfields had been converted into ranching country — the pioneers of '62 were honoured as living links with the past. Of them it was said, and always with awe, "He was an Overlander." There was no greater accolade.

18

The Ordeal of François Xavier Prieur

I have saved the story of François Xavier Prieur for the last because for me it is the most remarkable and the most touching. Prieur's own account of his seven-year exile to Australia following the abortive rebellion of 1838 is long out of print in Canada; yet it is the most Canadian of tales. I cannot read it without being moved by the intensity of longing that Prieur and his fellow convicts felt for their homeland. One does not encounter that same passion among the rebels from Upper Canada. With a single exception, all the French-Canadian exiles managed to return to Canada following their pardon. But their English-speaking counterparts scattered; some remained in the convict colony; some went to the United States; many more went back to the "old country," Great Britain. But to Prieur, Canada *was* the old country. When he was given a chance to go to France, he rejected it.

Another thread runs through Prieur's narrative — a devout Catholicism that goes deeper than the routine beatitudes of early French-Canadian documents. Prieur's unswerving faith did more than merely sustain him through danger, humiliation, uncertainty and suffering; for he not only survived his ordeal, he also prospered in exile and, when it was over, profited from what he had learned. His story, often hideous in its details, is essentially a love story — love of family, love of country, love of God. There is only one photograph of him extant, a rather muddy picture made in 1871 when Prieur was past middle age. It shows him surrounded by his family, plump, sleepy-eyed, bewhiskered — the typical Quebec bourgeois, by then a Conservative in politics. Nobody could know, gazing on that placid, domestic portrait, the trouble that François Xavier Prieur had seen. Nobody could know the despair he had suffered. Nobody could know the victories that were his.

Prieur was a fresh-faced farm boy in the parish of St. Joseph when the restlessness that led to the troubles of 1837 and 1838 began. At twenty-one, he set up a small store in St. Timothée, west of Beauharnois, on the south shore of the St. Lawrence. Business took him to Montreal and the bookstore of Edouard Fabre, a gathering place for Patriote leaders during the 1830s. There, Prieur met some of the great figures of the coming rebellions, including Louis Joseph Papineau, Louis Hippolyte LaFontaine and George Etienne Cartier. These men were to lead, in Lower Canada, a struggle for a fully democratic government that paralleled that of William Lyon Mackenzie in Upper Canada.

Prieur took no part in the rebellion of 1837, which saw Papineau driven into exile and the Patriote movement suppressed. But in 1838 he was sworn in as a *castor* in the secret society known as the Frères Chasseurs, an underground movement planning a second uprising. A *castor* was an officer commanding a company of ten platoons. Prieur became the rebel leader for his village of St. Timothée, mustering his men and his small hoard of munitions against the day of uprising. A less bloodthirsty youth cannot be imagined.

"I was young and inexperienced," he recalled, "a sincere lover of my homeland; I believed in the existence of all the evils enumerated; in the efficacy of the proposed remedy; I had read something of the heroism of my forefathers; I felt myself of good stock. Enthusiastically, I took part in the general training."

In St. Timothée, as in other parishes scattered throughout Lower Canada, the Patriotes awaited the call to arms. It came on the night of November 3. In the confused struggle that followed — scores of isolated skirmishes — the rebels, with their sporting guns, iron pitchforks and scythes, were no match for the better armed and disciplined British and Scottish regulars. The confusion of the Patriote forces was compounded by a lack of communication between parishes. The members of one community would prepare to resist while others were fleeing in disorder; one leader would be recruited while another was escaping across the border. It is not pertinent to detail Prieur's own tribulations — the early, brief successes; the rumours of defeat elsewhere; the uncertainty, the dissension and the desertions that weakened his own forces to the point where resistance became useless. It is only necessary to sketch in the final picture of the youth and his followers falling to their knees to tell their beads and repeat their litanies, as night falls and the rumbling of heavy gun carriages and cavalry swells in the distance.

All of Prieur's men melted quietly away into the night. Their leader went home, to find it a smoking ruin. Now François Xavier Prieur was a hunted man, hiding out in the haylofts of sympathetic farmers, to be betrayed, eventually, by an old comrade who turned him in to secure a pardon for himself.

The long ordeal began: forty prisoners, shivering in the bitter cold, living on bread and water in a flour mill at St. Timothée, hastily converted to a jail; fifty-two men now, almost all fathers of large families, chained two by two, and marched through the snow to Montreal to the infuriating skirl of bagpipes and the cries of an outraged mob; "Shoot them! Hang them!"; scores more men, jammed for five weeks in the gloomy prison of La-Pointe-à-Callières, watching while their comrades returned from their trials, condemned to die.

On January 9, 1939, Prieur and eleven others were taken in chains before the court martial, forced to walk directly under a scaffold spattered with the blood of two rebels whose hangings had been botched. The proceedings took place in English, a language few of them understood. They were not allowed French-Canadian lawyers because, they were told, this would prejudice the judges against them. The judges were prejudiced anyway: they insulted the prisoners and some amused themselves, during the sittings, by sketching little figures hanging from gibbets.

The case dragged on. Eight times the accused men were dragged into court handcuffed, to be abused and insulted by a rabble along the way. On January 18, as they arrived at the jail they saw the corpses of five of their comrades stretched out on the snow in their convict garb. One of the guards pointed out that all of them would shortly be in the same state.

Prieur's parents arrived to visit him. As he was led from the courtroom his mother rushed toward him, but a soldier thrust her back. Two hours later, when she was allowed to see him, she fainted in his arms: "At this moment," he writes, "I suffered the greatest anguish it has been my lot to endure during the course of a life which has suffered so much."

On the afternoon of January 24, Prieur and all his comrades were sentenced to be hanged. The condemned man told his parents to leave before the execution and to bury his body in the parish of his birth. In adjoining cells there were other tragic visits. Without breadwinners, most of the families of the Patriotes had nowhere to turn. Their homes and farms had been looted and burned; they were destitute.

Coffins were ordered; prisoners were led to the scaffold. Prieur, who knew his name was high on the list, waited for the fatal summons. It did not come. His own humanity had saved him; during the abortive uprising he had treated his captives with kindness. Among these were Jane Ellice and her husband, Edward, who was a nephew of Earl Grey and related to the Governor General, Lord Durham, and had until recently been one of his secretaries. They had successfully petitioned Sir John Colborne, the military commander at Quebec, to spare Prieur's life.

With fifty-seven others, Prieur remained in jail, not knowing from one day to the next what his fate would be.

He endured six months of misery. Then, on the afternoon of September 28, he and his fellow prisoners were told that their sentences had been commuted and that they would be transported the following morning to the penal colony of Australia for life. For many, there was not enough time to inform their families.

At eleven the next morning the fifty-eight men, shackled two by two, were led aboard the steamer *British America*. They were later joined by eighty-three rebel prisoners from Upper Canada and transferred, at Quebec City, to the big prison ship *Buffalo*. All were squeezed together in the unventilated hold, four and a half feet high. Each had about fifty cubic feet of air space. A row of packing cases ran down the length of their floating dungeon; on either side was a three-foot alley along which they could walk bent double. A bench, eighteen inches wide, flanked each walkway. Behind the bench lay a double row of compartments, nine on each side, six feet deep. These were their beds, each one holding four men on coarse mattresses with one blanket shared between two sleepers. Two small hatchways, covered by iron grilles and guarded by sentries, were the only source of light and air. For five months this was to be their home.

The English occupied the starboard side of the hold, the French the port. Prieur in his tiny corner at the far end slept well that first night, for he was exhausted. As he awoke, he heard the rattle of the anchors being raised; as the ship got underway, he realized that "we were leaving our native land without being able to cast a last glance at that beautiful landscape of Canada . . . so lovely; especially in this magnificent seaport of Quebec." With one accord, Prieur and his comrades fell on their knees to say their morning prayers, a ceremony from which they never wavered, morning and evening, throughout the long, distressing voyage.

At seven they were divided into groups of twelve to get rations. Their communal dish was a bucket, their only tableware a cup; there were no other utensils, although Prieur's group had a little pocketknife with which to cut meat. Breakfast was a pint of oatmeal soup; dinner consisted of four ounces of salt meat, a little suet pudding and some biscuit or, on alternate days, a pint of pea soup, three ounces of bacon and a little biscuit; supper was a pint of cocoa. Lest they die in the close atmosphere of the hold, they were allowed a daily two-and-a-half-hour walk on deck; the time was later reduced to one hour as punishment.

Now these men, most of whom had never seen the sea even from a distance, faced the horrors of an ocean voyage. After five days of calm, the waters grew rough and most of the passengers became ill. The decks became slippery with vomit. Forbidden to use the beds by day, the wretched prisoners huddled on the benches.

The crew and officers abused them, calling them cut-throats and sons of bitches. Prieur, one of the few who wasn't seasick, busied himself cleaning up after his less fortunate fellows.

When the storm ceased a week later, all were starving. Their clothes were infested with lice, their food buckets unbelievably filthy. During their hour of freedom on deck they tried to wash their clothes. As the ship neared the tropics, the heat below the waterline became stifling. One man died; others were desperately ill. Everyone suffered from a raging thirst. Two sailors who brought the sick men water and rum were flogged for that act of mercy. Other sailors sold water in return for some of the prisoners' few clothes. A brief respite on deck during a stop at Rio de Janeiro saved many lives. Here their rations were improved by the addition of lime juice; but in spite of this, scurvy was rampant, and the lice unbearable.

On February 13, the Upper Canadians were put off at Van Dieman's Land. Two weeks later, the ship reached Sydney. But Sydney did not want the rebels. Articles from the English-language newspapers in Montreal had arrived, branding them as bandits and roughnecks. They were rumoured to be destined for the hellish Norfolk Island, reserved for the worst criminals, hundreds of miles distant. They were held aboard the ship for two weeks while the Roman Catholic bishop, Monsigneur Polding, petitioned the authorities to allow them to stay, guaranteeing their good conduct. They were released at last from their floating prison, taken to Longbottom on the Paramatta River, eight miles out of Sydney, and marched for a mile inland. It was all they could do to make it.

"We were so weak, so worn out, and shaky on our legs that this short mile walk, taken at a slow pace, made us so tired that it gave us all pains in our limbs, pains that persisted with several of us for a few days. . . ."

The prisoners were lodged in four huts, just fifteen feet long and six feet wide, arranged with some out-buildings and barracks in a square. Anyone crossing the square without permission was subject to fifty lashes. For the first six weeks there were no beds, only bare boards to sleep on. The men awoke in the damp, chilly mornings with aching backs and heavy colds. Their food ration was as bad as that of the prison ship: por-ridge for breakfast, half a pound of rotting beef and twelve ounces of truly terrible bread per person for the rest of the day. The only available water came from rain holes dug in the ground. Each man's clothing was sten-cilled with the painted initials LB (for Longbottom) on back, legs, arms and chest. They worked under armed guards from early morning until six at night, smashing stones in a neighbouring quarry. The guards, it ap-peared, were terrified of them, having heard the rumours from Canada that these were dangerous, des-perate men.

But Prieur and his fellow prisoners were determined to justify Bishop Polding's trust in them by maintaining an impeccable behaviour. The prison superintendent, Henry Clinton Baddeley, a coarse and brutal man who had been discharged from the army for misconduct, tried his best to provoke them into open rebellion, which he knew he could quell with bloodshed. He failed. During "those long years of misery," Prieur was to write, ". . . one thing alone has supported me against the agonies of the heart and body, against the outbursts of temper; that thing believers will easily recognize, Religion." In the stable, which also served as a dining room, the prisoners set up a little chapel in which to receive the bishop when he visited them. They cleaned it, decorated it with fern leaves, built an altar out of sticks and covered it with a cotton cloth on which they hung all the little holy pictures their families had given them on departure.

One of the priests who visited them wrote to a local Catholic paper complaining about the food and conditions at the prison and urging that the men be allowed to find jobs for themselves. This only resulted in a vitriolic attack in the Sydney *Herald,* in which the Canadians were called cutthroats whose whole career had been marked by murder, pillage and arson.

But in the prison compound a bizarre turn of events helped alleviate the prisoners' suffering. The Canadians were guarded by one squad of police and one squad of soldiers. One night, the superintendent became involved in a drunken brawl with one of the policemen, whose wife he had insulted. The policeman was arrested and this touched off a wild mêlée, some taking the superintendent's side, others taking the policeman's side. In desperation, Baddeley released the Canadians and ordered them to arrest and lock up all the police and guards, except one sergeant. By obeying him they won his confidence, and completely changed his attitude toward them. After three months the authorities, in a remarkable gesture, removed all the guards and left the superintendent in charge. In effect the prisoners would guard themselves. Baddeley began to give those prisoners least used to manual labour easier jobs as overseers, cooks, servants and watchmen. Prieur became a night sentry.

The food improved slightly. The superintendent now trusted his prisoners, allowing them to leave their hut doors open at nights and to collect shells off the beach to sell to lime-burners to earn a few pennies for rice and sugar. Conditions were still execrable, but to a very real degree the prisoners were themselves given charge of their own prison.

A year passed. Life remained unbearably harsh. One man died of dropsy. Another, of colossal stature, expired from starvation because, though his friends shared their rations with him, he could not get enough to eat. The diminutive Prieur must have considered himself fortunate that he was under five foot five.

Under the Australian penal system convicts progressed by stages to become free citizens. In November 1840, twenty months after their arrival at Longbottom, the Canadians reached stage two of this progression: they were given permission to hire themselves out to residents of the country, a practice that meant they would no longer be a burden on the government. The rules continued to be strict: they were rationed to ten pounds of fresh beef, ten pounds of flour, a pound of sugar and four ounces of tea a week; they were quartered like plantation slaves in little huts adjoining their master's home; they worked a twelve-hour day and cooked their own food; and they could not leave their master's property except on Sundays, without a written permit. Nevertheless it was an improvement and, as Prieur wrote, "the only thing which troubled us ... was the thought that we were about to be separated from one another."

Man by man they were hired out. When all but one had left, Baddeley, the superintendent, sickened and died in the arms of the last Canadian prisoner. "No other person came to be present with him in his last moments, and not a single friend followed his coffin to the cemetery."

Prieur and a fellow prisoner, Louis Bourdon, were hired out to a Frenchman from Mauritius. They discovered that he had no intention of keeping them but proposed to rent them, at a profit, to another Frenchman and his German partner who had arrived in

Sydney to open a confectionery shop. The two Canadians worked and slept in a small shed, making syrups and candy. Compared to prison it was "an earthly paradise."

After three months, Prieur was suddenly denied his Sunday holiday and told he could not longer attend mass. To a devout Catholic this was outrageous. Prieur took the unusual step of striking. It was, he said, against his religion to work on the Lord's Day and also against penal regulations. Unable to get a hearing from his original master, the stubborn Canadian went to the government itself and was taken before the head of the department, a Captain McLean. Prieur attempted to tell his story in the halting English he had picked up in Australia. McLean responded politely that he might speak in French; he understood the language. A long man-to-man talk followed — for Prieur a "truly moral tonic." It was the first time in years that he had felt enough dignity to talk with ease to a man of superior intelligence, education and heart. "The interview reconciled me to my environment, and filled me with hope for the future."

Ordinarily, Prieur would have been sent back to the penal camp until a new master could be found. But McLean knew the difference between Canadian political exiles and criminals. He gave Prieur permission to seek his own job in Sydney and invited him to come back from time to time to let him know how he was getting along. Overcome with gratitude, Prieur felt that he had grown six inches.

But jobs in Australia were almost impossible to find; the colony was in the throes of a financial crisis brought on by land speculation and unhindered immigration. Prieur had a few gold coins from Canada hidden in the cover of a prayer book and a few shillings paid him by the confectioners, which he used to rent lodgings from a

man who had once lived in Montreal. Within a fortnight his money was used up and he found himself
without a roof over his head. He managed to get a job as
an assistant gardener from a man who had once been a
convict himself and was now a wealthy merchant. After
three months in this job he and the other Canadian
exiles were promoted again from the status of assigned
convicts to that of ticket-of-leave men. Now, although
he must always carry a pass and could be picked up by
the police whenever a crime was committed, Prieur
could work for himself.

He ran into his former partner, Louis Bourdon, who
persuaded him to go with him to a sawmill in the
bushland where ten of their comrades were working.
They bought some tools and set off a week later, walking the nine miles to the sawmill through dense, snake-
infested bush. Their welcome was warm and, in Prieur's account, there is a touching scene in which the
dozen exiles, seated at night in their frame hut on
mattresses stuffed with fern leaves, sing French-Canadian folk songs and talk among themselves about their
wives, children and parents in Quebec. In all this time
there had been no word from Canada. Prieur had no
idea whether his mother and father, brothers and sisters, were alive or dead; nor would he ever learn of them
during all the years of his exile. It was as if he had been
transported through a fourth dimension into a shadow
world.

Prieur and Bourdon decided to try their hand at
making laths. They worked desperately hard, felling
and splitting huge trees, their hands covered with blisters and their limbs stiff with fatigue. On a trip into
Sydney, Prieur encountered some officers from a
French whaling vessel who offered to help him escape
to France. He refused: he did not want these men to risk
fine and imprisonment for him and, as for France —

well, that, too, would be exile. Bourdon, however, sailed on the whaler and eventually made his way back to Canada.

For another year Prieur toiled in the forest, trying to make and sell laths. The work provided him with just enough funds to stay alive. Finally, he moved back to Sydney and went to work as business manager for three Frenchmen who wanted to set up a candle factory. He soon realized the business would fail and after four months resigned, went job-hunting again and finally got work clearing land.

Then a new venture beckoned. Two of the Canadians who had made a profit at the sawmill invited him to help them set up what was, in effect, a primitive shopping centre at a new village called Irish Town, twelve miles from Sydney. They would supply the capital and Prieur the business knowledge. They built their own shops from wood cut in the bush and within three days managed to erect a grocery, a bakery and a smithy. Near the bakery they built a Quebec-style oven, something that immediately drew curious spectators, for it was unknown in Australia. The bakery made money from the start; the shop broke even; the smithy failed and the blacksmith moved away. Prieur and his one remaining partner remained, making just enough to live on. And so another year went by.

In Canada, unknown to Prieur and his fellow exiles, attitudes had been mellowing. A new leader had emerged in Quebec: Louis Hippolyte LaFontaine, who had tried to pursue the French-Canadian cause by constitutional means. LaFontaine doggedly fought for an amnesty for the rebels of 1838. In 1843, Edouard Fabre, in whose bookstore Prieur had first espoused the cause of revolt, was helping to organize L'Association de la Déliverance to raise funds for the passage of the exiles back to Canada once an amnesty was proclaimed. The following year word of the first pardons began to filter to Australia.

Prieur had been at Irish Town for a year when he heard this unbelievable news. Two of the exiles had been pardoned. One of them was a close friend, Charles Huot, a former lawyer now in his fifties; Prieur had worked with him as night sentry in the prison camp. He rushed to see Huot, held the actual document of amnesty in his hand, read and reread it, finding it difficult to believe his eyes. Huot was overjoyed, even though for him the pardon was useless since he had no funds for passage home.

The following month, pardons arrived for half the Canadian exiles. Prieur was one of these. Nothing, he determined, would stop him from getting home again. "We were a-hungered and athirst for our homeland, we were consumed with the desire to return to Canada, to see again our families, our friends, our beautiful countryside, to salute the belfries of our parishes, to speak French, and to gaze on the sight of our good French-Canadian customs."

He, too, lacked the money for his passage. His partner in Irish Town, who had worked in the sawmill (which was far more profitable than lath-making) was able to leave. Again, Prieur went to Sydney to look for a job. By this time, the Canadians were in demand because their honesty and hard work were well known. Prieur had no trouble getting employment in a dry-goods store; the salary was the highest he had yet known in Australia.

In August, twenty-eight Canadian exiles embarked for England, where money raised in Lower Canada had been banked to pay for their passage home. These men promised to raise more money to pay for the later passage of those left behind. By this time, Prieur was fiercely homesick: "This disease threatened to bring me to my grave. Never, at any period of my exile, had I experienced anything approaching it. The boredom that I suffered is indescribable. I was very soon on the verge of falling into a state of melancholia, and of seeking only solitude, in the depths of which I nourished my sorrow. Every Sunday I spent my afternoon on a rock situated in the recesses of a solitary little bay overlooking Sydney Harbour; there I dreamed of my homeland and my family."

Prieur, who had now passed his thirtieth birthday, imagined he was watching the wake of the ship that had carried his comrades homeward. He saw himself aboard her, sailing home, up the St. Lawrence, finally reaching the parish where he was born — his mother's kisses, his father's joy, his friends' hand clasps. In anguish, he cried out, again and again, to the winds and to the sea: "When, oh when, shall I be able to set out for Canada?"

At this juncture he encountered a French merchant who was planning to sell his stock and return to Europe. He offered to take Prieur with him and to lend him the funds to go on to Canada. Prieur quit his job to help the Frenchman. In the evenings and on Sundays, he and seventeen other pardoned exiles, who also lacked funds, met and talked together.

More months dragged by. Prieur was summoned to see the Governor, Sir George Gipps, who told him that friends in several Quebec parishes had been requested by the British government to send money collected in Canada to Australia for the exiles' passage. Prieur and his friends were overjoyed. But more time passed and the money did not come.

At the end of January 1846, eighteen months after the first exiles had left Australia, Prieur and the French merchant finished selling all the stock and booked passage for England on the *Saint George*. They left in February. Prieur met one last time with his comrades and enjoined them to have courage: their turn would come. He shook hands with each one, the tears streaming down his face. Four months later (such was the slowness of ocean travel in those times) he reached England.

He began to search for the source of the funds said to be awaiting the return of the exiles. He had no idea where to look but after some days got in touch by letter with John Arthur Roebuck, an English member of Parliament, sympathetic to the cause. Roebuck sent him to see a Mr. Graham, who at once gave him the money to pay his London expenses and his passage home. There wasn't enough on deposit to bring the others back. Prieur was asked to help raise more funds in Canada.

On July 13, 1846, Prieur sailed from England for his homeland. At seven in the morning of September 2 he went on deck to see the Gaspé shores: "The Homeland! After more that seven years of exile!" It was so intoxicating that he reflected that the pleasures of entering Heaven must be beyond imagination. His fellow passengers were moved by his ecstasy. For two days he was too excited to sleep.

On September 10, Prieur touched the soil of Canada for the first time as he stepped off the ship at Quebec City. He took a carriage to his hotel. Every tiny detail moved him. "I cannot express . . . the effect that the sight of this carriage had upon me and the impression that I experienced when I heard French spoken around me . . . especially the simple words that the coachman addressed to his horse."

The news of his arrival spread through the city by a kind of moccasin telegraph. Strangers flooded into his room to congratulate him, to wish him well, to ask for news of those still in exile. They pressed invitations upon him but these he could not accept. He must go home; he still did not know whether his parents were alive.

He took the steamer to Montreal and there he heard the good news that his family were alive and well and, thanks to a letter from Roebuck, the British MP, expecting him. But before rushing home, he felt he must keep his promise to solicit more funds. He visited Fabre, who told him that sufficient money had been collected but a mistake in the methods used to transmit it to Australia had caused maddening delays. Prieur, with his experience in New South Wales, was able to advise him of better methods. Within sixteen months, fifty-five of the original fifty-eight exiles were back in Quebec: two had died at Longbottom and one had married and stayed in Australia.

The next day, Prieur took the steamer to his home parish. There was a frustrating hold-up in the Beauharnois Canal, which meant that he did not reach his parents' doorstep until two in the morning of September 4, 1846. By then everyone was in bed. It had been eight years since Prieur had stood on this spot: "Reader of my notes, put yourself in my place. Imagine it is you who stands waiting upon this threshold, and you will understand how I felt."

Suddenly the door was flung open. "It is he! It is Xavier!" His parents flung their arms around his neck. He knelt before his father to ask his blessing. Then, on their knees, the reunited family offered up their prayers, thanking their Maker for their son's return.

The word travelled like a fast-burning fuse. Old men in nearby cottages, getting up to light their pipes from the stoves, saw the lights in the Prieur house and woke their families. For miles around, men, women and children tumbled from their beds and set out to greet the returned exile, tapping on windows as they passed down the road, calling out, "Xavier Prieur has arrived. Aren't you coming to see him?" Half an hour after his return, the house was crowded with neighbours, with more arriving by the minute, the men in their caps, the women in their big woollen shawls, shivering in the cold but warmed by the miracle.

It was five in the morning before Prieur ceased shaking hands and even then his story was not told. He promised to relate the rest of it later; now he needed to go to bed — his own bed, which had been held ready for him for all those years. He felt indescribably happy. "It is good to be here, my Canada, parish of my birth. Here I find again my parents, the friends of my childhood and my youth. O God, full of kindness, blessed are Thou!" For François Xavier Prieur, rebel, patriot, ex-convict, devout Catholic, jack-of-a-dozen-trades, the eight-year ordeal was over.

Prieur settled down as a merchant in Chateauguay and later in Beauharnois. In 1849 he married. All during his exile, even in the Quebec prison "when over me hung the weight of the death sentence; when the dead bodies of some of the companions of my captivity hung suspended from the gibbet," the resourceful young man had recorded his experiences on loose sheets of paper. In 1864, he arranged these notes and published them. "I do not propose," he declared in his introduction, "to write history. . . . I wish to provide, for those who do, my share of the exact information concerning the things that I have seen with my own eyes, touched with my own hands, and suffered in my own person." He had long since begged God's pardon, he said, for disobeying the order of the church and he had long since forgiven all those who had done him wrong. "It is therefore in a spirit of calm that I write . . . without any desire to injure. . . ."

By the time his book appeared, Prieur had taken a new job. Thanks to the influence of his Conservative friends he was appointed Superintendent of the Reformatory at Ile-aux-Noix. One cannot imagine a man better experienced or more humanely equipped to run a jail. In 1875, he was promoted to Superintendent of all Canadian prisons. A man of great energy and perseverance (he lived to the age of seventy-five) he travelled widely across Canada, the United States and throughout Europe, visiting prisons and reform institutions, talking to wardens and jailers, investigating the latest methods of prison administration.

In his new job he saw a good deal of the world and also the inside of a good many prisons. But there was one part of the world he did not need to visit, one example of prison administration he had no further cause to study. There was no need for François Xavier Prieur to go back to the penal colony of Australia.

Index

Also in Penguin

Pierre Berton

THE NATIONAL DREAM

"One of the finest historical works ever written
in Canada, a genuine masterpiece."

Bruce Hutchison

The National Dream is the stirring story of a newlyformed
country's determination to build the world's longest and
costliest railroad. It is a tale filled with human drama —
politics, adventure, scandal, wheeling and dealing — the
story of larger-than-life individuals who rose to prodigious heights in the pursuit of a dream truly national in its
scope and vision.

"*The National Dream* is an amazing book. It is pure
excitement."

Hugh MacLennan

"...an exciting book, a book on the grand scale. Berton has
given us a superb history."

Vancouver Sun

"...a marvellous book."

Ottawa Citizen

Pierre Berton

KLONDIKE

"Pierre Berton writes 24-carat gold."
Edmonton Journal

Pierre Berton's *Klondike* is a dramatic tale which captures the full grandeur and sweep of the last great gold rush. It is first-rate history and a must read for anyone interested in the Canadian frontier.

"No one has told the story of the gold rush with the same fullness and readable authority as Pierre Berton."
Time

"*Klondike* is a fascinating book, whether considered as authentic history, which it is, or just as grand entertainment."
Montreal Gazette

"His entire tale has an epic ring, as much because of its splendid folly as because of its colour and motion."
New York Times Book Review

"A fascinating book of permanent value."
Globe and Mail

Pierre Berton

THE PROMISED LAND

"The Promised Land succeeds once again...."
Maclean's

The Promised Land is the final chapter in Pierre Berton's epic retelling of the opening of the Canadian West in the years following Confederation. After the pioneers, surveyors and entrepreneurs described in *The National Dream, The Last Spike* and *Klondike* came the settlers — a million people brought by government propaganda, ruthless boosterism and Utopian visions of a Promised Land. This is the compelling history of those lonely, often bewildered newcomers and of today's Canadian West, which was formed in the crucible of that tempestuous era when a thousand miles of prairie country was filled in a single generation.

"There's a vitality and life in Berton's writing that is particularly striking after re-reading other accounts of the development of the Canadian West. Berton readers have come to expect quality from him and, once again, he doesn't disappoint."
Toronto Star

"An engaging, lively and engrossing book."
Books in Canada

Pierre Berton

THE ARCTIC GRAIL

"There's enough riveting reading in *The Arctic Grail*
to last until spring breakup."

Globe and Mail

In *The Arctic Grail*, Pierre Berton follows the paths forged
by a handful of stubborn explorers, who risked life and
limb in their quest to find the Northwest Passage. This
quest is peopled with larger-than-life adventurers and
with the remarkable Inuit, without whom Arctic exploration would not have been possible.

"Berton's book is a thoroughly gripping read...by the time
Amundsen's little ship, *Gjoa*, finally reaches the Beaufort
Sea, most readers will inwardly shout hurrah at the
triumph."

Vancouver Province

"Berton's 34th book is rich and compelling enough to
keep the reader lost in cool adventures."

London Free Press

"A magnificent history...This should be the definitive
study of Arctic exploration for years to come."

The Kirkus Review

"Berton has produced a work that reads like a novel...it
presents explorers not as wooden heroes whose names
grace Canada's North, but as real men, many of whom
died in the snow and cold."

Hamilton Spectator

"*The Arctic Grail* is Berton at his best — careful research,
emphasis on the character of the Arctic explorers, and
clear vivid narrative."

Montreal Gazette

Pierre Berton

FLAMES ACROSS THE BORDER

"*Flames Across the Border* is drum-and-trumpet
history at its best."

The Washington Post

The Canadian-U.S. border was in flames as tensions
between the two countries flared. York's parliament
buildings were on fire, Niagara-on-the-Lake burned to the
ground, Buffalo was in ashes and Washington was put to
the torch. The War of 1812 saw one of the nineteenth
century's bloodiest struggles and in *Flames Across the
Border*, Pierre Berton brings the events to life in full colour
and vivid drama.

"Berton has the storyteller's gift, the novelist's insight, the
journalist's easy style and the historian's sense of time...
He writes history as it should be written."

Kingston Whig-Standard

"With the vividness of eyewitness reporting, Berton
brings us the heroes and heroines of this 'bloody and
senseless' conflict, as well as the cowards, the incompe-
tents and the eccentrics."

Publisher's Weekly

Pierre Berton

THE INVASION OF CANADA

"A wonderful historical work...a book of love,
ambition, guile, heroism, tragedy and cowardice."
The Detroit News

In this exciting and suspenseful account of the War of
1812 and the events that led up to it, Pierre Berton pulls a
dusty page from history and transforms it into an engrossing narrative that reads like a fast-paced novel.

"If history could be taught in the schools the way Berton
writes about it, there wouldn't be a more popular subject."
Globe and Mail

"...popular history as it should be written."
The New York Times

"If you are a military history buff, devoted to good old
fashioned drum-and-trumpet, blood-and-gore patriotic
history, *The Invasion of Canada* will satisfy your
appetite."

Montreal Gazette

"...a hell of a good book."

Kingston Whig-Standard

Pierre Berton

VIMY

"Vimy is Berton at his best and that's the best there is."
Peter C. Newman

On a chill Easter Monday in 1917 the four divisions of the Canadian Corps in France did what the British and French armies had failed to do — they seized the best-defended German bastion on the Western Front, a muddy scarp known as the Vimy Ridge. In his account of this great battle, Pierre Berton brilliantly illuminates the moment of tragedy and greatness that marked Canada's emergence as a nation.

"Vimy is a triumph. It stops the human heart and breaks it over and over again."

Timothy Findley

"Berton captures the horror of the front lines brilliantly."

Montreal Gazette

"I've read practically everything on Vimy and this is the best."

*William Pecover, soldier with
the 27th Battalion at Vimy*

"A book to make us proud, to make us weep."
June Callwood

Pierre Berton

WHY WE ACT LIKE CANADIANS

Our American neighbours wonder...
- Why we can't buy a six-pack in a Toronto deli
- Why our subways are so safe and clean
- Why we let movie censors tell us what we can and cannot watch
- Why nobody owns a gun
- Why the government owns so many corporations
- Why we didn't have a revolution like everybody else

Pierre Berton's *Why We Act Like Canadians* answers all these questions and more.

"*Why We Act Like Canadians* is light, amusing, and well-written. It is incisive and will cause the reader to roar with laughter, while at the same time think seriously."

The Sunday Sun

"Lively, provocative and wise."

Vancouver Sun

"Berton's book leaves nothing about our national character untouched. For that reason it should be recommended reading for every Canadian."

The Windsor Star

"Bright, readable..."

Montreal Gazette

Pierre Berton

THE LAST SPIKE

The story of the building of the great Canadian Pacific Railway brought to life in an epic tale filled with adventure, suspense and tragedy.

"No novel could surpass *The Last Spike* for plot; no western for wildness....This is a great book."

Vancouver Sun

"Lively, human and utterly absorbing..."

The Financial Post

"Outstanding."

Winnipeg Tribune